Remote Access Technologies for Library Collections:

Tools for Library Users and Managers

Diane M. Fulkerson
University of South Florida Polytechnic Library, USA

Managing Director:	Lindsay Johnston
Senior Editorial Director:	Heather Probst
Book Production Manager:	Sean Woznicki
Development Manager:	Joel Gamon
Acquisitions Editor:	Erika Gallagher
Typesetter:	Milan Vracarich, Jr.
Cover Design:	Nick Newcomer, Lisandro Gonzalez

Published in the United States of America by
Information Science Reference (an imprint of IGI Global)
701 E. Chocolate Avenue
Hershey PA 17033
Tel: 717-533-8845
Fax: 717-533-8661
E-mail: cust@igi-global.com
Web site: http://www.igi-global.com

Library of Congress Cataloging-in-Publication Data

Fulkerson, Diane M., 1957-
  Remote access technologies for library collections : tools for library users and managers / by Diane M. Fulkerson.
    pages cm
  Includes bibliographical references and index.
  ISBN 978-1-4666-0234-2 (hardcover) -- ISBN 978-1-4666-0235-9 (ebook) (print) -- ISBN 978-1-4666-0236-6 (print & perpetual access) (print) 1. Academic libraries--Information technology. 2. Academic libraries--Effect of technological innovations on. 3. Libraries--Special collections--Electronic information resources. 4. Libraries and distance education. 5. Online library catalogs--Remote access. 6. Digital libraries. 7. Copyright--Electronic information resources--United States. I. Title.
  Z675.U5F77 2012
  025.04'2--dc23
                                      2011046463

British Cataloguing in Publication Data
A Cataloguing in Publication record for this book is available from the British Library.

All work contributed to this book is new, previously-unpublished material. The views expressed in this book are those of the authors, but not necessarily of the publisher.

Table of Contents

Detailed Table of Contents

Chapter 1

Remote access technologies for library collections are the result of the growth of distance education programs in higher education. With the increased demand for online education, students needed a way to access library collections without coming to campus. As technology improved, the ability for students to use a library's database without coming to a physical campus became a reality. Through such technologies as virtual private networks (VPN) and EZProxy, students could use their ID and password to gain access to library collections. Distance education was the driving force behind the need to provide remote access to collections. As a result, students now have the ability to search a library's catalog or find articles in a database without coming to campus, anytime of the day or night. Librarians also have the opportunity to promote library resources and teach synchronous instruction sessions in online classes. Remote access technologies provide students, faculty, and librarians with the opportunity to meet user needs regardless of whether or not they are on campus. This chapter examines the growth of distance education programs at post-secondary schools, a trend expected to continue for the near future.

Chapter 2

Determining how a library can meet user needs can be accomplished through different methods. Libraries can use focus groups, surveys, or other means of assessment. Liquid+® is a survey available to all academic libraries from the Association of Research Libraries. Most libraries who administer the Liquid+® survey can use the survey results to do additional internal surveys with users or to meet with small groups of users to improve their services.

Chapter 3

Copyright plays an important role in not only print materials one finds in a library but also the resources accessed from off-campus through online course management systems and electronic, or e-reserves. This chapter provides an overview of copyright as it pertains to remote access of library resources.

The collection development policies of the library will determine the types of material included in the collection. Along with those policies are databases licensing agreements that determine who can access the materials and where they can be accessed from. Collection development policies are usually driven by the academic programs of the institution. Digital collections and digital libraries will often be created from materials at the university. Without collection development policies the digital libraries and collections may receive little use because they do not meet the needs of the students or are difficult to access on or off-campus.

Digital collections are found in most libraries. They include not only databases but also photographs, institutional repositories, manuscript collections, materials from the university archives, or special collections. Designing digital collections and making them available to users expands the resources users can access for a research project.

Technology to access materials remotely has gone from document delivery via snail mail to documents received electronically. No longer do users have to come into the library to find articles in scholarly journals, magazines, and newspapers. Books are not always available electronically, but users can search the library's online catalog to find print and e-books without going to the library. The primary technologies used to access materials off-campus are virtual private networks (VPN) and EZproxy. These technologies authenticate users through a password. Once they are authenticated they can access the library collections for their research.

In addition to electronic reserves, instructors can link database materials through course management systems (CMS). This type of software allows faculty to link articles from databases into their course materials. This chapter provides an overview of different course management software and explains how instructors or librarians can link course materials into these systems.

Social network sites such as Facebook and Twitter can provide another opportunity for users to remotely access library resources. The creation of a library Facebook page provides the library with the ability to promote licensed databases and the information users need to remotely accesses those resources and course or electronic reserve materials. Twitter accounts provide libraries with the opportunity to keep users informed about changes to licensed databases, in other words, anytime they add or discontinue resources or there is a problem accessing them remotely. Another option is foursquare. Foursquare allows you to find your friends and discover your city or library. Libraries can use foursquare to introduce students to it resources and services. The library could develop a contest for users to earn points and badges by discovering information about the library such as, new books, databases or services. Social networks provide libraries and users with new ways to promote and provide remote access to licensed databases.

Millions of people have a smartphone, and with smartphone technology comes the ability for Internet connectivity and with that the ability to access library resources. EBSCO, Elsevier, ProQuest, Gale/Cengage, and other database vendors have capitalized on the increased use of smartphones by developing the capability for library users to access EBSCO databases from their smartphones. Mobile technology extends beyond smartphones and includes technology gadgets such as e-book readers, the iPad, netbooks, and laptops. As technology that is more mobile becomes available, the ability and need to connect remotely will increase. Mobile technology has grown beyond cell phones and personal digital assistants to other types of devices most recently Apple's iPad. Gone are the days when the only computer available was the one on your desk. With better technology came laptops, and now netbooks and e-book readers. To access the Internet, campuses have wireless technology in most classrooms and libraries. The proliferation of mobile technology and the ability to gain access to the Internet from almost any place means libraries and database vendors need to make sure their websites and resources are compatible with mobile devices.

Virtual libraries are often considered the same as digital collections but in fact, they are different from digital collections given the fact they often contain links to reference sources or subject specific materials including reference books or web sites. Virtual libraries originally intended for distance education students but are available for any researcher or student.

With any remote access technology, problems can and do arise. Some of the common problems with remote access technologies are security, broken links, and privacy. Most remote technology is relatively stable, but unfortunately, problems occur from time to time. It is important that the library has someone monitor the technology to make sure there are no problems. Users become frustrated when trying to access a resource from off-campus only to find they cannot.

Remote access technologies for library collections encompass more than just the technology required to access the resources from an off-campus location. Users no longer have to enter the library to use journals or search the catalog to find books, and remote access technologies have moved the library beyond its physical space to reach a greater numbers of users. Is the library going to cease to exist because of this technology? It is doubtful. The number of electronic resources and collections continues to grow but libraries cannot subscribe to every journal electronically, and not every journal is available electronically. The same holds true for books. E-books can be found in the collections of almost every academic library, yet they are not very popular with students. As more online courses are offered by colleges and universities, remote access to library collections will continue to increase, and libraries will need to make sure their users will be able to access the resources and to offer instruction to students and faculty on how to gain access to the resources from off-campus locations.

Preface

The growth of the Internet over the past 20 years changed the way library materials are accessed. Gone are the days of the card catalog, print indexes, and making copies of articles available only in print. Remote access to library materials is the norm rather than the exception in 2012. A major factor for remote access was the growth of distance education courses and programs. What may have started out as a small portion of library services in academic libraries has increased in size and scope of services offered. Books and sometimes articles may be mailed to students who live off-campus; all campuses offer some type of remote access to their library resources. As more students enroll in online courses or programs at both for-profit and traditional colleges and universities the need for services and remote access to library resources increases. Remote access is not just limited to off-campus students. All students on or off-campus can access library resources through a remote connection. Some of the services available to students include chat reference, access to databases, virtual libraries, and the library catalog. A student working on a paper at two o'clock in the morning can now look for articles in one of the library's databases or check the catalog for books. The library is available to students 24 hours a day, seven days a week, regardless of whether or not the physical building is open. It is the growth and improvement of technology that has made all this possible.

Some of the first databases available required a mediated search with the reference librarian. Other databases and information were available on CD and had to be installed on a computer. As HTML became the standard language for the Internet database, vendors were able to provide content to libraries in either HTML full text or PDF (portable document format). Students could then print the articles while in the library. By the end of the 1990s virtual private networks (VPN) made it possible for remote connection to another location. The development of VPN and another technology, EZproxy in 1999, allowed students access to library resources from off-campus locations. EZproxy allowed libraries to create a password-protected environment that would authenticate students, faculty, or staff and provide them with access to library materials. As a new decade takes off, one can expect to see increased growth of mobile technologies from libraries and database vendors to improve remote access to their resources.

The ability to gain access to library materials on or off-campus brought about some problems for academic libraries. The primary one is copyright protection. Georgia State University in Atlanta was sued by Cambridge University Press, Oxford University Press, and SAGE Publications for copyright and fair use violations. The publishers claimed the university through the use of e-reserves or electronic reserves violated fair use because students or faculty members could print out multiple copies of the item or post them to a faculty website. As of the fall of 2011, the outcome of the case was still pending.

Today's library users want and need remote access to library resources 24 hours a day, and library managers and administrators want to ensure their users have access to library resources when they want and need them. This book is intended for library users and managers to gain a better understanding of remote access technologies currently available. So who are today's library users and managers? Library users can be students working individually or in a group on a research project. Faculty and staff need remote access to library resources. A faculty member could be writing a book or article and need to search the catalog or databases to find the information they need for their project. A staff member could be taking a class or need to obtain information for a project at work. Alumni of the school might want to find an old yearbook or photo from the year they graduated. It could be a community user or it could be a member of the "friends of the library" group who need to access library resources from home to find a book or article. You could also have one-time or first-time users visiting the library's website to find resources for a project. Visiting scholars are another group of library users and usually have remote access to library resources the same as faculty, staff, and students. All of these users need remote access to library resources to develop course content or to research a topic for a project. Some of the users might be technology savvy and able to navigate the library website and databases without any problems or the users might not be so technology savvy and require help from a librarian to understand how to access library resources while off-campus.

Library managers likewise can fall into anyone of a number of categories. They can be paraprofessional supervisors or professional librarians. Paraprofessionals, just like professional staff, need to know how users can obtain remote access to library resources. Managers, whether they are professional librarians or paraprofessionals, will often help users obtain the remote access they need to library resources. Managers and professional staff might lead focus groups or develop surveys to understand how users access library resources and how the library can improve access to its resources. It could be the manager for Interlibrary Loan or the Head of Access Services who need a better of understanding of how they can improve their services to users. Improving remote access services increases the library's role in the academic community and makes the library the prominent component of the academic life of the university.

CURRENT AND FUTURE TRENDS FOR REMOTE ACCESS

Technology changes rapidly, and new technologies will provide better access to library materials. Libraries will need to determine what technologies to adopt and how to stay up to date with new and emerging one. Some of the current trends and issues to explore regarding remote access to library collections include the following:

- Identifying new technologies
- The ability to implement and update new technologies
- Understanding copyright and fair use laws
- Creating metadata for access to digital collections
- Meeting user needs

Since the 2007 launch of the Kindle e-book reader, there have been a growing number of new products designed to access information from any location with Internet access. These include, but are not limited to, smartphones, the iPad2, iPod Touch, and netbooks. Smartphones and the Apple products all have a number of applications (or apps) that can be purchased or downloaded to access information for research or for entertainment. In early 2011 EBSCO launched a mobile application for access to their databases such as Academic Search Premier, Cinahl, and others. Other database vendors including Gale, ProQuest, and Elsevier, have developed and launched similar apps for their products. Their websites provides information on how to install and use their mobile apps. An issue related to mobile technologies is that some websites are not fully functional when accessed from mobile devices, or the Information Technology infrastructure may not be in place to provide access to information through a mobile device. This becomes a source of major frustration for users.

Determining which technologies to implement should be a direct result of the feedback from library users. There are a variety of ways to determine user needs, including focus groups, surveys, student advisory committees and user comment or suggestion cards provided by the library at their public service desks. The biggest mistake an organization can make is to not ask for user input before implementing a new service, or in this case, a new technology. One should never assume they know what the user wants and adopt a new technology only because everyone is talking about it. You might implement a new technology only to find out six months later there are a number of problems with it or it is too difficult for users to get used to it. It is also necessary to solicit feedback from library users about current services before implementing new ones. The feedback obtained from surveys or focus groups can be used by the library to develop or change their strategic plan.

Copyright laws govern fair use of any and all printed materials. Remote access to library collections allows students and faculty to gain access not only to databases but also to electronic reserves for classes. In addition to electronic reserves, materials can also be embedded into an online class through course management software, such as Blackboard/WebCT, Sakai, or Moodle. Electronic reserves and course management software require user passwords, but do not limit the number of copies you can make or distribute nor does it prevent you from sharing the link to an article or other copyrighted material with other outside of the class. It is an issue universities need to address through their policies regarding fair use of copyrighted material.

Metadata is the information that helps you find information in a database or other online resource. Without metadata you could not find information in a catalog, database or the Internet. The use of metadata provides the keywords, title, author's name, and other relevant information that allows you to find the information you need and to refine your search through additional search terms or metadata. It is the use of metadata that brings order to chaos. In a recently published article, the author indicated how Google uses metadata in several of its advanced search products (Beall 2010). The use of metadata in Google's advanced search options allows users to refine their searches to yield better results.

THE FUTURE OF REMOTE ACCESS

As the use of technology becomes more pervasive in society, it will become necessary for libraries to adapt to meet the needs of their users. Websites and databases will have to be compatible with mobile devices. Database producers will need to create mobile apps allowing users to access their information whether they are at home, in the library, or sitting in the local coffee house. As social networks gain in popularity, libraries will need to explore their potential for providing remote access to their materials. While they might not be able to place copyrighted materials on a social networking page, they can provide links to catalogs or tutorials on how to access materials. It may be possible to place a link to their databases that could link to EZproxy to verify the users' ability to access the libraries online materials. Another example of remote access is subject guides created with LibGuides. This product from

Springshare allows libraries to create subject guides and embed links to their catalogs and databases within those subject guides. Faculty and students then have the ability to gain access to library resources through the course subject guides.

Two additional sources for remote access include open access journals and digital repositories. Open access journals are digital literature put online free of charge and most licensing and copyright restrictions (Suber 2010). The Public Library of Science (PLoS) was one of the first open access scientific journals, and it uses a publication model requiring authors to pay production costs upfront so the information can be accessed free of charge (Suber 2010). Open access journals will never replace the scholarly journals published by the academic presses, but they do provide access to information, especially in the sciences and medicine, which may not be available to the general public without the open access initiative. The Directory of Open Access Journals provides links to open access journals grouped by categories. According to their website, there are now over 5400 open access journals available. Open access journals provide researchers with the opportunity to find peer reviewed articles without being affiliated with a college or university. As the cost of journals continues to rise, open access journals and the open access initiative may gain support from librarians and researchers.

One of the first digital repositories was a joint effort between the Massachusetts Institute of Technology and Hewlett-Packard, called DSpace (http://www.dspace.org/#). This open source software allows colleges and universities to preserve, manage, provide access to, and share their materials. The software allows colleges and universities to share documents, such as conference papers, video collections, and images. If one searches Google Scholar, you will find material from many large colleges and universities stored as PDF documents on the institution's digital repository. This provides researchers both on and off campus to access the digital repository without a password and opens up a world of scholarship that previously was not shared beyond a scholar's institution or a conference.

With the growth of social networks many libraries created a Facebook page, but the question arises: do students really want libraries on Facebook? Or to put it differently, how can libraries use social networks to meet the needs of their students? With half a billion users, Facebook certainly has the potential to reach almost every student on campus. Another option is Twitter, where users create an account and post what is happening in their world in 140 characters or less. The past two years, the American Library Association has provided Twitter feeds to some of their conference sessions. Feedback from ALA conference attendees has been very positive. They like the option of Twitter feeds and use Twitter to communicate with colleagues and follow conference sessions and events. Can this type of social network be used to provide remote access to library collections? Social media provides libraries with the opportunity to keep their students updated about new resources but to also interact with them by providing links to resources in places they work. Group work no longer has to take place in the library. Social media provide students with the ability to work remotely through Facebook, Twitter, and Google Docs. In order to make sure students access resources necessary for their projects academic libraries need to explore creating links for library resources through social media.

Security is an issue with remote access to library collections. Digital collections are often made readily available to the public. However, proprietary databases (i.e., those purchased by institutions) are not, which means students may only access databases off-campus with a password. In some cases, they use their student ID number and password or a password that is generated by the library or campus Information Technology that allows them to gain access to the proxy server or VPN. Depending on the policies of the institution, the password is changed at least every semester. Despite the improvements in technology users still encounter problems with remote access. In some cases, it is the firewall installed on the user's computer that prevents them from gaining access. Other times it can be a problem with the database vendor's server or the link to the database interface changed causing problems connecting.

Course management systems and distance education play a significant role in remote access to library collections. Online courses and programs are increasing in popularity and availability. Online course software allows instructors to embed links to articles from databases, videos, the library's catalog, or links to the library's databases and other materials students need. Another option in online courses is the "embedded librarian." A librarian works with the instructor and students to help them with their research assignments. Since most course management systems provide an option for synchronous instruction. Librarians can conduct library instruction classes in real-time allowing students to learn about and work with the library's resources. Blackboard is among the top proprietary course management software. In the open source course management software realm, Moodle and Sakai are the most widely used. Regardless of the course management system selected by the institution the software provides the library with the ability to embed their resources in courses for students. While synchronous instruction does not replace face to face library instruction, it provides the students with the opportunity for hands-on instruction using the library's databases and catalog.

ORGANIZATION OF THE BOOK

Chapter 1 gives an in-depth look at the evolution and development of distance (or online) education explaining how online learning lead to the need for remote access to library materials. As distance education evolved from correspondence courses to computer-based instruction students needed the ability to use library materials both on and off campus. As technology improved, the ability for students to access resources from home became a reality. Gone are the days when books and articles were mailed to students. Instead, students can now access the databases or library catalog from home or work. Articles found through the database can be saved or even e-mailed.

Chapter 2 addresses how libraries meet user needs to provide access to their resources. Not only is it important to provide remote access to students, it is equally important to have the resources they require. Libraries can use a variety of methods to determine how they will improve their customer service. Some of the most commonly used methods are surveys, statistics, and focus groups. Each of these methods provides libraries with the opportunity to address user concerns and improve their services.

Chapter 3 deals with copyright law as they relate to off-campus access. The recent lawsuit against Georgia State University in Atlanta brought this issue to academic libraries across the country. A primary concern of the lawsuit was the fair use of copyrighted material. This chapter focuses on fair use as it relates to remote access and the use of copyrighted material in online courses.

Chapter 4 explores collection development policies for off-campus licensing of databases. In negotiating contracts with database vendors, academic libraries include a section regarding off-campus access to proprietary databases, usually focusing on password protection and fair use of the resources. Most colleges and universities include a statement that off-campus use of databases is only available to current students and faculty.

Chapter 5 examines the development of online or digital collections. Digital collections include virtual libraries and usually go beyond the scope of the library's databases and catalog. A good example is the Digital Library of Georgia, which provides a number of resources, including photographs and documents that chronicle the history of Georgia. This is a project of the University of Georgia, and the collection was recently expanded to include the Civil Rights Digital Library. Both collections are available to the public and to anyone who is not a student at the university, which is a common feature of many such collections.

Chapter 6 examines the types of technology used for remote access to library resources, primarily EZProxy and VPN. Both make it possible for students and faculty to access a library's resources. EZProxy validates the user's identity as a current student or faculty member and provides them with access to a library's resources. Usually, the student or faculty member has to provide a password or other information that authenticates them as a member of the university. EZProxy is used to create links between databases and off-campus or remote access.

Chapter 7 focuses on the inclusion of library materials in course management systems, with the primary focus on embedding materials into online course software. This chapter explores the different course management software currently available, covering both proprietary and open source software for online course management.

Chapter 8 looks at social networks, especially Facebook, as another opportunity to provide remote access to library users. As the popularity and growth of social networks increases, the question arises: do they provide another effective means for libraries to reach their users? As this chapter shows, libraries may not be able to embed copyrighted material into a Facebook page, but social networks can provide opportunities for libraries to promote their electronic resources and provide links for students to access those resources off-campus.

Chapter 9 examines mobile technologies and their implications for library use. Recently the iPhone and other smartphones, tablet devices, and netbooks, for example, provide users with the ability to access the Internet remotely, which means users can access the library's resources anytime anywhere. Users can locate resources and e-mail a link to the article or save it to their device allowing them to access it whenever they need it.

Chapter 10 explores virtual libraries and the new technologies available to access them. The primary focus is on e-books and the technologies available to read them. Every academic library has one or more e- book collections, but even though many reference books are now available in e-format, it remains uncertain whether students really want to use e-book collections. EBSCO recently acquired Netlibrary from OCLC, and e-brary has one of the largest collections of e-books, allowing students to find e-books on any subject. There are, however, limitations to using e-books, which make them frustrating to use.

Chapter 11 examines some of the problems users may encounter with remote access to library collections such as for example, websites that are not compatible with mobile devices, and digital collections that are difficult to search, having to enter multiple passwords to access resources off-campus. The primary focus is security. The chapter explores the types of security used to make sure only authorized user have access to library materials. It also looks at proxy servers and virtual private network securities.

Chapter 12, the conclusion, serves as a summary of the whole volume, while also providing an overview of the opportunities for libraries to improve their service to library users through remote access to electronic resources. The chapter ties together all the previous chapters and explores some of the future possibilities for remote access technologies to provide an increased range of services in libraries across the United States and beyond.

REFERENCES

Beall, J. (2010). How Google uses metadata to improve search results. *The Serials Librarian, 59*(1), 40–53. doi:10.1080/03615260903524222

Suber, P. (2010). *Open access overview*. Retrieved from http://www.earlham.edu/~peters/fos/overview.htm

Acknowledgment

I would like to take this opportunity to thank everyone who encouraged me to become an academic librarian, which as a result lead to my writing this book.

First, I would like to thank my family for all their support through graduate school and the start of my second career as a librarian.

I thank the many wonderful faculty members I had in the Library Science program at the University of Buffalo—SUNY, and in particular Judith Robinson and John Ellison.

I thank Jenny Lloyd, a mentor and friend, whom encouraged me to apply to the program at the University at Buffalo.

I also want to thank my colleagues and friends whom provided me with feedback and encouragement as I wrote this book.

Finally, I want to thank my good friend and colleague Danilo Baylen whom encouraged me the entire year I worked on this book. His support, encouragement, and feedback were invaluable and greatly appreciated. You made me laugh and kept me going when I wanted to give up.

Diane M. Fulkerson
University of South Florida Polytechnic Library, USA

November 2011

Chapter 1
Distance Education and Library Services

ABSTRACT

Remote access technologies for library collections are the result of the growth of distance education programs in higher education. With the increased demand for online education, students needed a way to access library collections without coming to campus. As technology improved, the ability for students to use a library's database without coming to a physical campus became a reality. Through such technologies as virtual private networks (VPN) and EZProxy, students could use their ID and password to gain access to library collections. Distance education was the driving force behind the need to provide remote access to collections. As a result, students now have the ability to search a library's catalog or find articles in a database without coming to campus, anytime of the day or night. Librarians also have the opportunity to promote library resources and teach synchronous instruction sessions in online classes. Remote access technologies provide students, faculty, and librarians with the opportunity to meet user needs regardless of whether or not they are on campus. This chapter examines the growth of distance education programs at post-secondary schools, a trend expected to continue for the near future.

DOI: 10.4018/978-1-4666-0234-2.ch001

BACKGROUND

The first distance education programs were correspondence courses. Students enrolled in programs for everything from secretarial programs to cosmetology. Students were mailed the course material and assignments were returned to the instructor via mail (Hansen, 2001). Technology played a role in some of the forms of distance education. The development of the Linnebach lantern made possible the projection of images in public lecture tent shows. With the development of the phonograph and recorded sound after World War I university owned radio stations broadcast educational programs. The advent of movies with sound provided the opportunity for creation of educational films for training, especially during World War II. With the 1950s came the growth of instructional television courses (Berg, 2010). By 2000, web-based courses replaced correspondence courses. According to the most recent statistics from the National Center for Education Statistics (NCES), in the period from 2006-2007 there were 4,200 postsecondary institutions and 66 percent of the institutions offered some type of online or distance education courses (Department of Education, 2008). According to a report supported by the Alfred P. Sloan Foundation, over 5.6 million students took at least one online course in the fall term of 2008 (Sloan Consortium, 2010b)

Distance education is no longer the exclusive domain of traditional non-profit colleges and universities. In recent years, there has been a rapid growth of for-profit online universities. One of the leading for-profit colleges is Phoenix University. Others include Capella University and Kaplan University. The Department of Defense also offers military online universities such as Air University from the United States Air Force. Many major corporations offer online universities such as McDonald's Hamburger University that provides operation training and develops new leaders. There are also numerous online learning resources providing content for online courses.

MERLOT, the Multimedia Educational Resource for Learning and Online Teaching provides peer-reviewed online course materials. The materials on the MERLOT web site cover a variety of topics and include everything from tutorials to lectures (Rudestam & Schoenholtz-Read, 2010). Students who want to take online courses now have several options. They are no longer tied to traditional non-profit colleges. Regardless of which type of postsecondary institution the student chooses they need access to library materials.

MAIN FOCUS OF THE CHAPTER

Any faculty member who has taught online realizes there is a substantial difference between teaching in a traditional classroom and teaching via the Internet. Keeping the students engaged and on track to complete assignments is one major difference. The other is developing course content and materials to meet different learning styles. Online instructors, depending on the learning management system, have the ability to teach synchronously or asynchronously. The synchronous options works best for teaching students how to search the library's catalog or use their databases. The asynchronous option works best for lectures or tutorials to cover course topics. Online instruction based on a definition from the Sloan Consortium, 2010 report, *Class Difference$: Online Education in the United States, 2010,* "is any course where at least 80 percent of the course work is delivered online"(Sloan Consortium, 2010b, p. 5).

Asynchronous teaching requires the instructor to make their presence known in the online course they are teaching. Their presence is evident through PowerPoint slides, tutorials, discussion boards, assignments and exams. Having a presence in the online asynchronous class is important because students need to be aware the instructor is following their progress and can offer help when they have problems. The instructor's presence in the online course can lead to better student success given the fact students work in isolation from their fellow classmates (Rudestam & Schoenholtz-Read, 2010). Most students prefer asynchronous online classes because it allows them to complete the assignments and read the course material based on their schedule. Many instructors for face-to-face classes will use the course management system to upload lectures, web sites, or other course materials to supplement the textbook and classroom discussions. Students can then review the material if they missed a class. In addition to uploading additional course material, instructors can also use the course management system for test taking. Course management systems allow instructors to choose and create quizzes and tests (multiple choice or essay exams).

Synchronous online teaching allows students to talk to the instructor and their classmates. The synchronous learning environment provides the opportunity for real-time sharing of information whether through audio or video. For example, in Blackboard and WebCT, instructors have the ability to move students into breakout rooms and provide them with the opportunity for group work. Instructors can include video or audio clips and use webcams during a synchronous class. Even though students are not in a physical classroom, they can experience in-class learning. In order to have a successful synchronous class session, the instructor needs to create a schedule for the sessions to make sure students will attend. Another use of synchronous online teaching is virtual office hours. If students are off-campus or even in another country, synchronous teaching allows instructors to hold online office hours.

There are many benefits for colleges and universities to expand their distance education programs. As classroom space and computer labs or classrooms become more difficult to schedule because of increasing enrollment, online teaching becomes an attractive option for postsecondary schools. It provides students with the classes they need while providing faculty with an opportunity to incorporate new pedagogy into their classes.

Initially students and faculty are moved beyond their comfort zone of teaching and learning in a traditional classroom but online classes provide both with an opportunity to learn new technologies while also getting the needed education (Lei & Gupta, 2010). Students can increase their class participation through discussion boards, blog or wiki postings.

Students who live in rural areas also greatly benefit from distance education as it eliminates the need for them to commute great distances to attend classes. Since libraries with distance education programs are required to provide access to library resources, it is possible the library has a program that sends books through the mail and provides document delivery for articles in journals that are not available electronically. One factor to consider for those wishing to enroll in distance education programs that tuition is higher for distance classes than a class on campus. The additional cost is to cover the technology and other services provided to distance education students. Most universities indicate the cost per credit hour for distance education and face-to-face classes. Colleges and universities that offer a Masters in Business Administration (MBA) program usually provide an online program in addition to their campus program. Online MBA programs attract individuals with a full-time job but need the degree to advance their careers. Online education has given rise to for-profit colleges and universities in recent years, forcing non-profit public and private colleges to compete with them for students.

Not all faculty, believes online classes provide the same quality of education or teaching students receive in a traditional classroom. Some believe it is not an effective way to teach students. The Sloan Consortium Report (2010a) supports this sentiment. "Less than one-third of the chief academic officers who responded to the survey for the Sloan Report indicated their faculty members did not accept the value or legitimacy of online education"(Sloan Consortium, 2010a p. 3). According to the report, this figure has not changed since 2002. The same report found that most academic leaders believed learning outcomes for online classes were weak or inferior compared to the learning outcomes of face-to-face classes (Sloan Consortium, 2010b, and p.10.)

One issue previously raised is that online classes make it easier for students to cheat. Students can have their friends take the exam for them or they can collaborate while taking the exam. On the other hand, it is easy to catch people cheating in online courses. Most course management systems allow you to print exams and assignments making it easy for an instructor to compare answers from students on tests. Instructors can do the same for determining if the student plagiarized materials from a source or another student's work.

Another concern is students not participating in campus events are missing out on the college experience of interacting with their peers and professors. However, most online degree programs are offered at the graduate level and are designed for non-traditional students or working professionals. Rarely is a degree program at the undergraduate level offered completely online. Many distance education courses at the undergraduate level are hybrid classes requiring students to come on campus at different times during the semester for additional instruction beyond the online setting. Such on-campus instruction is not optional and students are required to attend.

In spite of some faculty members disdain for online teaching and learning reports from the U.S. Department of Education and the Sloan Consortium indicate distance education will continue to grow over the next several years. The report *Distance Education at Degree-Granting Postsecondary Institutions: 2006-07* published in 2008 by the Department of Education is based on a survey conducted in the fall of 2007 by the National Center for Education Statistics and had a weighted response rate of 87 percent. For the years 2006-2007 the survey indicated that 66 percent of two and four year Title IV degree granting postsecondary institutions offered some form of

online distance education courses. (Department of Education, 2008 p.2, 5) Of the schools that responded 67 percent indicated they offered distance education courses to provide access to students who may be limited due to work, geography or family situations. A majority of the institutions that responded indicated they developed their credit bearing online courses rather than purchasing them from a commercial vendor or developing them with another post-secondary school (Department of Education, 2008). So what does this mean for the future of online courses and programs? It seems to indicate that students who cannot attend class on campus are in need of online distance education classes and programs. It also indicates that most post-secondary institutions are seeking to increase their online distance course offerings. The report from the Sloan Consortium published in 2010 seems to support the increased demand for online learning.

The Sloan Consortium in 2010 published their report *Learning on Demand: Online Education in the United States, 2009*. At the time the report was published over 4.6 million students were taking at least one online course in the fall of 2008 and there was a 17 percent growth rate for online courses and programs. This report also indicated that the demand for face-to-face classes increased during the economic downturn but the demand for online courses was greater than the demand for face-to-face classes. Of the institutions, surveyed 66 percent indicated an increased demand for new classes and a 73 percent increase in demand for existing online courses. The report also indicated that the majority of students were enrolled in undergraduate classes while only 14 percent were enrolled in graduate classes. (Sloan Consortium 2010a). The economic downturn saw an increase in demand for college courses; unfortunately, most post-secondary institutions saw a decline in their budgets as states struggled to reduce budget deficits.

There are some disadvantages to teaching online. One is learning the course management or learning management software. Until students and faculty learn how to navigate the course software with greater ease, there can be problems or frustrations on both ends. Faculty members can be overwhelmed with messages from students who expect an immediate answer to their questions. Instructors have to adapt or completely change a face-to-face class for the online environment. This can be time consuming. Another issue is keeping students engaged and motivated to submit assignments and participate in online discussions, which requires instructors to create an online presence. This is accomplished through a variety of methods. Some of the methods used are effective course design, facilitating discussions, and direct instruction (Rudestam & Schoenholtz-Read, 2010). Many of these are accomplished through the creation of clearly stated course goals and objectives (Lei & Gupta, 2010).

Some other ways to create a presence in the online environment and make students develop an online learning community is to use the tools available in the learning management software. If the course is synchronous, instructors should take full advantage of the audio and visual tools in the software. In the asynchronous environment, creating breakout (or informal) rooms provide students with an opportunity to collaborate on assignments or class projects. These rooms are utilized in a synchronous class (Rudestam & Schoenholtz-Read, 2010). Utilizing the components of the course management software creates an online presence and a learning environment that will foster a sense of community and engage students in the learning process.

The following question arises: how does distance education affect library collections and access to those collections? Whether students are located on or off-campus, they still need access to library resources. If they cannot come to the library then the library needs to come to them. Distance education requires libraries to provide services to those students located off-campus such as document delivery, mailing books and with

electronic resources providing them with remote access with the use of proxy server and password.

As distance education programs grew in popularity, and numbers, traditional libraries had to change and adapt their services to meet the needs of distance education students. In order to meet the needs of distance education students libraries had to implement remote access capabilities. Students whether they lived on or off-campus needed the ability to access materials from their home or dorm room. According to a 2001 article in *CQ Researcher,* several universities saw an increase in electronically retrieved articles during the 2001 academic year. The University of Idaho had a 350 percent increase over a two-year period and the University at Buffalo during the 1990s had a six-fold increase in spending for electronic resources (Hansen, 2001).

Today almost every library has electronic resources that are accessible remotely. Academic libraries in particular subscribe to numerous subject databases, all of which is accessible remotely on or off-campus. Students can e-mail, print or save the articles they find electronically. Libraries can then track the usage statistics and know how many full-text articles users request. Before the advent of electronic library resources libraries would mail materials to students or students would come to the library to pick up the materials they needed or requested. Students may still be required to come to the library to get books or books may be mailed to them, but articles from many scholarly journals, magazines and newspapers may be obtained electronically.

Almost every college and university in the country provides library services to distance learning students. Many have a distance-learning librarian who works exclusively with distance learners or someone in access services is responsible for handling the requests from distance learners. In a 2005 survey of Association of Research Libraries (ARL) in the United States 21 percent of the libraries that participated in the survey, had a full-time distance librarian. Out of those 62 participating libraries, 35 had a person responsible for working with distance education students and faculty (Yang, 2005). Those librarians provided a variety of services, including the creation of online tutorials or multimedia courses for instructional services to helping distance learning students navigate library resources. Other services included bibliographic instruction, free document delivery, mailing books, and free interlibrary loan services (Yang, 2005). Most of the libraries have a web page designed specifically for distance learning students and faculty (Yang, 2005). In addition to libraries, providing materials through document delivery or ILL resources can be linked through course management systems.

Embedding library material into course management systems (CMS) provides students with access to the library's catalog and databases. Another option allows the instructor to link articles from the databases into the course content. Since all library catalogs are, online and all course management systems provide the option to include links to web pages an instructor can include the link to the library's catalog in their course content. Students can then use the link to search the catalog from the course management system while working on specific assignments. This provides students with the ability to determine if the library has the books, they need or if they will need to obtain them through interlibrary loan. Embedding links to library resources provides students with ready access to the resources they need without having to come to the library. Database articles, however, are a little more difficult to embed into learning management systems. Embedding database articles can result in copyright law violations and this issue will be discussed in Chapter 3. The reason for this is the fair use policy of copyright law. Essentially the faculty member would have to change the articles they embed into their online class every semester because fair use limits the number of copies that can be made of an article or limits the amount of the copyrighted work used in the class. While libraries and archives

can receive exemptions under copyright law for fair use of material, they cannot make multiple copies of an article for an online class or for use in electronic reserves. The copyrighted work must be in a password protected course management or electronic reserve system. This prevents unauthorized users from obtaining access to the materials especially if the article came from one of the university's licensed databases.

Database licenses limit access to current students, faculty and staff of a college or university. In order to embed a database article into a learning management system there needs to be some type of password protection. Without password protection, anyone can access the materials in violation of copyright law and the database licensing agreement. As Susan Gibbons stated in a 2005 article on integration of libraries and course management systems, "libraries need to be where the learning is happening even if this is the virtual environment of a CMS" (Gibbons, 2005 p.12). The CMS (Course Management System) provides libraries with the opportunity to expand their presence beyond their traditional borders and boundaries. The virtual learning environment provides new space for library resources and allows librarians to work with students in the CMS. There are some technological barriers to embedding materials from databases into a CMS. However, those barriers are being eroded thanks to new technological advances.

Anyone who has copied and pasted a link to an article from a database into a citation for a research project knows the link can be quite long. This may still be true but most databases provide persistence links at this point meaning that the link to the article will remain the same. It is a stable URL, that changes allowing a person to access the article again with the same link. Another addition that makes it easier to access articles is the inclusion of a digital object identifier (DOI). The DOI provides persistent identification of digital items on the Internet. According to DOI.org, the information about the digital object may change over time, but the name of the digital object will not. APA citation formatting requires the use of the DOI if one is available for the article or other type of digital object used in a research project.

Other issues raised in regards to embedding library materials into a CMS is the fact students have a difficult time searching multiple databases or resources. The first federated search options provided the ability to search multiple databases but often yielded too many results making it difficult for the user to narrow their search results to a manageable number. Over the course of the last two years, EBSCO introduced their Discovery Service and ProQuest the Summon Service making it easier for users to search a library's entire collection. Another option is Ex Libris's Primo, which allows users to search a library's entire collection including digital repositories. EBSCO's Discovery Service, ProQuest's Summon and Primo can be scaled to the size and needs of each library. The implications for embedding or linking library resources means it will be easier for users to search library collections without having to go through several screens or master different database search interfaces. Think of it as a Google-type search engine for library collections.

One issue that is a source of frustration for students accessing library resources off-campus is the need for multiple sign-ins and passwords. Most course management systems require a user name and password for distance learning students to access course materials or library resources. If there is a link to course reserves, students will need the password to read the course reserve material. Distance learning students may need at least three passwords-- possibly even more-- to gain access to library materials for a distance education course (Gibbons, 2005).

Despite multiple passwords required, it is still possible to link library resources to learning management systems. In order for librarians to embed library resources into course management systems, they need to be pro-active. Librarians have two different methods to incorporate library resources

into online courses. One is to incorporate library services such as virtual reference services and subject or course pathfinders. The second option is to work with specific courses and instructors and remain actively involved each course. This method is embedded librarianship (Black, 2008). Recent scholarship indicates that many libraries are selecting one or both of these methods to include library materials or information into online classes and course management software. Some link resolvers, such as, Metalib from Ex Libris allow libraries to embed materials into course management systems.

Duke University and Auburn University at Montgomery both integrate library resources into their course management systems. The public services librarians at Duke used the results of their 2007 Liquid+® survey to determine if the library's resources were underutilized and the decision was made to link library resources to their learning management system (Daly, 2010). Initially this consisted of including the contact information for the subject librarian and links to library resources for the subject areas. In order to add library resources to the learning management system the librarians requested course builder access to the learning management system. When Duke subscribed to LibGuides, web-based library guide software from Springshare, they designed subject guides they could link in the learning management system (Daly, 2010). Auburn University surveyed the faculty who had a WebCT course on the campus server. The survey allowed faculty to check the library services and resources they wanted linked to their online classes. The library created web pages with information about their resources and collaborated with the Technology Resource Center and the Faculty Development Institute to get the web site integrated into the WebCT course pages (Hightower, Rawl & Schutt, 2008).

Another example of linking library resources to course management systems is Ohio State University's Carmen Library link. The Carmen

Library link is designed to deliver a page of library resources to students through the learning management system. After the library implemented the link, the comments from a student survey indicated they found the link provided easy access to relevant library resources (Black & Blankenship, 2010).

In 2008 the Association of College and Research Libraries (ACRL) Board of Directors approved the *Standards for Distance Learning Library Services.* The underlying premise of the standards is equal access to information for library patrons. The standards provide details and guidelines for libraries to meet the needs of distance learning students. Some of the information includes needs and outcomes assessment, collections and technical requirements. Libraries must also keep documentation on file to indicate they are meeting the standards. Some of the services libraries need to provide are reference, online instruction, access to online resources, access to reserve materials, interlibrary loan and document delivery. (American Library Association, 2006).

Course Management Systems (CMS) provide librarians with the opportunity to provide virtual reference services, embed themselves in an online class, and provide links to relevant library resources for their research. Libraries can embed a link to virtual reference into a CMS. Students will have the opportunity to obtain remote access to library resources through different access points. Virtual reference regardless of the chat reference system used provide librarians and libraries with the opportunity to walk students through obtaining the password to remotely access library materials as well as to teach them how to search a database from off-campus.

Teaching distance education involves numerous types of technology. Students and faculty not only need a computer but also in some instances a web camera, speakers, a microphone, and a headset. Most importantly, to teach or participate as a student in a distance course requires a high-speed Internet connection. The CMS includes chat and whiteboard features and, the ability to

post videos and presentations, and instructors can divide students into groups for group work. Any method of teaching in a classroom can be adapted for the distance-learning environment. Teaching online is just as demanding, if not more so, than teaching in a classroom because students often do not see their instructor, unless you web camera is used, so the instructor needs to create an online presence and engage the students through course materials, online discussions and various assignments. Likewise, an online class can be just as time consuming, if not more so, than a face-to-face class. A rule of thumb is, for a three credit online course the student will need to spend six hours per week completing the work for the online class.

In order to have an effective and engaging online class faculty members need to know how to creatively integrate and use technology in the online environment. Some post-secondary institutions have a center for teaching effectiveness. Unfortunately, not all faculty members receive the necessary training before they start teaching online. According to the Sloan report, 19 percent of the institutions with online courses and programs offer no training to their faculty and just 65 percent of the institutions reported offering internal training programs for faculty (Sloan Consortium 2010a, p.3). Even if the instructor's institution does not offer a class or seminar on instructional design for online classes, there are books, such as, *Teach Beyond Your Reach, Teaching Online and Empowering Online Learning,* and the American Library Association and the Association of College and Research Libraries offer webinars and online class that instructors should take advantage of whenever possible.

The lack of teacher training can lead to poor instructional design and an online class that does not engage students or keeps them motivated. Likewise, a poorly designed course can increase the number of students who drop out of the class, which leads to lower retention in online classes. If a class is properly designed, it will contain all the components of a face-to-face classroom including a syllabus, attendance and participation policies, and learning outcomes or learning objectives. Students in an online class should know at the start of the semester the instructor's expectations of them as students. It is the instructor's responsibility to work with students who fail to complete assignments on time; or appear to have stopped logging into the CMS.

Distance learning students can also obtain reference services through remote access. Almost every library uses some form of chat reference, where students can ask and obtain an answer to a question in real time. There are many options to choose from for virtual reference services. Some of the major chat reference services are Meebo, Ask-A-Librarian, OCLC's QuestionPoint, and Libraryh3lp. Online reference services meet the needs of students both on and off-campus. QuestionPoint from provides 24 hour-a-day chat reference services to students. Each library using the service must provide a set number of reference hours for their home institution; in addition, they must provide a set number of hours each week for the cooperative where they answer questions for colleges and universities from around the country.

Libraryh3lp (http://libraryh3lp.com/docs/h3lp) provides both instant messaging and web chat services to users. It is also mobile device friendly, allowing students to text the library's phone number for help. The software has an easy to use interface and is ADA compliant. Virtual reference services like remote access to library resources are the rule rather than the exception. Every academic and many public libraries offer some form of virtual reference services. The 24 hour-a-day option QuestionPoint is convenient because many students working in the early hours of the morning have someone they can contact for help. If the librarian who takes the question cannot answer it during the chat session, the question is sent to a librarian at the student's university and they can follow-up with the student to provide further assistance. With the increase in mobile devices, especially smart phones, texting will be the next option for reference services that will increase both demand and use.

While still used, blogs are being replaced with wikis and social networking sites especially Facebook. RSS feeds also still exist, but many organizations and corporations are now mostly using Facebook to update information on their products and services to reach their perspective clients and audiences. Social network sites can already replace the discussion board in a course management system. Students can use it for group work more effectively rather than having to post to a discussion board. As mentioned previously, the one problem with social networking sites is providing links to copyright protected material, which could lead to violations of not only copyright laws but also the licensing agreement with the database publisher.

Faculty use wikis to supplement the CMS because of the ease to create and update assignments and the syllabus. Faculty can post their syllabus and assignments to the wiki as well as create a space for group work or discussion. One difference between wikis and CMS is the ease to update. While many CMSs require you to upload files from a computer or use their platform to develop course materials, wikis make it easy to cut and paste material or to add an attachment for the class. The faculty member can provide the students the link and students, by creating an account; have access to update or change the existing wiki.

The reality is that most faculty members who teach online use a combination of course management systems, blogs, and wikis to deliver course materials to their students. Course management systems are currently the primary method for embedding library services into an online class. The software is used to create a link to library resources and information on how to contact the librarian who works with that particular subject area. Since most CMSs require a password for access, current students of the school may only use resources from the library's licensed databases. Blogs and wikis, on the other hand, allow faculty members to create group projects and group study space that is easier to access than via the CMS. Further, they also allow the instructor to quickly change, add, or delete materials for the course. They have potential for use as a method for electronic portfolios for students to store all their work related to a particular course or major.

Most course management systems have a link to software that provides users with the ability to meet virtually in real time. Some examples of this type of software are Wimba, Elluminate, Adobe Connect and Skype. Regardless of the software, used synchronous instruction allows librarians to demonstrate how to access electronic resources remotely and provide links to electronic resources. During a synchronous instruction session, students have the opportunity to either ask questions through a chat feature or sound feature of the software allowing them to have hands-on participation during the class. Another benefit of synchronous instruction is the ability to record the session and an archive of the session is available in the CMS. The librarian can send the link to the archive directly to the professor, who can post it in the CMS. Students' who were unable to attend can watch the session at a later time or students who did participate can use it as a refresher.

Another aspect regarding distance education (and consequently remote access to library resources) not to overlook is accreditation standards. In other words, the question to ask is, what are the requirements from accrediting agencies such as for example, the Southern Association of Colleges and Schools (SACS) or the Middle States Commission on Higher Education for an institution to receive accreditation in order to qualify for federal funding. When an institution comes up for accreditation it is required to provide specific information on whether it meets the needs of the students both personally and academically. Everything from counseling services to library services is included. The library needs to provide information about

meeting the needs of distance education students, especially those enrolled in completely online programs. Programs or services that do not fully meet the students' needs, particularly when it comes to academics, are noted in the final report from the accrediting agency. The institution is then required to correct the problem. SACS, for example, has specific accreditation standards for distance education students, programs and library services. (It may be accessed online here: http://www.sacscoc.org/pdf/Distance%20and%20correspondence%20policy%20final.pdf)

The accreditation standard clearly states that schools need to provide not only access to library materials but that they also need to make sure the distance student can effectively use those materials. In order to comply with this, accrediting agencies requires each school to have a librarian or someone in access services devoted entirely to the needs of distance students. Services could include anything from document delivery, to mailing out books, but the most important service is training students how to gain access to library resources without having to set foot in the physical library. Video tutorials can walk students through the process of how to obtain the password and connect remotely. Libraries can also post written instructions on the library's web site.

FUTURE TRENDS

Based on recent reports and studies by the U.S. Department of Education and the Sloan Consortium distance education will continue to grow in the coming years. As a result, technology for distance education courses will continue to improve and new methods for instruction and delivery of course material will surface. The use of wikis and social networking sites will see continued growth for use in online courses. In addition, there will also be new or vastly improved course or learning management systems. The current proprietary systems available such as WebCT and Blackboard use a Java-based platform that can be difficult for both students and faculty to navigate. Students using WebCT often complain they have a difficult time uploading assignments or opening materials in the course pages. Systems such as, Moodle are becoming more popular and will continue to grow owing to their easy-to- use interface, robust features of its modular based system allowing for easy customization when compared to other proprietary systems.

If the number of students in online programs continues to increase at current rates of approximately 13 percent a year (Sloan Consortium, 2010b); this will have a significant impact on institutions. Faculty will need adequate training in instructional design for online courses and universities will need to consider adding faculty to teach in online programs, especially for those programs offered exclusively online. The growth of online programs over the next several will have a significant impact over the next years. Instead of one librarian or paraprofessional providing services to distance learning students the library may create a distance library services department, consisting of at least two and possibly more people with the responsibility to meet the growing virtual needs of those students.

Libraries will need to improve the methods currently provided to help students take full advantage of library resources. Connecting to online resources should not require the student to enter multiple passwords to connect to library materials. The links provided on library web sites for distance library services should indicate how to connect to library resources and start the research process. The University of Florida link (http://guides.uflib.ufl.edu/distancelearners) provides a PDF brochure about their distance learning services that students can print or save to their computer or flash drive. Brochures of this nature provide students with an online guide for off-campus access to library resources.

Libraries will need to continue to adapt to the needs of distance education students. They will also need to determine how to use social media and similar software to their advantage. The information commons model adopted by libraries has done much to attract students to come into the library and study or work on group projects. Libraries need to recognize that as distance education enrollment increases they need to find a way to make sure those students are not forgotten and their needs are go unfulfilled.

Discovery tools such as, Primo, Summon and Discovery Service will continue to grow in use in academic libraries. Mobile applications for databases will also grow. Whatever can be accessed off-campus from a home computer will need to be adapted for mobile technologies. Adapting database interfaces, for mobile devices, will make it easier for students and faculty to search through library resources when they need them and access information from different types of mobile technology. The implications for library collections are significant. Technology for mobile devices will probably lead to increased use of electronic resources while print collections and resources will continue to see a decline in their use. All this also implies that the number of students who will physically need to be at the library to do research will continue to dwindle. Therefore, academic libraries will need to offer more services beyond books, journals, a café and a quiet place to study to attract students to the confines of their walls. Academic libraries will never cease to exist because many campuses are positioning their library to be the center of the academic community, but remote access of their materials will increase and their physical space will become quiet study space and more.

CONCLUSION

Distance education began as correspondence courses. Students paid money to take classes at a college or university and the assignments and course materials were mailed to them. When they completed their assignment or exam they mailed, the material back to the school. It was a time-consuming process and if they had questions along the way, they needed to send a letter back to the school, or as time progressed, they would reach out to the instructor directly. With the development of the Internet and affordable computers, distance education classes moved from a paper format and correspondence courses to a completely online environment. Instead of waiting for days to receive new material for their class, materials were received the same day. Students no longer had to send their instructor a letter or call if they had a question, they could send them an e-mail and, once again, receive an answer the same day. Course management systems provided instructors with the ability to place course materials in one place and a method for students to submit assignments and exams back to the instructor. As course management systems improved, the types of materials instructors can upload also changed. Instructors were no longer limited to paper materials. They had other options including web sites, podcasts and videos. Then discussion boards were added and, the ability to teach synchronously, and provide students with the ability to work in groups on a project.

The growth of distance learning will increase demand for remote access to library resources. As more resources became available electronically, students access to the library's collection without having to be physically present at the library. Allowing students and faculty to access library materials remotely provides students with the opportunity to work on a research project anytime of the day or night, which can increase their overall productivity as learners. As technology improves and grows in the coming years, students will have more resources to select from and use. In addition to the many databases offered by the library, there will be new opportunities for students, faculty, staff, community members and alumni to use digital collections, institutional repositories

and electronic dissertations and theses by other scholars and peers.

Libraries already see more Internet activity to their web sites and electronic resources than 10 years ago. In order to meet this increased demand, libraries will need to make sure they have the information technology infrastructure as well as the staff to, to meet the demands of the distance-learning students. The types of services they offer will depend on the programs and courses offered by their institution. A completely online degree program may require the librarian be embedded in the program, and offer library instruction synchronously to students. Other online degree programs provide more flexibility, such as those that may require students to come to campus at the start of the semester, and then, after the initial meeting with other classmates are not required to be on campus anymore. In those cases, students may have an appointment with an instructor occasionally but do not regularly come to campus. Students in hybrid classes are required to come to campus a number of times during the semester and the number of times they are on campus is determined by the instructor. In those cases, the instructor may require students to use the library when on campus and will include an instruction session with the students and the librarian, so that they had better understand how to access materials when they go home. Once students receive an instruction session, they have the contact information of the librarian, who they can ask for additional help by contacting them at any time throughout the semester. Another option is remain in contact with the library using the library's virtual reference services.

Every academic library has some type of virtual reference service in place whether through chat, text, e-mail, or instant messaging. The days of needing a physical reference desk to answer students' questions are long gone. At some point in the near future, face-to-face reference services will be on-call rather than a set schedule at a desk in the library. As technology changes and improves, more transactions can be facilitated remotely rather than requiring the student to come into the library. There are exceptions to this. A student with a detailed reference question, which requires them to browse a number of different sources at once or a student working on a thesis or dissertation will need to work face-to-face with a librarian. Detailed or lengthy reference questions do not lend themselves to the virtual environment. However, most chat reference programs allow librarians to copy and paste a URL into the session or links to search results from the catalog or databases. Using all the features available in the chat software will allow librarians to help students or faculty learn how to use the electronic resources available to them.

There are different options available for students to access library resources from an off-campus location. One is by logging into a student portal that allows students to connect remotely to library resources without using multiple passwords. The University of South Florida (USF) is one example of this, where students can log into Blackboard and use the link to USF Libraries to gain access for the library at the campus they attend. It is similar to a virtual private network (VPN) because the system only authenticates them one time and they are only required to enter one user ID and password.

EzProxy is used by most academic libraries to authenticate users who try to access library resources off-campus using a password. Once the password is entered, the user is able to search the electronic licensed resources of the library. If the user stays logged into the session, they will not need to enter the password each time they attempt to access a different database. If they leave the session and come back several hours later, they will be required to enter the password again. Another option is a virtual private network (VPN). EzProxy is the most stable proxy server software available and easiest to configure providing users with seamless off-campus access to library resources.

Virtual private networks (VPN) give the appearance you are working at your desk or on campus. Once you log in using VPN, you will not have to enter any additional passwords because you logged in using an e-mail address or some other form of identification associated with the institution. The information the user provided when they logged in verified them as a person who can be a student, faculty, or staff member of the institution. A VPN is more secure than EzProxy because it requires better authentication of users. EzProxy requires an accurate and up-to-date list of authorized users. If the list is not regularly updated it can result in people no longer affiliated with the institution to gain access to licensed electronic resources. Another problem with EzProxy is it can be hacked into, resulting in unauthorized users gaining access to the libraries licensed resources. Firewalls can help prevent attacks of this nature, but skilled hackers can always find a way around any system.

Libraries can embed links to their web sites through course management systems such as, Blackboard, WebCT, Moodle, and Sakai. An instructor working with the library and librarian associated with their department or program can embed library materials or a link to the library web site through the course management system. Embedded librarian programs serve a dual purpose. The first is to allow the students to work with the librarian through the CMS. They can contact the librarian for help with research for the class and the librarian can recommend sources for the students to use. The librarian will also be able to offer instruction sessions for the students either synchronously or asynchronously. In the end, the students and the library both gain something from the experience. Students get one-on-one library instruction and the library is able to promote and market their resources through the online class. Students then have a way to connect remotely to library resources. While this might not be the best way for all students to connect and use library resources when off-campus it s an option many libraries and students opt for.

The second purpose of embedded librarian programs is to link library resources to students through electronic course reserve. These are materials instructors either link through the course reserve system or submit in print to the library to scan and upload to the course reserve system. If the item is linked electronically, the instructor can use the persistent link from the database. When students log into the course reserve system they will be able to access the article from the database without having to log into the database. Every database provides users with the options to e-mail, print, save or export to a bibliographic management software such as, RefWorks or EndNote. If the student e-mails the article, they have the option of sending a link to the article or if the article is available as a PDF, they can include the PDF in the e-mail. Students can save the PDF version of the article to their computer or flash drive.

Just as instructors need training on how to use CMS and how to be effective teachers and instructional designers, librarians should receive the same training so they can effectively navigate their institution's CMS and work with students through synchronous or asynchronous instruction. They also need to know how to embed links to library resources or provide effective tutorials for students during the semester. If the instructor or librarian's institution does not offer, workshops on how to teach effectively online or instructional design there are many books and online seminars available in lieu of traditional workshops. They can also check with other institutions in the area to see if workshops are offered to faculty outside of the host institution.

The growing importance of digital collections from university archives and special collections should not be overlooked. Since they do not have the same hours as the library, it is often difficult for researchers to use their materials. Digital collections continue to be developed, allowing researchers to have access to materials without needing to go to the archives. Even when an entire collection may not be available online, remote access will provide the researcher with the opportunity to look at some of the material before making an appointment to look at the entire collection at the library. Digitized materials will continue to be more prevalent as libraries, museums, archives and special collections seek grant funding or donor contributions for digitization of resources. This, too, remain an integral part of the topic of remote access technology to library collections.

At some point in the next few years all libraries will have a web site for the mobile web, along with an app for their catalog, and database publishers will provide mobile applications for access to their products (some already do). Researchers-- both students and faculty--will be able to access the materials when and where they want and any time they are in transit. This is an improvement from the days of print materials. Researchers had to use microfilm for newspapers and magazines, or documents from Interlibrary Loan were photocopied. Today documents are scanned and converted into a PDF (portable document format), then e-mailed to the student in a matter of minutes.

While technology provides library users with the ability to access materials 24 hours a day; it can also fail. When technology does not work properly, or a library user cannot connect remotely, the research process becomes highly frustrating. The issue becomes, does the library have the right technology and resources to meet its users' needs? It is imperative for libraries to keep up with what their users want and listen to and act upon their complaints. Over the course of the next several years, libraries will have a tremendous opportunity to make improvements to their information technology infrastructure, and adopt new technologies at their institutions. The new technologies will fit their user's lifestyles as well as research habits. It will require systems librarians to identify technology that will benefit users.

Once new technology is identified, it is important to determine how it will be implemented and, most importantly, what the associated cost will be. In this sluggish economy, libraries need to remain open to all sorts of alternatives, including exploring open- source software or identifying software and other technology that will allow users access to resources without costing the library thousands of dollars each year on subscriptions and maintenance. In today's world of shrinking budgets libraries need to adapt and change, to meet the needs of their users but also to find ways to satisfy those needs without busting their budgets. It is in an exciting and challenging time to work in libraries, and remote access to library resources is just one area where libraries will be able to meet the changing needs of their users. Remote access to library collections will provide them with the opportunity to reach a broader base of patrons and turn their physical space into a more vibrant part of every academic community.

REFERENCES

American Library Association. (2008). Guidelines for distance learning services. Retrieved from http://www.ala.org/ala/mgrps/divs/acrl/standards/guidelinesdistancelearning.cfm

Encyclopædia Britannica. (2011). Distance learning. Retrieved from http://www.britannica.com.ezproxy.lib.usf.edu/EBchecked/topic/1482174/distance-learning

Gibbons, S. (2005). Course management systems. *Library Technology Reports, 41*(3), 12–20.

Hansen, B. (2001, December 7). Distance learning. CQ Researcher, 11, 993-1016. Retrieved from http://library.cqpress.com/cqresearcher/

Lei, S. A., & Gupta, R. K. (2010). College distance education courses: Evaluating benefits and costs from institutional, faculty and students' perspectives. *Education, 130*(4).

National Center for Education Statistics. (2011). Fast facts: How many postsecondary institutions offer distance learning programs? Retrieved from http://nces.ed.gov/fastfacts/display.asp?id=80

Rudestam, K. E., & Schoenholtz-Read, J. (2010). *Handbook of online learning.* Thousand Oaks, CA: SAGE Publications.

Sloan Consortium. (2010a). Learning on demand: Online education in the United States, 2009. Retrieved from http://sloanconsortium.org/publications/survey/learningondemandsr2010

Sloan Consortium. (2010b). Class differences: Online education in the United States, 2010. Retrieved from http://sloanconsortium.org/publications/survey/classdifferences

United States Department of Education. (2008). Distance education at degree-granting postsecondary institutions: 2006-07. Washington, DC: National Center for Education Statistics. Retrieved from http://nces.ed.gov/pubs2009/2009044.pdf

Yang, Z. Y. (2005). Distance education librarians in the US: ARL libraries and library services provided to their distance users. *Journal of Academic Librarianship, 31*(2).

KEY TERMS AND DEFINITIONS

Asynchronous Instruction: The type of instruction in an online course that allows students to read course materials, submit assignments and exams either at their own pace or by the assigned due date.

Bibliographic Management Software: Provides users with the ability to save citations for articles and books. The software formats the citation in the proper format for MLA, APA, Chicago and other format styles. Students can use the stored information to create a bibliography for their research project.

Course Management System (CMS): Software, either proprietary or open source that allows faculty to teach online by providing them with the resources to upload course content, assignments, quizzes and exams. Students use the CMS to submit assignments and exams.

Distance Education: Any course taught completely or partially online.

Synchronous Instruction: The type of instruction using the CMS that simulates an actual classroom allowing students and the instructor to work together in real time.

Virtual Reference Service: Librarians provide research help to users through e-mail, chat or text.

Chapter 2
Meeting User Needs

ABSTRACT

Determining how a library can meet user needs can be accomplished through different methods. Libraries can use focus groups, surveys, or other means of assessment. Liquid+® is a survey available to all academic libraries from the Association of Research Libraries. Most libraries who administer the Liquid+® survey can use the survey results to do additional internal surveys with users or to meet with small groups of users to improve their services.

INTRODUCTION

Libraries now compete with online and digital resources. In order to make sure they are meeting their user needs, they must work with their users to identify areas for improvement and to build on the services they do well. Assessment of library services through surveys and focus groups are two methods available; another assessment is to match library services with the overall strategic plan of the institution. The information obtained through focus groups and user surveys is a way to align the library's strategic plan to meet user needs. Assessment of library services is an ongoing process

DOI: 10.4018/978-1-4666-0234-2.ch002

and provides the library with the opportunity for continuous improvement of their services. Ease of remote access to library resources is one of the services that can and should be assessed on an ongoing basis.

BACKGROUND

Database vendors supply usage statistics to libraries, allowing them to determine not only the number of times the database is used but also the number of full-text results selected by users from their database search results. The combinations of statistics help libraries determine the amount of use for the database. As database subscription costs increase, the usage statistics become important in determining which databases to discontinue versus which ones to keep in the collection. Usage statistics can also be used to determine need and as a way to promote a particular database or service. The statistics combined with user surveys can address gaps in the collection and the need for new services or resources. In the last five years, libraries and other organizations such as, for example, EDUCAUSE, have surveyed or examined how students study and find information. In other words, how they engage in the research process. Other studies have examined student use of federated search options, using LibQUAL+® to identify student and faculty satisfaction, how a catalog interface design can influence catalog use and library service perceptions, and how to improve library services to graduate students.

MAIN FOCUS OF THE CHAPTER

Assessing and meeting the needs of users are the topics of discussion in most academic libraries these days. User-centered and student-centered libraries are the goal of all library renovation projects. The question to answer is; how do libraries know if they are meeting the needs of their users? The only way to know for sure is to ask users directly. In 2007, Georgia Institute of Technology was one of three recipients for the Association of College and Research Libraries (ACRL) annual Excellence in Academic Libraries award. Throughout the design and implementation process, Georgia Tech met with users from across campus to learn about their vision for the library. In the end, numerous focus group sessions and a partnership with Georgia Tech's Office of Information Technology transformed the library into a space that people want to use and come back to day after day (http://www.lita.org/ ala/mgrps/divs/acrl/publications/crlnews/2007/ mar/07awardwinners.cfm).

Robert Fox and Crit Stuart in a 2009 article in *EDUCAUSE Quarterly* provide an in-depth look at the renovation and transformation of the Georgia Tech library through collaborations other departments on campus, students, and faculty (Fox and Stuart, 2009). The renovation of the Georgia Tech library resulted in the creation of an East and West Commons and each of the commons provides different services. The West Commons provides over 100 computer stations, a presentation practice studio and a multimedia center. The West Commons was designed in collaboration with the campus Office of Information Technology (OIT) but without input from students and faculty (Fox & Stuart, 2009). The East Commons was designed and created in collaboration with students and faculty.

The renovation and design of the East Commons at Georgia Tech library used focus groups of students and faculty to obtain information of their needs for the renovated space. A variety of methods was used to solicit ideas and generate discussion about the proposed renovations. Some of the methods used were inviting students and faculty to lunch, focus groups, and affinity focus groups with different populations of students, faculty, and staff, web-based surveys, student advisory council guidance, campus and outside experts to comment on their findings (Fox and Stuart, 2009). Using the different methods provided the library's administration with a list of attributes they wanted in the East Commons. The attributes included for example, mobile chairs and tables, group productivity tools, easily adaptable space, and assistance when they needed it. The result was two collaborative computing areas with 40 workstations and several printers plus comfortable and movable furniture (Fox & Stuart, 2009).

While not every library will win the ACRL Excellence in Academic Libraries award, Georgia Tech has proven how any library can be transformed through collaborative efforts between the library and the user community. Georgia Tech in renovating their library used some of the methods from the University of Rochester study to obtain student input for the renovation. The purpose of the study undertaken by the University of Rochester library was to discover how students complete a research project and use the library. The study is discussed further in this chapter.

One approach to determining if user needs are being met is to use a customer service model to determine how well the library is meeting the needs of users to obtain information. In 2008, a survey was conducted at Purdue University that was based on core questions from the LibQUAL+® survey. The survey used a primary variable of information with independent variables of access, facility, knowledge, and attitude. The results of the survey indicated there was a correlation between the adequacy of access to information and the adequacy of the information sources (Saunders, 2008). The University of Idaho undertook a similar study in 2004. The university used the results of the LibQUAL+® survey to focus on graduate student satisfaction and expectations of the library. The graduate student results were compared to the faculty, staff, and undergraduates at Idaho (Jankowska, Hertel, Young, 2006). Analyzing the survey results by using the graduate students as a benchmark to compare them to undergraduates, faculty, and staff provided the University of Idaho with the opportunity to identify their strengths and weaknesses. It allowed them to make changes to improve the quality of their services to library users and in particular graduate students (Jankowska, Hertel, Young, 2006.).

The University of Notre Dame conducted an internal survey in the spring of 2008 to determine how well the Hesburgh Libraries were meeting the needs of its graduate students. A survey was e-mailed to all 1,861 students and of those students, 920 respondents completed the survey for a response of 49.4 percent. The survey questions focused on various aspects of library services and student access of library resources. When the survey results were analyzed, they indicated the majority of graduate students used the library

for their own research and not that of a faculty member (Creaser, 2006). Over 40 percent of the students found the library to be a useful resource for their research programs and overall the graduate students were generally satisfied with library resources. An analysis of LibQUAL+® survey results at four universities in the United Kingdom indicated users seldom expressed their dissatisfaction with services offered by their library. The analysis did indicate that different user groups required different services from their library and their needs did influence their perception of the services they received (Creaser, 2006).

An examination of the LibQUAL+® survey questions indicated the survey has some strength and weaknesses and its focus on customer service is applicable to libraries, but the survey should expand to examine library effectiveness from an operational perspective. Questions should be included that focus on an academic library's operations, funding, library users, and the users' need for assistance from a librarian (Edgar, 2006). Examining the questions that make up the survey reveals the strengths and weaknesses of each section of the survey. The LibQUAL+® survey instrument is just one of many tools libraries should use when determining user satisfaction and their effectiveness as an academic library. A revision of the survey should focus on the academic library's overall effectiveness in meeting user needs (Edgar, 2006).

Most of the literature focuses on the use of LibQUAL+® to determine library users' satisfaction with library services. As the literature notes, once the survey results are received, libraries then need to do additional internal surveys of users. The survey results provide an opportunity to create focus groups to discuss the services users are dissatisfied with and work together to improve those services. The survey results also provide the library with the opportunity to develop new services to meet user needs. In order to determine what information students are accessing remotely libraries need to examine how they use the catalog, interlibrary loan statistics, and federated searching. A study by the University of Rochester examined a number of factors influencing student research and the use of library resources. Smaller case studies and surveys have examined student use of library services and resources. These smaller studies and surveys conducted at the local level provide libraries with better indicators of user needs and expectations of the library.

One study by two academic libraries in North Carolina replicated the five major questions from the OCLC survey of *Perceptions of Libraries and Information Resources.* The replicated questions focused on the library as place and what students thought was the purpose of the library. The conclusion the two institutions drew from their replicated survey was that their local responses differed from the national survey conducted by OCLC. Overall, the two academic libraries determined it was more important to use local information to determine and assess local needs (Sutton, Bazirjian & Zerwas, 2009).

Whether libraries use surveys or focus groups, they must determine if they are meeting their users' needs. Surveys can provide libraries with information on broad issues or concerns of their users. Focus groups allow libraries the ability to work with small groups of students, faculty, and staff to obtain specific information about library services and user needs. Both methods help libraries improve their services, including remote access to library resources. As people increase their use of mobile devices to access the Internet, libraries and database vendors need to adapt their web sites and resources to be accessible by users through their mobile devices. If libraries and database vendors fail to adapt and recognize the growth of mobile technologies, users will turn to other sources such as Wikipedia or websites for their information needs.

The seminal study on undergraduate research is the 2006 study undertaken by the University of Rochester, which used anthropological and ethnographic methods to examine what students do when they need to write a research paper (Foster and Gibbons, 2007). This study began with a planning session in 2004 and in 2005, the librarians surveyed students at the reference desk. The study is unlike most others because it focused on how students conducted research. It used anthropological and ethnographic methods to explore how undergraduates researched and wrote their papers (Foster & Gibbons, 2007). It went beyond the level of satisfaction with library services because it explored what students thought would be the ideal library space. This survey serves as a benchmark or standard for determining how the students not only conduct research but what they envision would be the best way to utilize library space. The focus of the study was to determine how to create a student-centered library. Most library research focuses on the standard surveys available through the Association of Research Libraries but in this case, the University of Rochester used the library literature and developed a research study that focused on students and student needs (Foster & Gibbons, 2007). The study is important because it is the first to look at how students undertake a research project and how their daily lives influences their research and their use of library resources.

Statistics are another way for libraries to determine if they are meeting the needs of their users. Depending on the size of the library, librarians may use hash marks on a sheet of paper to track the number and types of transactions that take place at the reference desk or other public service areas. Another option is to create a database where staff members can input the transactions. A database will allow the library to collect more information about the transaction. For example, if it was a reference question, the person at the desk can enter the question and the answer they provided along with the amount of time they spent working with the person. There is also software available. Some of the software is open source such as Libstats; others are proprietary, such as RefTracker.

Libstats, originally developed by the University of Wisconsin-Madison, is available through Google groups, and libraries can download the software onto their server. Once the library downloads the software, they can customize it for their institution. The library can determine the question types, patrons, and locations. It allows librarians to enter examples for question types. For instance, if someone is unsure if the question they answered was an instruction question or a research question, they can use the examples provided to help them determine the type of question. Once statistics are gathered, libraries can use them to determine when the library receives the most questions at the public service areas, the types of questions asked, and the amount of time spent with a library user. Using the information provided through statistics helps the library determine staffing needs. Just as database usage, statistics will help libraries determine the most widely used resources.

In 2007 two academic librarians, from different institutions, used the READ Scale (Reference Effort Assessment Data) to analyze over 22,000 transactions from 14 different academic libraries with 170 individual participants. The purpose of the READ Scale is to develop qualitative statistics from a reference transaction. Each reference transaction is assigned a number from one to six, with one being reference transactions that require the least amount of effort and 6 being reference transaction that requires an extensive amount of time and effort to complete (Gerlich & Berard, 2010). Librarians coordinating the study performed a pre-study calibration and submitted sample questions to the libraries participating in the study. This provided the study coordinators with a baseline sample of how the participating libraries graded their reference question transactions.

The participating libraries could make adjustments based on the feedback from the study coordinators. All of the participants elected to participate in the study for three weeks and seven of the institutions elected to continue the study for the entire semester. At the conclusion of the study, the individual participants were given an online survey designed to solicit feedback about using the READ Scale for keeping statistics at the reference desk. The comments received from the study indicated the participants learned a great deal about the types of reference transactions and opportunities to improve training and provide outreach to their subject areas (Gerlich & Berard, 2010).

Two librarians from the University of Colorado at Boulder (UCB) used the results of their LibQUAL+® survey to determine student satisfaction with the electronic resources at the UCB libraries. The purpose of the study was to determine if there was a relationship between the physical space and use of the library and their electronic collections. Students were asked which library they used most often on campus, their subject discipline, and their age. The results concluded students used the libraries' web sites to discover electronic resources and because of study, improvements were made to the web sites to make it easier for students to find electronic resources. In addition to making it easier to discover e-resources, the libraries implemented an open URL resolver to help students find resources either in print or electronically (Gerke & Maness, 2010). The study concluded that there was a correlation between the use of the library's web site and its physical place. The same study also concluded that the physical and virtual spaces of the library worked in direct correlation of each other and students expected they would be able to find the electronic resources they needed through the library's web site as well as the physical library (Gerke & Maness, 2010).

A similar study conducted at Tennessee State University with 30 social sciences and humanities faculty and doctoral students. Through a series of interviews, the faculty and students were questioned about their use of electronic resources for research (Ge, 2010). Xuemei Ge in her study examined a number of electronic resources used for research. She included everything from e-mail to web portals. She also used the information-seeking model created by David Ellis in the 1980s that focused on how social science researchers searched for and interacted with the materials versus how the sources used and how the research obtained them (Ge, 2010). During the interview process, which averaged about an hour per interview, she discussed with the participants their use of electronic resources, their perceptions of print and electronic resources, problems they encountered, how they sought help, and whether they sought information based on the model developed by David Ellis (Ge, 2010). What Ge discovered through the course of her interview was that 96.7 percent of the researchers used the web for research purposes and 90 percent of those interviewed used databases for their research (Ge, 2010). Of the researchers who used the web as a basis for information gathering for their research, 48 percent visited the web daily or multiple times during the day to search for information (Ge, 2010). Most of the respondents used a combination of the web, databases, e-journals, e-mail, and online catalogs to search for information for their research project. Over 50 percent of the researchers indicated their research needs were met through electronic information.

The reason researchers preferred electronic over print sources was because they were easier to use, print, and store, and they could be accessed from any computer from anywhere on or off-campus anytime of the day or night (Ge, 2010). The one factor they cited as an obstacle to using electronic resources was the lack of accessibility (Ge, 2010). While electronic resources are accessible on or off-campus users indicated they could not find full-text articles through the library's databases or could not access the databases because the library's system were down (Ge, 2010). Another issue cited was usability, which focused primarily on finding the necessary resources through the library web site (Ge, 2010). Because of the study, the library at Tennessee State University implemented changes that improved and helped students and faculty use the library's electronic

resources more successfully. One change was implementation of a new online library catalog system, another was a 2007 implementation of an embedded librarian program and orientation classes, offered to new faculty at the start of each semester (Ge, 2010). Another factor improving library services was the growth and development of social networking sites such as Flickr, Facebook, and Twitter (Ge, 2010).

In the spring of 2010, Project Information Literacy compiled a report, based on the survey results from over 8,300 college students on 25 campuses across the United States that examined how college students evaluated and used data in the digital age. Some of the findings from the report indicated that 96 percent of the students used their course readings to find information for research related to their courses, but for everyday life research 95 percent of the respondents used search engines like Google to find the information they needed (Head & Eisenberg, 2010). When asked how they evaluated information from a web site for their courses, 77 percent of the students responded they used the publication date, followed by the author's credentials, the domain of the web site, and the interface design. They used the same criteria when evaluating information for personal use but at lower percentages. Of the students surveyed, only 54 percent reported using the publication date as criteria for evaluating web content. Only 48 percent used the author's credentials to evaluate web content for personal use (Head & Eisenberg, 2010). When asked whom they turned to for help with evaluating web sources for course work, 49 percent reported they asked their instructor for help, but when it was for personal use, 61 percent responded they asked family and friends for help with the evaluation (Head & Eisenberg, 2010).

Students were asked the criteria they used to evaluate library sources versus a source from the web and 67 percent reported they used publication date for library materials versus 77 percent for web sources. When asked if different viewpoints were included or acknowledged in library sources, 50 percent responded it was used as criteria versus 59 percent for web sources. Essentially, students had higher standards for evaluating web sources or content than they did for library sources. Almost two-thirds of the students interviewed stated they used evaluating sources as a way to narrow down the sources they would use for their research project (Head & Eisenberg, 2010).

The survey also asked students about the difficulties they encountered in the research process for both course-related and personal research projects. For course-related research, 84 percent responded they found it difficult to get started and for personal research projects, 41 percent stated it was a matter of filtering irrelevant results (Head & Eisenberg, 2010). The final question of the survey asked participants to state the most important outcome for completing course-related research. Ninety-nine percent stated it was to pass the course. Another 97 percent stated it was to finish the assignment, in order to receive a good grade (Head & Eisenberg, 2010). One of the conclusions drawn from the study and follow-up interviews with students was instructors should emphasize the research process for course-related research projects and students needed to be held accountable for the research they conduct (Head and Eisenberg, 2010).

Database vendors provide their subscribers (i.e., libraries) with usage statistics for licensed products they purchased from the vendor. The statistics usually include the number of times the database was accessed, the number of searches completed, and the number of full-text articles accessed. These usage statistics allow libraries to determine which databases get the most traffic. While these stats do not tell the library who the user was that accessed the information each time, they do provide information on where the database was accessed. When budgets are cut, as they have been during the economic downturn, libraries can and will use the statistics to determine what databases they will continue to subscribe to or

look for lower-cost alternatives if a database is not being used frequently enough. Briefly, statistics provide libraries with a better understanding of what their users need and want when they come to the library.

Three librarians at the University of Illinois-Chicago examined the database usage statistics from 2002-2004 and compared the differences in COUNTER-compliant statistics versus search alert services versus federated searching on vendor supplied search and session data. Most database vendors supplied usage statistics for the e-resources purchased and licensed to the university. However, as the authors discovered in the analysis of the database usage statistics, a consistent methodology for gathering and reporting database usage statistics needs to be used by all vendors (Blecic, Fiscella, Wiberley, Jr., 2007). This led to the creation of Project COUNTER (Counting Online Usage of Networked Electronic Resources) in March 2002. The main purpose was to develop a consistent method for libraries and database vendors to capture and report usage statistics for e-resources licensed to or purchased by the institution.

Consistent reporting of statistics supplied for all databases licensed to a library will provide librarians with better ability to make purchasing decisions for electronic resources. The analysis of database usage statistics by the three librarians from the University of Illinois-Chicago looked at COUNTER compliant statistics versus use statistics supplied by the database vendor. Their research and analysis indicated differences in the vendor specific search counts versus the COUNTER search counts. In other words, the number of searches by database users at the University of Illinois-Chicago supplied by the database vendors did not match the COUNTER-compliant statistics (Blecic, Fiscella, Wiberley, Jr., 2007).

The difference between vendor-supplied statistics and Project COUNTER statistics in part is explained in how different types of database sessions are recorded by the two groups. An example of this is a session that times out after 30 minutes is included in the sessions by Project COUNTER but is not included in the vendor-supplied statistics. Federated searching is another variable that influences the search result statistics. The search results from the use of a federated search such as WebFeat or Metalib indicate an increase in database searches whereas vendor and COUNTER-compliant statistics indicate a lower number of database searches (Blecic, Fiscella, Wiberley, Jr., 2007). With consistent statistics for use of electronic resources, librarians will be able to make informed decisions about electronic resource use and purchases. It will also provide them with the means to compare vendor-supplied statistics with those supplied through Project COUNTER (Blecic, et al., 2007). The conclusion of this analysis by Blecic, Fiscella and Wiberley indicates libraries need to understand what information vendors are reporting in the database usage statistics supplied to them in order to make informed decisions about their electronic resources and how often users access them.

In 2004, Brigham Young University (BYU) conducted a study comparing the use of federated searching by undergraduate students at BYU-Idaho and BYU-Hawaii. The purpose of the study was to determine if undergraduates preferred federated searching of databases versus non-federated searching (Belliston, Howland, Roberts, 2007). Federated searching allows a researcher to search multiple databases at one time and it groups the results by database and relevancy. Some of the better-known federated search engines are WebFeat, 360 Search, and Metalib. Federated searching is sometimes referred to as aggregated searching because it searches multiple databases and aggregates the results. The results from the survey of students indicated they were happy with federated search results versus the non-federated searching, mostly because it took less time to complete their assignments (Belliston, Howland, Roberts, 2007). A similar study conducted at Sam Houston State University in Texas indicated

students will use federated search options but the study also indicated the students had a lower level of satisfaction with the federated search results (Korah & Cassidy, 2010). What does this mean for remote access to library collections? It means that students can use federated search options when they access their library's resources off campus. Most academic libraries include some type of federated search option from their list of databases. Using information provided from the database publishers and from the federated search engine allows libraries to access valuable search statistics.

The University of Notre Dame (ND) used the comments from their 2006 LibQUAL+® survey results to determine student and faculty needs. The comments included statements about accessing library resources from home as well as campus. After the survey was completed, the comments were downloaded into an Excel spreadsheet, and were coded by user group, faculty or student, and their subject discipline (Jones & Kayongo, 2008) coded them. By coding the comments by user group and subject discipline, the ND library was able to find common threads in the comments and group them together (Jones & Kayongo, 2008). The biggest concern for undergraduates was adequate hours of service, for graduate students their primary concern was that the library needed to have the resources for their research either in print or electronically, the primary concern for faculty was the same as it was for graduate students (Jones & Kayongo, 2008). Comments related to the adequate hours of service were the ability to access library resources on or off campus (Jones & Kayongo, 2008). By compiling the comments from the survey and grouping like responses together, librarians were able to meet with student groups and make changes to the library policy to accommodate their needs (Jones & Kayongo, 2008).

This is just a sampling of the many surveys undertaken by librarians over the course of the past seven years. What they all seem to indicate is that access to e-resources does have an impact on research by faculty and students. Another aspect highlighted by some of the studies is the impact the library's web site can have on the ability of researchers to find the electronic resources they need. Once the study or survey is complete, whether it is an in-house survey or LibQUAL+®, it is important for the library to use the results to make improvements. Comments from a survey can provide the library with additional information about users likes or dislikes about library services. One of the biggest mistakes an organization can make is not using the results from a survey to make changes that will enhance services offered to patrons.

Another way to utilize survey results to improve library services is through focus groups. Focus groups usually consist of a small number of students, faculty, and staff who originally participated in the survey. Usually the participants are randomly selected but should be a representative demographic of the institution. Ideally, focus groups should consist of a broad range of ages and disciplines and incorporate a diverse group of students and faculty. Focus group sessions can explore in detail the survey results that indicated areas the library needed to improve in or areas where the library was missing an opportunity to meet the needs of their users. Focus group sessions can be spread out over a series of weeks or days, however, it is important to be mindful and respectful of other obligations students, faculty, and staff have. Their time and commitment are vital to the success of the project.

Often focus groups are broken into smaller groups based on demographics. For example, undergraduate students meet separately from graduate students and faculty members meet separately from staff members. By separating the groups and listing the results from their sessions, it is easier to find common threads or themes in their comments or needs. After the focus group sessions are completed, and the library has identified common areas for improvement and change, a follow-up session can be conducted and potential solutions to the issues needing improvement can be discussed with the focus group members. Feedback from the follow-up session will allow the library to identify ideas or areas not included in their solutions. In addition, users are more than likely to make better use of a service or change in service if they feel they have a stake in the outcome.

Can libraries apply just one method to determine user needs as opposed to several. Libraries could probably use one method, but to obtain the most effective results, libraries should use more than one method. Taking a survey of user habits is a good start, but focus groups allow libraries to further improve or add services at the institutions. Using the survey results without user input may result in less-than-satisfactory results and the library may still offer services that are not entirely meeting their patrons' needs.

FUTURE TRENDS

In order to continue to meet the needs of their users, libraries will continue to rely on surveys and focus groups for patron feedback. The LibQUAL+™ survey developed by the Association of Research Libraries has become the survey all academic libraries use to determine how satisfied students and faculty are with their services. Once the library has the results at hand, they should conduct their surveys to explore in-depth issues related to areas users indicated they were dissatisfied. In the future, the types of questions may change but the survey will continue to be a primary method for libraries to gather information about user needs and satisfaction about their services. Focus groups will continue to be used and will possibly be used largely than surveys because they provide first-hand information from actual users. One challenge with focus groups is it can be time consuming to plan such gatherings in advance and it can get difficult to get participation. However, most libraries offer incentives to prospective participants, such as food during the discussion or gift cards.

In addition to conducting them at the library, librarians may opt to conduct surveys and focus groups online with such tools as Google forms, Survey Monkey, or Zoomerang, which allow them to create their own surveys and send links to them directly to the participants. The same goes for focus groups. Using online meeting software like Wimba, Elluminate, and Adobe Connect librarians can conduct focus groups with participants online to discuss how to improve library services. A Facebook page can also accomplish the same thing. Many libraries have a Facebook page and they can use the students who are friends of the page to create a virtual focus group. Students can leave comments, or start a discussion regarding library services. The library's Facebook page provides a more convenient method to obtain feedback. It can also be used to schedule a focus group event and invitations can be sent to the subscribed users of the page.

Surveys and focus groups will not disappear as means through which librarians obtain valuable feedback from their users in the near future. What will change is the methodology by which they are accomplished. This is especially true for focus groups. Face-to-face meetings in a library room may cease to exist down the line. A much greater emphasis will be placed on "meeting" students where they are (whether at their dorm, in the dining hall, or any other common area), i.e., bringing the survey to them (which is, in essence, another way of meeting their needs). Using technology to work with users is a trend that will continue to grow in popularity. Utilizing social media outlets to conduct focus group meetings will evolve in the future by providing libraries with the ability to connect to users through Facebook, Foursquare, Twitter, LinkedIn and now Google+ as will video conferencing through such popular tools as Skype. To find out what users want and to improve services to users social networks and technology can and will provide the most effective method to connect with users.

Libraries need to learn how to leverage social media sites to meet student research needs. This means much more needs to be done than to merely create a Facebook page or a Flickr site. Libraries need to determine how such Web 2.0 tools can be used to their advantage for training students and faculty to use their resources or for promoting such resources so that patrons are more aware of the library's holdings. Before the library undertakes an initiative to add new technology or change existing technology, libraries need to have a thorough understanding of how students use each new technology.

EDUCAUSE (http://www.educause.edu), a non-profit organization that focuses on the use of information technology in higher education, publishes an annual study of undergraduate students and technology. In 2010, it conducted the *ECAR* (EDUCAUSE Center for Applied Research) *Study of Undergraduate Students and Information Technology,* whose purpose was to examine how students were using technology in higher education and compare responses to previous years to highlight changes and trends in IT use amongst undergraduates. The study's 36,950 participants included freshmen and seniors at 100 four-year institutions in the United States. It also included general students from 24 two-year schools in the United States and Canada. Focus groups consisting of 84 students from four institutions were also included in the survey results (ECAR Study, 2010). The study examined a broad range of information technologies and their use by traditional and non-traditional students. EDUCAUSE divided the technologies used by students for their course work into two groups. The first focused on older PC-based technologies and the second group focused on newer, web-based collaborative technologies. According to the study, a majority of the students used the library's web site and course management software. The study also indicated that 53 percent of the students used some type of cloud computing software such as Google Docs, Zoho, or Microsoft Office Live. The results indicated cloud computing-based applications are becoming more prevalent and more widely used on college campuses (ECAR Study, 2010).

Just as distance education drove the need for remote access to library resources, meeting the user's needs is just as critical to the library's success in achieving the goals of their strategic plan. Involving the user in determining the types of services or access to resources provides libraries with the ability for continuous improvement and user input means the user has a stake in those services and will more than likely use them. The LibQUAL+® survey is the primary survey used by academic libraries to study service quality. Offered through the Association of Research Libraries (ARL), it has been around since 2000 and since its inception, more than 1000 libraries have participated in the survey. Survey participants receive training and support throughout the process. Once the survey is administered and the institution receives the results, it is the responsibility of the library's administration to use the results to improve the quality of their service. One option for improving service quality is to ask users to complete a follow-up survey based on the results received from LibQUAL+®. While this might seem redundant, it will allow the library to ask specific questions about ways to improve their services. The follow-up survey provides the library with the opportunity to use the results of their internal survey to create focus groups. The process can be time-consuming and require a monetary commitment from the library. However, the end results are the library will better serve its community. Surveys not only help improve library services, they can also be combined with other statistics to determine the purchase of electronic resources.

Database publishers provide libraries with usage statistics, which capture the number of searches and full-text article results. An effort is currently under way to provide more consistent recording and reporting of database use statistics through Project COUNTER. Consistent reporting of usage statistics will help libraries determine the databases widely used as opposed to the ones underutilized. It will also help libraries determine the cost per user of a database. While there is still work to do be with Project COUNTER, more database publishers are expected to participate in the future. With improved statistics, libraries will be able to spend their shrinking budgets on the resources users want and need for their research, as opposed to those that get very little to no traffic. This kind of targeted purchasing is important in light of the fact library resources now compete with free Internet sources. Using surveys and focus groups in combination with such vendor-supplied statistics will provide libraries with a much broader picture of the electronic resource landscape.

Two very different studies one from the University of Rochester and the other from Project Information Literacy explored how students conduct research and how they evaluate and use the information they find. The University of Rochester study combined anthropological and ethnographic research methodology using faculty and student interviews, surveys, workshops and mapping diaries, allowing the librarians to develop a better understanding of how students not only conducted research but also to envision the types of features and services they wanted for the library in the future. Research of this nature goes beyond the traditional survey of students because it explores the steps students take for the research process. The study included steps that librarians overlooked such as, for example, where and when they like to study or how they used the Internet. One aspect of the research process librarians did not take into consideration before the start of their study was students discussed their research projects with their parents, even going so far as to provide their parents with a rough draft of their assignments for them to critique (Foster & Gibbons, 2010).

The common thread through all of the various studies is how to make any library more student-centered. At least two of the previous studies mentioned in this chapter used survey results to make changes to their library and its services, both physical and virtual. They did not use the same type of methods as the University of Rochester, but they still focused on meeting student needs and making the library more student-centered, since its services were being more and more based on student feedback and through observation of students' evolving research habits. Because of the survey, which explored the electronic methods, faculty and graduate students used for research projects, Tennessee State University implemented changes that improved services to students and faculty alike.

The survey conducted by Project Information Literacy (PIL), as discussed previously, is important for a number of reasons. The primary reason is it examines how and where students search for information and how they evaluate the sources they select for course-related and personal research. One of the more interesting survey results had to do with how students used different criteria for evaluating sources for course-related versus personal research. Students turned to professors for help evaluating sources for their course-related research but turned to family for help evaluating a source for personal research (Head & Eisenberg, 2010). Students who participated in the study at the University of Rochester, however, indicated they turned to their parents to help them edit their research papers (whereas the students in the PIL study turned to parents for personal research only). In some ways, the answers are not contradictory because if students were surveyed further, the results would probably indicate that course-related research projects are often based on personal interest. Future research studies may help determine how often personal research becomes the topic for a course-related research project.

One of the conclusions drawn from the PIL study is that libraries need to continue be aware of how students access and use information and where they are obtaining help when they cannot find the information they need on their own. The study also took note of the fact that with the ex-ception of Google Docs, most students did not use Web 2.0 tools to collaborate on research projects (Head & Eisenberg, 2010). The most concerning aspect of this study was that it did not really convey how students shared, collaborated, and used the information they found to create new knowledge or information (Head & Eisenberg, 2010).

Librarians and professors have often down-played the significance of free research sources such a Wikipedia, but the truth is that it remains the first place students turn to when they need information about any topic, whether for a course project or their personal research. While academia prohibits its use, it might be time for them to reconsider that idea. It may be more effective to teach students how to properly use Wikipedia and regard it as just one source to be used in conjunc-tion with other sources of information. Studies like PIL point to the need to begin teaching students effective and efficient methods to find informa-tion by teaching them first to recognize reliable sources of information.

CONCLUSION

Understanding the types of resources available for research—whether free or purchased through a vendor or publisher—and understanding where and how students access them is at the core of any discussion related to remote access. This is because electronic resources provide students with the ability to download and store the information on their computer or a flash drive. It does not re-quire them to be physically present at the library or to take up space in their apartment, dorm, or house for copies of articles (or heavy print tomes) they need for research. Needless to add, studies repeatedly point to the fact that students prefer electronic resources to print for their research projects. This means that the library's web site becomes *the* portal through which they access library's e-collection. Students can use that web site to navigate and find the electronic resources they need. Alternatively, they can also use Google Scholar as a basis for finding materials within the library's database. Students or faculty can set their search preferences in Google Scholar to their university library. When they search Google Scholar, it will identify articles located within their library's databases with a link "Find@." Clicking on the link will take them to the link resolver with the databases containing the article.

The number of transactions at the reference desk may be in decline, but the reference desk (as a physical object) will never truly disappear. Students will always need someone there to ask if they have a problem with the copier, a computer, or cannot figure out how to search the catalog or a database while they are at the library. However, over the past several years, virtual reference services have dramatically grown in both size and scope, having already moved from e-mail to instant messaging to chat and now to text messaging. This trend will continue. As technology continues to evolve, so will the methods for libraries to connect with students virtually. With chat reference, for example, students can be sitting across the room or on another floor in the library and chat or text the librarian in the same building to obtain the information they need. They no longer have to leave their seat in the library to get the help they need when they need it. Services such as OCLC's QuestionPoint, for example, already provide users with 24-hour-a-day reference services. All this is another indicator that students want remote access not just to library collections but also to library services.

Statistics are also a vital part of any discussion of remote access. Libraries need statistics to help them determine how their collections are being used and how many reference transactions are conducted daily. Database vendors supply such statistics to the subscribers of their databases, including information about the number of searches, the number of full-text articles accessed, and information on how the database was accessed. Such usage statistics allow libraries to determine if the cost of the database equals the amount of use, it receives (in other words, it helps them determine if they are getting enough bang for their buck). If a resource is underutilized or not used at all, the library can choose to promote the resource to the departments and programs who should be aware of it to help give it another boost, or it can consider not renewing their contract with the vendor when the subscription expires.

In light of the rapid rise in remote access technologies, libraries constantly need to re-valuate not only their services but also their tools. If a library web site is difficult to navigate, electronic resources may be underutilized because patrons may find it a challenge to locate them online. Using a link resolver helps users find the materials they need, especially journal articles, by redirecting their inquiry to the database where it is located, or if it is in print, to the record in the online catalog. Online catalogs are also crucial to helping researchers find resources when they are off campus. Having a link to the catalog in a prominent location on the library's web site will lead users to find books in print, e-journals, and possibly e-books. An online catalog that contains records for electronic resources helps lead researchers to the resources they need.

The PIL study drew attention to the need for information literacy instruction in grades K-12 so students graduate high school with the research and information literacy skills for college. It is important for students to have the necessary research and critical thinking skills when they enter college. How to find and evaluate material for a research project is crucial for the success of the project. Students are mostly concerned with passing a class when undertaking course-related research, but if they do not know how to gain remote access to library resources, their success may be limited, or they may not receive the grade they hoped to receive. Instructing library users on how to access materials remotely is just as important as showing them how to use e-resources. This can be accomplished in many ways. Providing a video tutorial or screen captures with text is one way to help users connect remotely to library resources.

As mentioned previously, the topic of remote access is closely tied to the topic of meeting user needs. In fact, one cannot exist without the other. Using a combination of statistics, surveys, and focus groups help libraries determine areas for improvement. This information can help libraries determine how they will implement changes so that students access their resources remotely without much effort or complication. Sometimes an adequate improvement involves something as simple as changing the library web site or the online catalog's interface.

Studies conducted by organizations such as EDUCAUSE help colleges and universities determine the technologies students use and how they use them for their courses. While not every institution can adopt the technologies to keep up with students, it helps universities to identify technologies students do use or underutilize. For example, course management software (CMS) is used by 90 percent of the students surveyed by EDUCAUSE, yet just a little over 50 percent of those students reported a positive experience with CMS (ECAR Study, 2010). Faculty and students alike from a range of institutions have already reported on CMS not always being user friendly (Chapter 7 discusses the positive and negative aspects of CMS and its impact on remote access to library collections). Still, early adoption of new technology is critical for libraries because it allows them to collaborate with their patrons and, perhaps most importantly, create new knowledge through technology. This has broader implications for higher education because while it can lead to the creation of new knowledge posting copyrighted materials in the CMS can result in copyright issues for the institution.

In order to meet user needs, institutions of higher education need to continue surveying their students or look at surveys from institutions comparable to theirs to determine how to meet the research needs of their users. Meeting user needs is critical to the institution because without periodically surveying the landscape, libraries will miss opportunities to grow, adapt, and change. Students will eventually find other avenues to obtain the information they need for their course-related research and they will turn to someone other than a librarian with their research questions if they feel their library is no longer a reliable place for up-to-the-minute information. With the advent of new technologies like cloud computing, libraries have an opportunity to help students take advantage of this type of technology by showing them how they can share research or other information for group projects. It is also an opportunity for librarians to work with students to get a better understanding of how they use all these emerging technologies.

The use of technology by students, academic libraries, and institutions of higher education needs to be a coordinated effort in order for all sides to take full advantage of what new technologies have to offer. Without a coordinated effort (i.e., without all sides participating in the process; libraries by remaining aware of student habits, students providing necessary feedback, etc.), libraries could find themselves outpaced by their students' knowledge of new technologies. It is true that libraries cannot implement every new technology or Web 2.0 tool. Libraries need to remain aware of what students want and need to help institutions develop a cohesive and comprehensive strategic plan for the implementation of new technologies across campus. This will reap great benefits for students in the end. As for libraries and libraries, it will help keep them an integral (and irreplaceable) part of current and future research in academic and beyond.

REFERENCES

Belliston, J. C., Howland, J. L., & Roberts, B. C. (2007). Undergraduate use of federated searching: A survey of preferences and perceptions of value-added functionality. *College & Research Libraries, 68*(6), 472–486.

Blecic, D. D., Fiscella, J. B., & Wiberly, S. E. Jr. (2007). Measurement of use of electronic resources: Advances in use statistics and innovations in resource functionality. *College & Research Libraries, 68*(1), 26–44.

Creaser, C. (2006). User surveys in academic libraries. *New Review of Academic Librarianship, 12*(1), 1–15. doi:10.1080/13614530600913419

Edgar, W. B. (2006). Questioning Liquid+™ expanding its assessment of academic library effectiveness. *Portal: Libraries and the Academy, 6*(4), 445–465. doi:10.1353/pla.2006.0050

EDUCAUSE Center for Applied Research. (2010). ECAR study of undergraduate students and Information Technology 2010. Retrieved from http://www.educause.edu/Resources/ECARStudyofUndergraduateStuden/217333

Foster, N. F., & Gibbons, S. (Eds.). (2007). *Studying students: The undergraduate research project at the University of Rochester*. Chicago, IL: Association of College and Research Libraries.

Fox, R., & Stuart, C. (2009). Creating learning spaces through collaboration: How one library refined its approach. *EDUCAUSE Quarterly, 32*(1). Retrieved from http://www.educause.edu/EDUCAUSE+Quarterly/EDUCAUSEQuarterlyMagazineVolum/CreatingLearningSpacesThroughC/163850

Ge, X. (2010). Information -seeking behavior in the digital age: A multidisciplinary study of academic researchers. *College & Research Libraries, 71*(5), 435–455.

Gerke, J., & Maness, J. M. (2010). The physical and the virtual: The relationship between the library as place and electronic collections. *College & Research Libraries, 71*(1), 20–31.

Gerlich, B. K., & Beard, L. G. (2010). Testing the validity of the READ scale (Reference Effort Assessment Data) ©: Qualitative statistics for academic reference services. *College & Research Libraries, 71*(2), 116–137.

Head, A. J., & Eisenberg, M. B. (2010). *Lessons learned: How college students seek information in the digital age*. Retrieved from http://projectinfolit.org/pdfs/PILFall2009finalvYR1122009v2.pdf

Jankowska, M. A., Hertel, K., & Young, N. J. (2006). Improving library service quality to graduate students: LibQual+™ survey results in a practical setting. *Portal: Libraries and the Academy, 6*(1), 59–77. doi:10.1353/pla.2006.0005

Jones, S., & Kayonga, J. (2008). Identifying student and faculty needs through LibQual+™: An analysis of qualitative survey comments. *College & Research Libraries, 69*(6), 493–509.

Korah, A., & Cassidy, D. E. (2010). Students and federated searching. *Reference and User Services Quarterly, 49*(4), 325–332.

Saunders, E. S. (2008). Meeting academic needs for information: A customer service approach. *Portal: Libraries and the Academy, 8*(4), 357-371. DOI: 10.1353/pla.0.0020

Sutton, L., Bazirijian, R., & Zerwas, S. (2009). Library perceptions: A study of two universities. *College & Research Libraries, 70*(5), 474–494.

KEY TERMS AND DEFINITIONS

EDUCAUSE: A nonprofit association that explores effective use of technology in higher education.

Federated Searching: A search tool that allows library users to search multiple databases with a single search.

Focus Groups: Groups of library users who meet with library administrators to provide feedback about library services and resources.

Library Student Advisory Council: A representative group of the student population that works with the library to identify opportunities to add or improve library services and resources.

Project Information Literacy: An ongoing study by the University of Washington's Information School to examine the research habits of students enrolled in community colleges and private and public colleges and universities in the U.S.

Surveys: Questionnaires administered either on paper or electronically to library users to determine satisfaction with library services and resources

Chapter 3
Copyright

ABSTRACT

Copyright plays an important role in not only print materials one finds in a library but also the resources accessed from off-campus through online course management systems and electronic, or e-reserves. This chapter provides an overview of copyright as it pertains to remote access of library resources.

INTRODUCTION

The United States Constitution under Article 1 Section 8 makes provision for the creation of copyright protection for authors. With or without the copyright symbol any work that is produced has copyright protection. Copyright grants the author the right to disseminate or make changes to their original work Copyright laws and protections have changed through the years and are often confusing for educators, students and the general public. The concept of fair use is the cause of most problems with copyrighted materials. The underlying premise of fair use allows students or researchers to use copyright protected materials without requesting permission from the author

or creator of the work for research or educational purposes. In the case of electronic reserves and course management systems even with password protection there can still be questions as to whether or not the posting of copyrighted materials violates fair use. This chapter will explore some of the issues surrounding copyright materials as they relate to remote access of library collections.

BACKGROUND

The first copyright law in the United States passed in 1790. The law established author rights to publications, fines for publishing the document without the author's consent (fifty-cents per page) and the length of copyright protection at 14 years. An author, their heirs, or executors could extend

DOI: 10.4018/978-1-4666-0234-2.ch003

the copyright on a document for another 14 years providing they registered the publication again with the copyright office (http://www.copyright.gov/history/1790act.pdf). Through the years as different media were developed the law was amended and the length of copyright protection afforded the author was increased. A change to copyright law extended protection beyond the original 14 years to the life of the author plus 70 years after the author's death for any works created after January 1, 1978 (United States Copyright Office, 2011a). It is the concept of fair use that is the gray area for most users.

There is a fine line between fair use and copyright infringement. For materials available to researchers off-campus this is the where libraries and faculty members can encounter problems. It was the concept of fair use that resulted in the lawsuit against Georgia State University library for copyright infringement. A settlement has yet to be reached in the case but, may be settled in 2012. Another factor pertaining to copyright is distance education and the Technology, Education, and Copyright Harmonization (TEACH) Act. The act allows a broader range of materials for use in distance education courses but, specific criteria must be met by the institution to qualify for TEACH Act exemptions. One of the criteria is use of material must be limited to a "specific number of students in a specific class" (Copyright Clearance Center, 2011a). Copyright law is not user friendly. Most of the current literature indicates there is confusion about copyright law and how to apply it. Remote access to library materials whether through a distance education class, e-reserves, course reserves, or the library's databases must follow the law's requirement for fair use.

MAIN FOCUS OF THE CHAPTER

What is Copyright and why do we need it? Copyright was established with the Constitution of the United States (Article 1, Section 8). The provision provides copyright protection for authors and grants them the right to deny or grant permission for any reproduction, public distribution, display, performance or works derived from the original. The protections afforded to an author or creator of a work is limited and copyright law does allow exceptions for fair use and compulsory license where a set royalty is paid allowing limited use of copyrighted material providing it complies with current copyright law (United States Copyright Office, 2011a). At the time the first copyright law was passed in 1790, there were limited types of publication and mediums of publication. In the intervening 222 years, how and where materials are published has changed substantially. The way we access those publications has undergone radical change. No longer are people restricted to going to a library, bookstore or mapmaker to obtain the material or information they need.

There are numerous electronic resources available. We have e-books, web sites, blogs, wikis, databases, digital collections and virtual libraries. All of the previously mentioned resources are either readily available for free or through a subscription paid to a database vendor. With blogs, wikis and web sites it is important to make sure copyright materials used within those sites are properly cited. Researchers using materials from blogs, wikis, or web sites must cite the source. Using material from the Internet does not mean the information is free, or is not copyright protected. It is a published document and therefore is subject to copyright protection and falls under the fair use for scholarly or personal use.

There are two web sites researchers can use to learn more about copyright. The first is (http://www.copyright.gov/) the U.S. Copyright Office at the Library of Congress. The second and equally informative web site is (http://www.copyright.com/) the Copyright Clearance Center that provides information on obtaining copyright permission. So how does one determine if a publication is in public domain or still under copyright protection? The U.S. Copyright Office website contains a chart with copyright expiration dates. According to their website, any works unpublished or unregistered have a copyright term of life of the author plus 70 years. So as of January 1, 2012 authors of such publications who died before 1942 their works are in the public domain. Works that were registered and published prior to 1923 are in the public domain because the copyright has expired. Anything published and registered from March 1 1989 to 2002 is still under copyright protection for 70 years after the death of the author and if it is a corporate publication, it is 95 years from publication or 120 years after creation whichever expires first (Copyright Office, 2011b). This is why copyright law becomes confusing for librarians, faculty and students. Copyright expiration is based on publication date or date of creation, which results in numerous dates for the expiration of copyright.

There are different types of copyright infringement. The types of copyright infringement are direct, contributory, vicarious and innocent. Direct copyright infringement interferes with the copyright holder's exclusive right of the work (Lipinski, 2006). Contributory infringement is the library or school is not directly involved in copyright infringement but contributes to copyright infringement through their knowledge of inappropriate use of copyrighted materials and therefore held legally responsible for the infringement (Lipinski, 2006). Innocent copyright infringement is the user claims they did not know they were committing copyright infringement (Lipinski, 2006). While this may seem like a specious claim, it often results in the person receiving a reduced penalty for violating copyright law (Lipinski, 2006). Vicarious copyright infringement is the library or similar institution is held accountable for copyright infringement because they were supposed to supervise the activity responsible for copyright infringement (Lipinski, 2006)

The first step to understanding copyright is to know the basics about copyright law. As daunting as that might seem knowing the basics can help libraries make sure they comply with copyright law when providing remote access to copyright protected materials. In a discussion about copyright there are four terms everyone should know because it is the primary components of copyright. The first is copyright. Copyright is the owner's legal right to reproduce, display, transmits, perform and modify a work. In the case of sound recordings, it includes the right to perform the music via digital audio transmission. Copyright exists from the time a work is created in fixed form (United States Copyright Office, 2008).

The second term is exemption. An exemption is an exception to the legal rule and is granted to benefit the public not the individual (Hobbs, 2010). Fair use is the next term and it allows people to use copyrighted material without payment or permission. Most of the material used under the principle of fair use is for scholarship, teaching and learning, or news reports (Hobbs, 2010). The fourth and final term is public domain and it applies to materials no longer under copyright protection (Hobbs, 2010).

Why does copyright cause problems for people doing research or students taking an online class or for a professor teaching online? The confusion is the result of the concept of fair use. If you use the same articles or book chapters semester after semester for an online class is it fair use or an infringement on copyright? A literal interpretation of the TEACH Act indicts you can only use the materials for a "specific number of students enrolled in a specific class" (Copyright Clearance Center, 2011a). Because copyright is complex, it often leads to confusion by educators and students on the "fair use" of materials for research or other course projects.

Fair use of copyright materials is not as simple as it might seem. Even if the material is being used for research or academic purposes does not necessarily mean permission is not required to use the material. There are four criteria used to determine whether the doctrine of fair use applies to the material being used for academic purposes. The first criterion is how the material will be used. Is it being used for commercial purposes or by a nonprofit academic institution for educational purposes? The second criterion is based on the nature of the copyrighted work. What type of work is it? Is it a book, video, audio recording, an article or an image? The type of work will affect fair use of the material. The third criterion is how much of the work will be used in proportion to the size of the original work. The larger the portion of a work that is used in proportion to the size of the original work determines if it complies with fair use. The last criterion is what impact does the use of the copyrighted material have on the value or rather the potential profit from the original work. If the use of material from the original work cuts into the profitability of the original then it will not meet the criteria for fair use (United States Copyright Office, 2009). All four criteria are used to determine if the use of copyrighted material constitutes fair use. If the intended use fails to meet the fair use criteria for in a publication, work or educational use the person or institution can be accused of copyright infringement.

The TEACH Act signed into law by President George W. Bush in 2002 provides improvements in copyright law regarding the use of material for educational purposes. It focused on the areas of distance education and course management systems. Instructors for distance learning classes use some type of course management system to teach the course. These systems allow instructors to provide links to videos, music and articles from licensed electronic resources. The copyright law as written prior to the enactment of the TEACH Act had the potential for instructors to be in violation of copyright law by including such materials in their course management systems. The TEACH Act allows accredited non-profit educational institutions with the right to use copyrighted materials in distance education courses. The law amended sections 110 and 112 of the U.S. Copyright law it exempted certain performances and displays for educational purposes and ephemeral recordings. The amendments to the law do not allow the conversion of analog or print materials into a digital format (American Library Association, 2011).

Some of the other stipulations of the act require the material to be used as part of mediated instructional activities. Its use must be limited to the specific number of students in the class, it must be used with synchronous or asynchronous instruction and last it must not be materials from the textbook or materials intended to be used specifically for online courses (Copyright Clearance Center, 2011a). A key exception under the TEACH Act does not supersede fair use or existing digital license agreements. This is crucial for institutions with distance education courses to make sure they comply with this section of the law. Instructors for distance education courses cannot include materials from course packs, electronic reserves or interlibrary loan. It is also the institutions responsibility to make sure instructors understand the provisions and comply not only with the provisions of the TEACH Act but also with institutional policies regarding the use of copyrighted materials from licensed sources such as databases and fair use of copyrighted materials for educational purposes.

The American Library Association (ALA) created a section within their web site specifically addressing "Distance Education and the TEACH Act." This section provides a history of the legislation but more importantly it lists the benefits and requirements of the TEACH Act and provides information on the duties of policymakers, information technology officers, instructors and the role of librarians in complying with the TEACH Act. The ALA points out the primary benefit of the act are the expanded range of copyrighted works that can be used for distance education courses. One point the ALA notes is educational institutions must have clearly established copyright policies and make those policies available to members of the academic community. Information technology officials at the institution must determine the length of time students will have to access materials transmitted digitally and ensure only students enrolled in the course will have access to the materials. Instructors for distance education courses will have a broader range of materials they can include in their distance education courses (American Library Association, 2011)

The provisions of the TEACH Act, according to the ALA web site, materials from a licensed database or electronic resource may be uploaded to the course management system but, the materials can only be available for a specific period of time. Instructors working in conjunction with the institution's information technology department must implement controls that prevent unauthorized access to copyrighted materials. At the end of the course, the material must be removed from the course management system (American Library Association, 2011). Instructors must work in conjunction with the policymakers and information technology officials to ensure they comply with the law. Finally, yet important, is the role of librarians in this process. The TEACH Act will provide librarians with the opportunity to work with faculty, administrators and information technology staff to create copyright policy for distance education courses. Librarians will also have opportunities to work with faculty to ensure they are in compliance of the law by offering alternative delivery methods for course materials so they are not in violation of the law. Alternative delivery could be expanding electronic reserves, purchasing the material in an alternative format and putting multiple copies of an item on course reserve (American Library Association, 2011)

Librarians could enhance or improve access to databases needed for a distance education course. An example would be working with a database vendor to arrange for additional simultaneous users for a specific period during the semester. If the students are working on a project and the database allows three simultaneous users the library could ask for the number to be doubled, or provide access to all students in the class for

a limited period such as, two weeks, or until the project is completed. The benefits of the TEACH Act will improve the quantity and quality of materials available for instructors and students in distance education. Yes, not all material can be included in the course management system but if administrators, information technology staff, instructors and librarians work together they will be able to craft policies and develop practices that will work for all parties involved while meeting the provisions of the law and improving distance education courses (American Library Association, 2011). Digital materials in the course management systems became the basis of the lawsuit against Georgia State University in the spring of 2008 by Cambridge University Press, Oxford University Press and Sage.

As of this writing the judge in the case has decided the trial against Georgia State University will go forward. The list of allegations against Georgia State University were numerous and included excessive amount of a copyrighted work included under "fair use," no password protection for electronic reserves, excessive portions from copyrighted books downloaded and available every semester through the university's course management system. The lawsuit against Georgia State became a wake-up call for colleges and universities across the country to re-examine their policies and procedures regarding copyrighted materials and their user in course management systems and electronic reserves. By the time this book is published in March of 2012 a decision will probably be rendered in the case.

Even with the provisions from the TEACH Act excessive use of copyrighted material is prohibited. The Copyright Clearance Center has a short five-page white paper that provides guidelines and best practices to use with course management systems. Some of the highlights from the guidelines include using small excerpts from copyrighted materials. Providing links to articles from databases is acceptable providing the users are still at the institution, using materials semester after semester requires a new copyright permission each semester, copyright notices be posted and copyrighted materials must be removed from the course management semester at the end of the semester (Copyright Clearance Center, 2011b)

Copyright law can be confusing and there are a number of requirements and exceptions to the law. When in doubt instructors and even librarians should check their institutions policies before scanning large portions of a book for an electronic reserve. If an instructor asks for the same materials to remain on electronic reserve for the next semester they need to provide the library with new copyright permission documentation. Password protection of materials in course management systems prevents unauthorized users from gaining access to the material; however, the instructor is still responsible for obtaining copyright permission before uploading the material to the course management system. In addition to the guidelines for course management systems the Copyright Clearance Center has, guidelines posted for electronic reserves and interlibrary loan. Like course management systems both of these areas can cause problems for libraries.

The TEACH Act provides libraries with the opportunity to create up-to-date copyright policies. Having up-to-date policies prevents the library and instructors from facing allegations of copyright infringement. While the TEACH Act is not perfect it does make exceptions for some digital materials used in distance education courses. Digital materials are used exclusively in distance education courses and at some point this law will need to be revisited as digital materials become more widely used in on-campus and distance education courses. In addition to keeping up with changes in copyright law it will be important for libraries to keep up with changes in technology to prevent unauthorized users from using copyrighted materials available in distance education and e-reserve systems (Carter, 2008).

Electronic reserves, just like course management systems, allow instructors to place materials in a digital format for students to use for their course work during the semester. Think of electronic reserves as an online version of a course pack. A course pack is usually a collection of articles and/or book chapters copied and compiled for use by students in a class and sold through the institutions bookstore. Copyright permission is required for the materials included and sold in the course pack. The same permissions are required for electronic or e-reserves. Without those permissions, the material be scanned or made available for students through the e-reserve system. The permission must be obtained before the material can be posted in the e-reserve system (Copyright Clearance Center, 2011d).

Many of the rules pertaining to course management systems apply to materials used for e-reserves and that includes using original materials owned by either the library or the instructor. If it is the original work, it should be scanned and used for e-reserve. Another similar guideline between the two systems is the licensing agreement to reuse materials subscribed to by the institution's library. If the subscription stipulates how the material can be re-used and includes e-reserve or course management, systems the institution will not have to pay twice for the right to post materials (Copyright Clearance Center, 2011b).

For interlibrary loan requests the focus should be on the library lending the material as opposed to the library borrowing the material. It is the responsibility of the lending library to ensure the interlibrary loan request complies with copyright law. Some of the key components of complying with copyright law for interlibrary loan include both libraries must be open to researchers from outside the institution or the public. Licensing agreements for licensed materials may include limitations on their reuse. The requests must be evaluated in terms of their purpose. If the material being requested will not be used for personal use, research or scholarship then the request will be denied. A copyright notice should be included with each request and interlibrary loan rights must be negotiated with subscriptions to licensed resources (Copyright Clearance Center, 2011c).

Guidelines from the National Commission on New Technological Uses of Copyright Works (CONTU) require the library to check the date of the publications being requested. Any publication less than five years old is limited to five copies from a single periodical during a calendar year. Anything older than five years is left to the discretion of the lending library to determine the number of copies that can be made during the calendar year. Another requirement under copyright law is borrowing libraries must keep their records of all borrowed materials for three years after the request was made. Once limits are exceeded under CONTU libraries must request permission through the Copyright Clearance Center (Copyright Clearance Center, 2011c).

A survey of the 786 collections and twenty-nine institutions that are part of the Digital Library Federation examined the copyright statements attached to the collections created by the member libraries. When the authors examined the digital collections for copyright statements, they found the statements were inappropriately labeled. They also discovered the statements could be found anywhere in the collection. Slightly more than 50 percent of the collections had copyright statements associated with the collection or located at the item level. What the authors found was the institutions within the Digital Library Federation omitted an important element that would help users understand copyright law and provide them with a better understanding of how to use the materials within the collections. Any library undertaking a digitization project needs to provide a copyright statement indicating who owns the collection, how the material may be used or if the collection is in the public domain and does not have any copyright restrictions. As more libraries undertake digitization projects it will be necessary for them to provide this type of information. Digitization projects create an opportunity for libraries to gain a better and more

thorough understanding of copyright as it pertains to digital resources (Schlosser, 2009).

Along those same lines is the issue of Digital Rights Management or DRM. Digital rights management technology is also referred to as technological protection measures (TPM). A position statement from the American Library Association (ALA) indicates ALA has fundamental disagreements with DRM and its impact on libraries and users. Digital rights management is the result of the Digital Millennium Copyright Act of 1998 (DMCA). The passage of the law had to purposes. One was to address the growth of digital materials and the other was to make the U.S. copyright law conform to the requirements of the World Intellectual Property Organization (WIPO) (American Library Association, 2006).

The law favored copyright holders rather preserving the balance between accesses to information and protecting the copyrighted materials. The passage of DMCA led to the creation of digital rights management and the technologies to prevent their copying and hinder access to the resources. According to the American Library Association (2006), "The purpose of DRM technology is to control access and limit uses of digital works." (Digital Rights Management & Libraries, paragraph 1) The American Library Association's primary concern is the control DRM technology has over consumer use of the work once it has been acquired. Their position is DRM technology alters the relationship between the creators, users and publishers of the work to the detriment of all three groups. This technology will severely restrict libraries and schools to meet the information needs of their users. Digital Rights Management technologies are a by-product of the Digital Millennium Copyright Act of 1998. The law provided for the creation of technological protection measures that would prevent the unauthorized use of digitally created material. One example would be photographs containing the logo of the company that created or owns them or materials in an online digital collection that have the institutions watermark or other logo in the background of the image. Music downloaded from iTunes is another example of material containing DRM technology (American Library Association, 2006).

Digital rights management (DRM) creates a significant problem for libraries because it prevents users from gaining full access to digital resources. The technology used in digital media or materials also prevents users from having full functionality while using the electronic resource. In some instances, they cannot download the item, copy and paste, or print. This form of technology is intended to prevent the pirating of digital materials, especially music and videos but its use in academic resources prevents faculty and students from using materials that would enhance their course work or research (Puckett, 2010). Legitimate use of digital materials within the academic setting is hampered through DRM. Libraries need to address and voice their concerns with digital rights management embedded in digital resources. One way is to voice their concerns to vendors selling digital content embedded with DRM technology. Another way is for libraries to make their users aware of limitations placed on their access and use of digital content because of DRM technology. Libraries need to address this issue because students and faculty (Puckett, 2010) use digital content every day.

The Free Software Foundation (FSF) (http://www.fsf.org/) advocates for free software and media formats. By free software, they mean the freedom of users to download and run the software, make modifications to it, redistribute copies of the software and distribute copies of modified versions of the software created by the user. This organization seeks the removal of DRM from eBooks and movies. Their web site provides an extensive list of free software and a list of campaigns supporting and advocating free software development and implementation. Organizations of this nature while providing alternatives to licensed software and advocating for an end to DRM can also serve as a partner to libraries in their effort to combat the effects of DRM technology limiting access to digital materials. The purpose of an organization such as FSF is to seek an end to DRM technology by the media and entertainment business.

Because of the complexity of copyright law in the United States and other countries in the world it becomes confusing for librarians and their users to determine what constitutes fair use and what does not. Producers of movies and music and other digital materials push for further restrictions on access to digital materials increasing the problems with access to and use of digital materials. Copyright law should be and needs to be re-examined to make it easier to understand for all involved and to reduce the restrictions currently in place to digital materials. In a January 2010 article published in *portal: Libraries and the Academy* the author lists seven steps that would help alleviate the confusion over copyright protection and make it easier for libraries to understand and comply with copyright laws (Smith, 2010).

One of the steps suggested is expanding the exceptions for faculty members, other than those teaching film and media studies classes, with the ability to circumvent the digital rights management technology for digital content used in their classes (Smith, 2010). He also suggests the creation of a "first sale" doctrine for digital materials (Smith, 2010). The doctrine of first sale applies to physical objects such as books, CDs or DVDs (Smith, 2010). An original copy once purchased can be lent multiple times or sold in the second-hand market (Smith, 2010). Materials in digital format cannot be sold or copied because they would fall outside of the scope of the first sale doctrine. The current law protects distributors and publishers of digital materials. It is a way to guarantee their control over sale and distribution of digital content. The author concludes that librarians should advocate more user and library friendly copyright laws (Smith, 2010).

Digital Rights Management has led to digital restrictions management. Essentially libraries, librarians and faculty have numerous restrictions placed on how digital content can be used in courses or electronic reserves or distance education courses. This results in user frustration and limiting the types of digital content or materials that can be used for a class. E-books are just one example of digital rights management technology preventing users from downloading or printing materials from an e-book. A work protected under digital rights management does not have an expiration date like copyrighted materials. At some point, copyrighted materials will enter the public domain not so for software and other digital content protected under DRM. With digital content copyright has become a quagmire in which they continue to struggle to understand what does or does not constitutes fair use.

A 2008 study examined digital rights management use restrictions a library user will encounter while trying to access a digital collection. The types of restrictions were divided into two categories, soft restrictions and hard restrictions (Eschenfelder, 2008). Soft restrictions included extent of use that limits the "suspicious or excessive" patterns of use for a digital collection (Eschenfelder, 2008). Another is restriction by frustration where the user can only print and save portions of the material at one time (Eschenfelder, 2008). It takes several times before they obtain the information they need and increased frustration with the material and resource. Some digital resources place restrictions through warnings in the database leading the user to believe they cannot print or save because they will be in violation of their institution's copyright policy. An example of a hard restriction is the inability to copy and paste text from a digital collection. This seems to be the most prevalent hard restriction in digital collections (Eschenfelder, 2008). Digital rights management technology while clearly intended to protect the intellectual property rights and copyright of publishers and authors becomes a source of frustration and problems for users in the academic community. The restrictions prevent

them from gaining the full use and functionality of the electronic resource they are using. Librarians need to advocate for changes in the law in this area because it hinders access to information (Eschenfelder, 2008).

There are several different types of DRM technology and each is embedded in specific types of media. Each type of media uses a different DRM technology to prevent unauthorized use or access of the digital material. One of the DRM technologies used by the film industry is Advanced Access Content System (AACS) used with HD DVD and Blu-ray discs. This form of technology uses encryption to restrict access and prevent copying of HD DVDs and Blu-ray discs. When the video is played, the player decrypts it. The television employs two different forms of DRM technology known as CableCard standard used by the cable industry to control access by cable television subscribers to the channels that are part of their subscription package. Another DRM technology employed is broadcast flag that requires every HDTV to "obey a stream specification." The stream specification determines whether or not a program can be recorded using a digital video recorder (Wikipedia, 2011).

Audio or music CDs are no longer released with DRM technology. Conversely, all music purchased on the Internet contains DRM technology. Each of the Internet music services employs a different DRM technology and prevents users from downloading music and using it with different types of technology such as Microsoft Media Player or MP3 players. Music purchased through iTunes no longer uses DRM technology. EBooks use DRM technology to prevent printing, copying or sharing of the eBook. Currently there are four e-book formats, Mobipocket, Topaz, ePub and PDF. Each of the formats is used by the different e-book DRM technologies of which there are four. Adobe Adept applies to ePub and PDF format, Fairplay from Apple applies to ePub books and can only be read by its iBooks app on its iOS devices. Barnes & Noble DRM technology uses

Adobe's Adept and Amazon uses an adaptation of Mobipocket DRM technology (Wikipedia, 2011). As you can see, there are a number of different DRM technologies employed by each segment of the media and entertainment industry. Consumers and end users of digital materials all encounter DRM technology of one form or another depending on the media they are using.

The Copyright Clearance Center (CCC) based in Danvers, Massachusetts provides services for libraries, faculty or individuals to obtain copyright permissions for materials. Publishers and authors can license their copyrighted materials with CCC. In turn, CCC keeps track of the permissions requested, collects royalties, and sends payments to the copyright holder. Business and academic institutions can pay an annual licensing fee that will allow them to use copyrighted materials in course packs, reserves, e-reserves and distance education courses. Obtaining an annual license prevents the library from non-compliance with the use of copyrighted materials. Another service recently introduced by CCC is "Get It Now." The service provides academic library patrons with the ability to obtain copies of articles from journals not subscribed to by their institution 24 hours a day and seven days a week. The application is integrated into the interlibrary loan system used by the library or can be integrated into the library's link resolver. Another benefit is this service can be included in the annual license purchased from CCC by the library. Copyright Clearance Center is the source for obtaining licenses to use copyrighted materials and to register copyrighted materials. They do the work of determining the licensing needs for the material and provide libraries with the necessary guarantees they will comply with copyright law (Copyright Clearance Center, 2011e)

Creative Commons on the other hand is a non-profit organization that focuses on digital creativity within copyright law. It works with users to help them develop and use digital materials by providing them with the necessary copyright licenses and tools to use materials from the Internet. They are providing the necessary infrastructure for users to draw from a collective pool of digital content and use it for their projects while at the same time comply with copyright law. The materials they provide can be copied, edited, distributed, and remixed by individuals, corporations and academia (Creative Commons, 2011). This is an alternative to using the Copyright Clearance Center. The materials available under the Creative Commons licenses must be used according to the requirements within the license. If the owner of a Creative Commons license does not approve of the way the content was used by someone the owner can ask his or her name be removed from the derivative work. There are four different types of licenses each with different requirements. The most basic is providing attribution for materials obtained from Creative Commons to prohibiting derivative works based on the original without permission from the creator (Creative Commons, 2011).

Libraries are responsible for ensuring the materials used for reserves, e-reserves and distance education courses comply with copyright law. In order to ensure the library complies with copyright law conversations need to take place across campus with administrators, information technology staff and faculty. Clearly defined policies need to be established and included on the library's web site provide everyone concerned with acceptable and unacceptable use of copyrighted materials. As more digital content is created and used in the academic setting makes it crucial for everyone using copyright protected content to know, understand and comply with copyright law. At some point, libraries will need to advocate for copyright law that provides users with access to the materials and resources they need without fear it was obtained and used in violation of current copyright law. This is one of the premises of the Google Books lawsuit that Google will provide access to copyrighted material and deprive publishers and authors of royalties. Over the course of the next few, months and possibly years it is a lawsuit that once settled could possibly bring about changes in copyright law.

FUTURE TRENDS

Copyright law is not going away anytime soon. A provision for copyright protection was included in the constitution. Unfortunately, it was at a time when there were only printed materials. The growth of digital content and media will result in more challenges and questions as to what constitutes fair use of copyrighted materials. The Digital Millennium Copyright Act brought about a new challenge for libraries in the form of digital rights management (DRM). This technology restricts the use of digital content and limits its use in the academic setting. This is a copyright law supported by the music and video industry because it prevents pirating of music and movies. As technology changes and with the growth of mobile technologies such as the iPod users and libraries will challenge this law.

Mobile technologies bring about new challenges to copyright law. Users will be able to access materials from their phones and can then share that information with others. Students will be able to download an article from a licensed database and store it on their phone. Nothing can prevent them from sharing the article. While DRM cannot be removed from music or videos, it does not prevent the sharing of articles or web content by users. The Library of Congress will have to adapt and change copyright law to meet the growing use of mobile technology and digital content. As we make our way through the 21st century, the Library of Congress will need to expand their list of exceptions for use of copyrighted materials in academic settings.

One area that comes up repeatedly is the use of videos in the classroom through services such as Netflix. Companies who supply videos will need to develop policies for institutional use or create institutional accounts that will allow their videos to be used in academic settings through either classroom use or streaming them to students. Librarians who are often the keepers of copyright information will need to keep up with changes in the law but also share those changes with people across campus. Copyright policies will need to be included in a section on the library's web site. Copyright education classes will become part of new faculty orientation and libraries will need to hold classes for current faculty to remind them of the requirements under existing law and inform them of any changes to the law. Students will be provided with an overview of copyright requirements in library instruction classes and should be directed to the copyright resources available on the library's web site.

Use of the Copyright Clearance Center to obtain licenses and permissions will increase as the types of materials in digital formats grow. Database publishers will need to include contract terms that include remote access for digital content through mobile devices. Nonprofit organizations similar to Creative Commons will grow in size in an effort to make more content available to users. Organizations such as, Creative Commons will challenge copyright law while at the same time promoting the creation of new knowledge and digital materials. The Google Books lawsuit will eventually be settled but, in whose favor is anyone's guess. Google will continue to challenge publishers and authors. They will also collaborate with libraries both public and academic to make sure people have access to information. The copyright laws of the future will be vastly different from current laws. The focus will be on digital content and creation as opposed to print materials.

Creative Commons and the Copyright Clearance Center will continue to grow and their demand for licensing and licensed products from users and libraries alike will increase. Libraries and users will look for a source that can provide them with materials that can be used and remixed to create new knowledge without having the fear of violating someone's copyright protection. Licensing is crucial for using copyrighted material and if colleges risk being sued for copyright violation or infringement they will need to review and revise if necessary their current copyright policies. Libraries will also need to review their processes and procedures for interlibrary loan, reserves, e-reserves and materials used in distance education classes. Librarians will need to make sure they understand copyright restrictions and digital rights management and share their information with their users. User education classes about copyright will increase and be necessary to prevent lawsuits. With increased quantities of digital materials, libraries will need to have the information about copyright to answer their users' questions.

CONCLUSION

Many books and articles have been written about copyright and more will be written as the laws change. This chapter is a brief overview of the many nuances of copyright law and its impact on remote access to library materials. Distance education led to the need for library materials being made available to students when they were off-campus. Off-campus access grew from e-reserves to EZproxy and VPN allowing students access to the library's databases and catalog. Students could access the resources they need using their ID and password. Electronic resources are embedded into online courses through course management systems.

Course management systems allow faculty members to include different types of material, everything from music to videos to articles. The course management system is password protected and allows only currently enrolled students to gain access to the materials. There are other stipulations and requirements for materials used in a course management system as Georgia State University discovered when some of the major academic publishers sued them. This lawsuit is a wake-up call for every college and university using course

management and e-reserve systems and allowing faculty to include copyright protected materials in those systems. One of the allegations against Georgia State was the lack of password protection for their systems. Another issue was the use or re-use of material from one semester to the next by faculty in their online classes and e-reserves.

While this lawsuit makes its way through the courts, it provides other academic libraries around the country the opportunity to re-examine their own copyright policies. As academic libraries look at their policies to determine whether they comply with the fair use doctrine of copyright law they can also review their policies regarding materials faculty can place on reserve or e-reserve. If they find a faculty member reusing the same, materials each semester without obtaining a new permission they are violating copyright law. Most students attending college are digital natives and to them copyright hinder their ability to create projects for the courses. The question becomes when the remixing and reusing of materials becomes a violation of copyright.

Use of copyright materials in course management systems is also tied to intellectual property rights of faculty members who create original content for the online courses. The debate centers around who owns the intellectual property rights to the material within the course management system. The American Association of University Professors (AAUP) supports the faculty in asserting their claim the content created by them for their online classes is their intellectual property and is not owned by the university where they teach. Unfortunately, current copyright law grants the intellectual property rights for materials created for distance education courses to the university. There is no easy solution to this problem and it will require negotiating by both parties at a university to resolve the issue (Kranch, 2008).

One of the Association of College and Research Libraries information literacy standards requires students to use information ethically and legally when incorporating it into their work. The problem becomes for most students is if they take a small portion from one work and a couple of words from another and some images from a web site a small piece of music from a favorite song and mix them together is it really copyright infringement? If the material does no longer resembles the original then they might not be in violation, however, others will say they are because they did not provide proper attribution for the material they used in their digitally remixed project.

Copyright law has serious implications for remote access to library resources. Course management systems and e-reserves are two technologies allowing students to gain access to copyrighted materials. Instructors must work with the library to place materials on e-reserve because articles or book chapters may need to be scanned from originals converted to a PDF then uploaded to the e-reserve or course management system. Password protection to both types of systems prevents unauthorized users from gaining access to the materials. This alone does not mean the university is protected from copyright infringement.

The Copyright Clearance Center noted in their white paper there are other protections that must be taken by instructors and librarians to make sure the material meets the guidelines for fair use and the correct permissions and licenses were obtained. Faculty members cannot reuse the same materials year after year without obtaining a new copyright permission. Copyrighted material must be removed from the system when the semester ends. If the material was in a course management system all copyrighted material must be removed because once the semester ends users are no longer authorized to access it. The same holds true for e-reserves. Students would no longer be considered an authorized user because the semester ended. Another issue is fair use. Distance education has a few more exceptions than reserves or e-reserves because of the TEACH Act. Under this act, there are still restrictions and guidelines that must be met in order comply with copyright law. The TEACH act is more library friendly than other aspects of copyright law (Copyright Clearance Center, 2011b).

The TEACH Act does make a difference for libraries and instructors to provide materials to students in distance education classes. While there are restrictions and limitations, it does provide some expanded rights and uses for distance education courses and their instructors. The American Library Association through their web site provides an excellent overview of the TEACH Act as it relates to distance education. Their web site includes responsibilities for instructors, information technology departments, and librarians. It also includes a section on opportunities for librarians to work with distance education programs.

Digital rights management (DRM) technology in digital content creates numerous problems for librarians and their users. Simply explained DRM is technology embedded in digital content that controls the way the information is used. It controls the functionality available to library users preventing them from unauthorized use of the information. The creator of the content views all users as potential thieves of intellectual property. Digital Millennium Copyright Act (DCMA) of 1998 allowed creators of digital content to embed DRM into their products. The driving force behind this was the movie and music industry in an effort to prevent peer-to-peer file sharing of music or pirated copies of movies. Unfortunately, in an effort to protect their profits they failed to take into consideration the impact it would have on libraries and their users. Digital materials are a large part of library resources and over the next several years, their growth will continue. While the law that enacted DRM will probably not change, in the near future libraries will need to address the problem of DRM and its impact on library resources. Circumventing the technology is not an option because the law includes penalties for anyone who bypasses the technology. There are no exceptions for distance education or remote access.

The original intent of copyright was to protect the works of an author to make sure their works were not reproduced without their consent. In the intervening years, since the first copyright law was passed in 1790 the types of materials produced both in print and digital have grown substantially. The growth of the publication and entertainment industry brought about changes to the copyright laws in the United States and around the world. Changes in the copyright laws have become the means by which publishers, authors and entertainment companies can protect their profits while impeding the right to fair use. One group, The Electronic Frontier Foundation (EFF) (http://www.eff.org/) is working to protect the rights of individuals using digital materials. Their web site provides a wealth of information about a person's rights to use digital material and includes information about copyright laws not only from the United States but also at the international level. The web site covers everything from privacy to fair use. One section includes a checklist of your rights when using a digital book. There are many other examples listed on the EFF web site.

Remote access technologies for library materials need to comply with copyright law provisions. As laws and technologies change, it will be the responsibility of instructors, librarians and information technology departments to make sure they comply with the law. Training for all concerned will be very important. Copyright law affects not just students taking a distance education class but also faculty members who upload course material to course management systems or request the library place an item on reserve in the library or in the library's e-reserve system. Interlibrary loan departments have copyright law requirements they must comply with or they can be accused of copyright infringement. Interlibrary loan has stipulations about the number of copies they can provide from a journal title based on the year it was published. Copyright notices must be included with all interlibrary loan requests. Course reserves and e-reserves also require copyright notices. Libraries should provide copyright notices on their web sites. Ever changing copyright laws and requirements cause problems for libraries, librarians, students and instructors.

The common theme throughout this chapter has been two fold. One is to provide an overview of copyright law and its use in protecting the rights of authors and publishers. The second is to illustrate how copyright laws and protections can hinder access to library resources. With the proliferation of digital materials, laws were changed or new laws passed to protect the copyright holder but also limit access to digital materials. Alternatively, how digital materials are used in the academic environment. The Georgia State University lawsuit currently making its way through the federal court system is just one example of how copyright law was used against an academic institution. The suit alleges the university's policies and procedures regarding the use of copyrighted materials in reserves, e-reserves and course management systems did not comply with current copyright law. As the lawsuit progresses academic libraries across the country will follow it in an effort to ensure they comply with copyright law. The outcome of the lawsuit will construct library copyright policies regarding reserves, e-reserves and materials for online classes. In the meantime, colleges and universities will need to work within the current copyright law to meet the needs of their users.

REFERENCES

American Library Association. (2006). Digital Rights Management. Retrieved from http://www.ala.org/ala/issuesadvocacy/copyright/digital-rights/index.cfm

American Library Association Public Libraries Interest Group. (2011). *Distance education and the TEACH Act.* Retrieved from http://www.ala.org/Template.cfm?Section=DistanceEducationandtheTEACHAct&Template=/ContentManagement/ContentDisplay.cfm&ContentID=25939

Carter, H. V. (2008). Why the Technology, Education, and Copyright Harmonization Act matters to librarians. *Journal of Interlibrary Loan. Document Delivery & Electronic Reserves, 18*(1), 49–56. doi:10.1300/J474v18n01_06

Copyright Clearance Center. (2011a). *The TEACH Act*. Retrieved from http://www.copyright.com/content/dam/cc3/marketing/documents/pdfs/CR-Teach-Act.pdf

Copyright Clearance Center. (2011b). *Using course management systems: Guidelines and best practices for copyright compliance*. Retrieved from http://www.copyright.com/content/dam/cc3/marketing/documents/pdfs/Using-Course-Management-Systems.pdf

Copyright Clearance Center. (2011c). *Interlibrary loan: Copyright guidelines and best practices*. Retrieved from http://www.copyright.com/content/dam/cc3/marketing/documents/pdfs/ILL-Brochure.pdf

Copyright Clearance Center. (2011d). *Using electronic reserves: Guidelines and best practices for copyright compliance*. Retrieved from http://www.copyright.com/content/dam/cc3/marketing/documents/pdfs/Using-Electronic-Reserves.pdf

Copyright Clearance Center. (2011e). *Get it now*. Retrieved from http://www.copyright.com/content/cc3/en/toolbar/productsAndSolutions/getitnow.html

Creative Commons. (2011). *Frequently asked questions*. Retrieved from http://wiki.creativecommons.org/FAQ

Eschenfelder, K. R. (2008). Every library's nightmare? Digital rights management, use restrictions, and licensed scholarly digital resources. *College & Research Libraries, 69*(3), 205–225.

Hobbs, R. (2010). *Copyright clarity: How fair use supports digital learning*. Thousand Oaks, CA: Corwin.

Kranch, D. A. (2008). Who owns online course intellectual property? *The Quarterly Review of Distance Education, 9*(4), 349–356.

Lipinski, T. A. (2006). *The complete copyright liability handbook for librarians and educators*. New York, NY: Neal-Schuman.

Puckett, J. (2010). Digital rights management as information access barrier. *Progressive Librarian, 34/35*, 11–24.

Schlosser, M. (2009). Unless otherwise indicated: A survey of copyright statements on digital library collections. *College & Research Libraries, 70*(4), 371–385.

Smith, K. L. (2010). Copyright renewal for libraries: Seven steps toward a user-friendly law. *Portal: Libraries and the Academy, 10*(1), 5–27. doi:10.1353/pla.0.0089

United States Copyright Office. (2009). *Fair use*. Retrieved from http://www.copyright.gov/fls/fl102.html

United States Copyright Office. (2011a). *Copyright basics*. Retrieved from http://www.copyright.gov/circs/circ1.pdf

United States Copyright Office. (2011b). *Duration of copyright*. Retrieved from http://www.copyright.gov/circs/circ15a.pdf

Wikipedia. (2011). *Digital rights management*. Retrieved June 8, 2011, from http://en.wikipedia.org/w/index.php?title=Digitalrightsmanagement&oldid=432654426

KEY TERMS AND DEFINITIONS

Copyright: The law granting authors the right to deny or grant permission for reproduction, public distribution, display, performance or works derived from their original work. The United States law grants copyright protection for the life of the author plus 70 years.

Course Reserves: Books or other materials placed on reserve for use by an instructor's class. The works placed on course reserve must the original work.

Digital Millennium Copyright Act: This law passed in 1998 made provision for the creation of technological protections to prevent unauthorized use of digitally created materials. It is Public Law number 105-304, 112 Stat. 2860 signed into law on 28 October 1998.

Digital Rights Management: Is the technology encrypted into digital materials preventing unauthorized copying or altering of digital materials.

E-Reserves: The same as course reserves except printed material is scanned into an e-reserve system. The system is password protected. Video materials require the library to purchase streaming rights before it is made available in the e-reserve system.

TEACH Act: Technology, Education, and Copyright Harmonization Act signed into law in 2002 expanded the provisions of existing copyright law for use of copyrighted materials in course management systems.

Chapter 4
Collection Development Policies

ABSTRACT

The collection development policies of the library will determine the types of material included in the collection. Along with those policies are databases licensing agreements that determine who can access the materials and where they can be accessed from. Collection development policies are usually driven by the academic programs of the institution. Digital collections and digital libraries will often be created from materials at the university. Without collection development policies the digital libraries and collections may receive little use because they do not meet the needs of the students or are difficult to access on or off-campus.

INTRODUCTION

All libraries have collection development policies regarding the materials they will include in their collections. For example, some libraries will not purchase textbooks; others may not purchase bestselling books or movies for their circulating collection. Databases are usually purchased based on the academic programs of the institution and may be needed for a particular program's accreditation. Databases include a licensing agreement and the agreement determines who can access the

database. The collection development policies extend to digital collections and libraries. Since many digital collections are based on the resources of special collections or archives and possibly an institutional repository of theses, dissertations, and faculty scholarship, the collection development policy for the digital library will be based on the needs and collections of the institution. Since digital collections may fall outside of database licensing agreements they may be considered open access collections allowing anyone to use the materials. Even with open access materials there should be copyright information provided (See Chapter 3).

DOI: 10.4018/978-1-4666-0234-2.ch004

BACKGROUND

Every library whether it is academic or public has collection development policies that cover print and electronic resources. Contracts between academic libraries and database vendors limit remote and on-campus access to licensed databases to current students, faculty and staff. Many states have a collection of databases available to state residents that can be accessed remotely. For example, the New York State Library databases are accessible to anyone with a valid New York State driver's license. The Alabama Virtual Library uses geo-location technology that authenticates Alabama resident's IP address and allows them to access the resources remotely without the need for a username and password. Access restrictions are a key component of the licensing agreement between the library and the database vendor. The policy regarding access should be posted on the library's web site.

Access policies provide current students and faculty with a clearly defined statement of what is acceptable use versus commercial use of copyrighted materials. There are a variety of licensing agreements for library collections. The licensing agreements are statutory, "shrink-wrap (used for consumer software) and negotiable (Chou & Zhou, 2005. The primary purpose of licensing agreements is for copyright protection and the licensing agreements while necessary often conflict with the purpose of libraries to provide access to information to everyone. Negotiation of licenses is a primary component of making sure users have remote access to library collections. When negotiating the licensing agreement the library staff needs to know the terminology involved and the types of negotiating techniques. Part of the licensing agreement should include clauses for interlibrary loan. When negotiating the licensing agreement or contract interlibrary loan should be part of the agreement from the start of the negotiations rather than later. Another aspect of licensing and copyright protection is digital

images. If a library or publisher has a digital collection of images copyright information and licensing for those images need to clearly state what constitutes fair use.

MAIN FOCUS OF THE CHAPTER

Collection development policies for many libraries were created before digital content from publishers became the norm rather than the exception. Often times they focus on the print collection of books and journals. While those aspects of collection development need to be maintained libraries need to update their policies to include information about digital materials and how they will be purchased and accessed. Collection development focuses on the types of materials to be collected, the scope, and purpose of the collection. The collection development policies usually state they will be used in support of student and faculty research but, the limitations for example, such as, the major academic disciplines of the collection should be included. If it is a major research institution then the focus on the collection may be for doctoral students in some areas but undergraduate in others. Collection development policies should provide users with an idea of the types of resources they can find and use for their area of research.

The first step in creating collection development policies is to build a core collection of books and journals that meet the needs of students in undergraduate core curriculum courses. The materials in the collection to meet the needs of lower level undergraduate students become the basis for determining additional resources for the collection in the various subject disciplines. Another factor to consider is faculty research. If the academic library supports the research of students and faculty the library should collect the seminal works in the area of research for faculty. Collecting for faculty research then extends to student research because faculty will include materials they are familiar with from their graduate research. Electronic resources are part of collection development policies but, they require separate licensing agreements.

There are several key components of any licensing agreement for electronic resources. Most contracts have the same terms and will vary from one database vendor to another (Crawford, 2008). Some of the key terms are user license allowing the library a non-exclusive and non-transferable license to use the database (Crawford, 2008). The authorized use clause of the agreement states how the library can use the database consistent with copyright laws pertaining to fair use (Crawford, 2008). Another clause is restrictions which state what the library cannot do with the database under the agreement. The contract also defines who will be authorized to use the database. Most agreements include currently enrolled full or part-time students, faculty, staff, affiliated researchers, distance learning students, visiting scholars and the general public who are in the library to use its resources (Crawford, 2008).

Delivery and access to the materials in the database are spelled out in the contract. Essentially the product will be in digital format and authorized users will have access to the material as long as the library has a paid subscription to the product (Crawford, 2008). Another aspect of the contract is making sure the library is not responsible for unauthorized use and the agreement should not include any clause that would violate the privacy rights of the users. The terms in the agreement are the only terms that can be enforced if there is a later contract dispute with the vendor (Crawford, 2008). Contract negotiation begins the process of remote access to library collections. It is the contract that defines the authorized users allowed to access the collection on or off-campus. It is the contract that defines how the collection can be accessed and most importantly it determines if there will be perpetual access to materials within the collection. These components are essential for granting remote access to library resources. Unauthorized access to licensed resources can

result in the library not only violating the terms of their licensing agreement but can also be accused of copyright infringement. Most contracts for electronic resources stipulate the resources are to be accessed only by people currently affiliated with the university. Under the agreement they are entitled to fair use of the materials under current copyright law. When an unauthorized user gains access to the licensed resources it is considered a violation of the fair use clause of copyright law. Unauthorized access to licensed resources was one of the accusations in the lawsuit against Georgia State University Libraries in Atlanta, Georgia.

Remote access to library collections begins with the contract or licensing negotiations between the library and the database vendor. The negotiation should include remote access and interlibrary loan clauses because without it library users will have limited access to the collections. A primary reason for licensing agreements is copyright protection. The first of the three most widely used licensing agreements is a statutory or compulsory licensing agreement. This type of agreement allows a library to use copyrighted material with the author's permission and the payment of royalties (Chou & Zhou, 2005). A "shrink-wrap license applies to consumer software such as, Microsoft Office once you open the package you agree to the licensing agreement for the software (Chou & Zhou, 2005). A negotiable license where both parties, in this case a library and a database vendor come to an agreement of terms that are acceptable to both parties (Chou & Zhou, 2005). Libraries and database vendors have conflicting values when it comes to access to information. Librarians support access to information all people to help educate all people. Their doctrine of fair use supports public libraries as educational institutions.

Publishers and database vendors, on the other hand, view fair use as a defense of copyright infringement rather than as the means to provide access of information to all people. In order to access digital resources libraries require a licensing agreement. Without an agreement they would not be able to access the resources and could not provide access to the digital content to their users without an agreement. Interlibrary loan requires the ability of the library to supply digital content to users at other libraries. The conflicting values between librarians and publishers regarding access to resources are an ongoing issue that needs to be addressed. An example is the announcement by EBSCO approximately two years ago that they purchased the exclusive rights to some of the most popular magazines such as, *Time, Forbes, Fortune, and Harvard Business Review*. By acquiring the exclusive rights they are able to charge what the market will bear for libraries to gain access to those materials.

A core value of libraries is providing equal access to information for all users. Database vendors, on the other hand, believe the information should be accessible to library users but, there is a cost associated with the information (Chou & Zhou, 2005). Libraries and in particular academic libraries bear some responsibility for allowing publishers to gain control over large portions of scholarly journals published in the United States and across the world (Chou & Zhou, 2005). As the cost to gain access has risen and libraries have smaller budgets for subscriptions the conflicting values, between libraries and database vendors, become even more apparent (Chou & Zhou, 2005). This phase of shrinking budgets will probably not result in lower prices from publishers but it might result in libraries becoming more creative with providing users access to resources they need while at the same time controlling their costs (Chou & Zhou, 2005).

Interlibrary loan statistics serve another purpose because they can be used by the borrowing library to find the gaps in their collections and purchase materials where they are needed most. Three librarians from the University of Colorado at Boulder completed a study comparing their interlibrary loan statistics with the English language holdings in their circulating collections. The librarians at the end of their study stated they

would gather statistics of this nature every year and provide the information to their subject bibliographers so they could determine what books needed to be purchased. They also plan to use the statistics as a way to determine low circulating items that could be moved to remote storage (Kneivel, Wicht & Silipigni, 2006). Interlibrary loan is another method for determining resources to purchase for the collection. Depending on the interlibrary loan system used by the library it can provide subject librarians with information about the books and journals requested in the subject areas they purchase for. One rule of thumb for subscribing to a journal is if the library requests articles from a journal more than six times they should subscribe to it. The copyright costs will eventually equal the cost of a subscription and at some point it becomes more expensive to continue to request articles through interlibrary loan rather than subscribing to the journal.

Contract negotiations for electronic library resources are critical not only to the library but also to its users. Making sure authorized users are clearly defined in the agreement is important. The group of people authorized to access the database will be included in the technology used to create remote access. For example, if the library uses EzProxy they will know the list of users they need to draw from in order not to exclude users from off-campus access to library resources. However, the Digital Millennium Copyright Act of 1998 included new provisions that must be addressed in contract negotiations for licensed electronic resources.

As Chou and Zhou point out in their article libraries and database vendors have different perspectives on how information should be accessed libraries want a fair use doctrine that supports teaching and research activities while database publishers want a system based on licensing agreements that limit access to only those who have the money to purchase the licensed materials. In other words licensed products go against the core value of libraries of access to information for everyone

(Chou & Zhou, 2005). In some instances the cost can be prohibitive for a library to purchase the digital content. Pricing agreements for licensed products at academic institutions is based on the number of full-time enrolled students. Consortial agreements may help to reduce the cost because larger schools in the agreement would pay a larger share of the cost making the licensed product more affordable for the smaller schools in the agreement.

As library collections, especially in the area of journals, magazines and newspapers, have moved from print to digital database publishers moved from selling information to licensing of information. The licensing of information allows database vendors or information providers to package information. No longer can libraries choose the publications they want to subscribe to (Cotter, et al., 2005). Instead the database vendors provide a list of the resources available in the subscription package they want to purchase. Just as libraries have collection development or acquisition policies for their printed materials they also need policies for their electronic resources (Cotter, et al., 2005). Just as there is a cost associated with print materials there is a cost associated with electronic resources. The cost is based on the type of subscription the library obtains. It can be a bundled subscription where they purchase more than one product or a print and e-journal subscription, or one based on the maximum number of users (Cotter, et al., 2005). Each of the different types of subscriptions has a different cost associated with it. The licensing of information rather than the sale of information is the same as renting property rather than buying property. A number of organizations including the American Library Association and the Association of Research libraries are just two of the many organizations offering help to libraries to negotiate contracts for database licenses (Cotter, et al, 2005).

While many think the Internet will replace libraries it will not. Instead it is just another information resource. The deep web, the part hidden behind firewalls and password protection, is not accessible by using a search engine. Metasearch or federated search tools are designed to search across different databases and provide the results in one location. Search tools of this nature can also search institutional repositories and would be included in the results (Cotter, et al., 2005). While these tools are able to search many resources at once a downfall is users may end up with too many results and are unable to refine the results to a manageable number. Electronic collections and the licensing of information have changed the nature and scope of library collections and their collection policies.

The cost of licensed electronic resources increases every year requiring libraries to budget for those cost increases for electronic and print resources. As a result some journals or databases may have to be eliminated to meet budgetary constraints. A reduction in the number of titles in print coupled with a reduction in access through electronic resources has an impact on collection management and policies. A 2005 article by Karen Hunter of Elsevier, discusses access management issues as they related to electronic resources and collections. Hunter examined the difference in orthodoxies between libraries, librarians and database publishers. She began with the basic orthodoxy that increased use will lead to increased value. As a result of the increased value because of increased use the database vendor sees the opportunity to make more money through the increased value because it means it will continue to be purchased (Hunter, 2005).

Libraries and librarians, on the other hand, want the same functionality and increased content as a result of the increased value or use for the same amount of money (Hunter, 2005). The point Hunter makes throughout her paper is all aspects regarding access to and the cost of information must be examined. The distribution of scholarly materials through database vendors is not going to change. Licensing agreements will continue and open access will grow but not will not provide competition to database vendors that would warrant them reducing their costs. The purpose of Hunter's article was to challenge the orthodoxies and beliefs about licensed resources and the access to materials in the hope of changing the beliefs (Hunter, 2005).

The access to electronic resources leads to new opportunities as Lehigh University discovered when their collection of electronic resources increased. It was an opportunity for them to ensure students knew how to access library resources off-campus. This was especially important for distance education students. Improving access meant improving the library web site and implementing the link resolver SFX. The implementation of SFX and an electronic resource management system (ERMS) led to improved access to off-campus students and effectively using library staff (Wiles-Young, Landesman, & Terrill, 2007).

Contract negotiation for electronic resources is just one part of collection development policies for remote access. Making sure users know how to access the materials and having the technology in place is just as critical. Electronic resources are managed either by the acquisitions or the serials librarian. This person may work in conjunction with the systems librarian to make sure users can find and connect to resources through the library's web site and SFX and EZproxy. (Wiles-Young, Landesman, & Terrill, 2005) It is crucial for contracts for licensed resources indicate who will have access to the material contained in the database. Access should also include providing materials to other institutions through interlibrary loan. As libraries reduce their serials collections interlibrary loan demand will increase as users ask for resources the library does not have in their collection.

Any licensing agreement for vendor databases should include a clause for interlibrary loan. When negotiating a license with database vendor libraries can ask the vendor to include a clause that allows interlibrary loan to supply digital content to other libraries. Libraries might reconsider sub-

scribing to a database if the digital content cannot be provided to other library patrons. The key to provide access to digital content from licensed databases is negotiation. Database vendors will consider reasonable requests from libraries, but if a library does not negotiate a contract that provides remote access and interlibrary loan access to digital content then there will be very limited access to library users (Croft, 2005).

Liblicense software is a free software that can be downloaded from (http://www.library.yale.edu/~llicense/software.shtml)The website provides information on specifying the terms the library will need to meet interlibrary loan requests to database vendors (Croft, 2005) The web site also provides an overview of contract terms and contract examples that can be helpful when negotiating with the database publisher (http://www.library.yale.edu/~llicense/table.shtml) As costs increase negotiations will focus on what is needed versus a bundled package of resources where some may go unused or underutilized.

One issue that has been repeated throughout many of the articles is the issue of perpetual access to a journal. This is particularly important of the journal ceases publication, the library cancels their subscription or the journal is sold or transferred to another publisher. Libraries are left to resolve issues of this nature when they occur. While perpetual access is included in the contract it is not clearly defined. When the contract is canceled will the library still access to the journal? Depending on the wording of the contract the library may have access to the journal (Waller & Bird, 2006). Waller and Bird's article focuses on the creation of the Canadian National Site Licensing Project (CNSLP) whose purpose is to build the infrastructure by licensing online content for all the participating institutions, there were 64 in 1999 when the project began, in the areas of science, technology and medical fields.

The Canadian government has ended the funding and the project is now the Canadian Research Knowledge Network (CRKN). The licenses obtained by CRKN all contain a perpetual access clause in the contracts (Waller & Bird, 2006). In 2005 a survey was conducted of the participating libraries to determine if they were making sure they had perpetual access to the journals they no longer subscribed to or had been sold to another publisher. What the authors discovered through their survey was libraries are not following up on the journals they have perpetual access to but are no longer included in their subscription. This has a tremendous impact on users who are expecting access to the journal when searching off campus only to find they cannot access it. If perpetual access is part of the licensing agreement then libraries need to make sure they have access to the resources in the contract (Waller & Bird, 2006)

The digital age provides challenges and opportunities for collection management. Libraries core belief is access to information for anyone needing it. Open access to scholarly resources is an area librarians have embraced because of the value it provides to the library users. However, because of licensing agreements open access to scholarly materials is limited. Along those same lines information stored digitally can also disappear because of changes in technology both hardware and software. The dissemination of scholarly material has changed through the years. At one time libraries owned the journals in their collection. Through licensing agreements with database vendors libraries now rent their journal collections instead of owning them. Respecting author rights and copyright permissions in addition to determining access to library resources is part of collection management in libraries. In order to meet the needs of users' new approaches and ideas need to be explored to meet the growing demands of library users (Horava, 2010).

Libraries in order to meet user needs will have to redefine collection management practices and policies in the digital world. Some areas for consideration are the purpose of the collection rather than focusing on what the collection is. Libraries will have to determine the media formats they will support. Since they cannot support all formats successfully they will need to focus on the combination of formats that will meet their user needs. Most importantly libraries will need to develop creative partnerships with publishers and vendors. In addition to developing partnerships with vendors and publishers collection librarians will need to develop new skills in order to keep ahead of changes in collection management. Without adapting and changing collection management policies will not keep up or meet the needs of users (Horava, 2010).

Some libraries in an effort to better manage their electronic resources use electronic management tools for their collections. Before libraries implement an electronic management tool for their resources they need to identify the problems that need to be fixed. This is basic project management. Identify the problem areas and you will then be able to select the right tool to fix the problem. In this case it is identifying how to improve your electronic resources and more specifically how to manage access to those resources. Electronic management tools do affect the end user because they standardize access to the library's electronic resources. For the end user they should be able to access electronic resources from different access points and receive the results they want and need from the search of the library's catalog or databases (Emery, 2007). Washington State University Libraries discovered after they implemented an electronic resource management tool it was easier to manage their resources. It also brought about changes in their cataloging and acquisitions procedures and policies established long ago were examined and changed to meet the new workflow. For end users and the library it resulted in the information for electronic resources residing in one system rather than the multiple systems previously in place (Chisman, et al., 2007).

Link resolvers will be discussed further in Chapter 6, also provide end users with access to library resources and in particular through Google Scholar and journal portals. James Madison

University conducted research study with their students and faculty to determine which method or tool worked best for users trying to find journal articles. The research focused on using the library's web site versus using Google Scholar. The result of the study lead to changes in the library's web site making it easier to locate journal articles and it also indicated sites such as Google Scholar can be an effective way for users to find journals for their research (Dixon, et al., 2010).

One of the major factors currently driving collection development policies for electronic resources is price. According the most recent periodicals price survey published in Library Journal both academic and public libraries will need to look at not only their print subscriptions but also their electronic packages. The link to the survey results is below:

http://www.libraryjournal.com/lj/home/890009-264/periodicalspricesurvey2011under.html.csp

Some of the major trends from the survey include, 80 percent of librarians who responded to the survey indicated they were likely to move print with online subscriptions to a completely online subscription and 78 percent of the respondents said they will reduce the number of print journals in their collection. As libraries reduce print subscriptions and re-examine the pricing structure will change to a tiered structure, where pricing is based on the amount of back file included, full-time enrollment, and possibly the Carnegie Classification for the institution (Bosch, Henderson, Klusendorf, 2011). The era of the "Big Deal" where pricing was based on print subscriptions combined with electronic subscriptions is on the decline. Publishers need to re-examine their pricing structure as more publications are available electronically as opposed to print. Budget constraints due to continuing reductions in collection development funding will force libraries to discontinue large journal packages, use more pay-per-view content delivery and provide links to more open access

content (Bosch, Henderson, Klusendorf, 2011). Another factor having an impact on libraries and periodicals cost is the need for mobile content. Tablet devices resulted in the need for e-content availability for periodicals. Many publishers are working to develop the applications (apps) needed for mobile access to content but, the cost of the mobile apps should be included in the subscription cost not an additional charge to libraries. The result of new mobile technologies and their increased use means librarians and publishers need to evolve in order to meet the needs of their users (Bosch, Henderson, Klusendorf, 2011).

FUTURE TRENDS

Collection development policies for electronic resources focus on the key components of authorized users, perpetual access, interlibrary loan and electronic resource management tools. Contract negotiations will no longer focus on large bundled packages of journals or combinations of databases to libraries because of cost. Libraries will look for a package that contains the journals and electronic sources their users need and want. Pricing will become the driving force behind the types of contracts libraries negotiate and the package of journals they will include in the contract. Mobile apps and technology will play a bigger role in how users connect to library resources. Libraries will need to develop their own apps for users to find the resources before they come to the library. No longer will users need a laptop or desktop computer to find materials at a library. The development of mobile technology by publishers could result in libraries paying a higher price for their subscriptions. Print collections of periodicals will decrease as collection development funding and overall library budgets are reduced.

Another trend will be increased use of electronic resource management tools (ERM). Tools of this nature provide libraries with the ability to manage their resources through one interface instead of multiple tools and it will provide user with better and more efficient access to electronic resources. While the initial set-up requires a considerable amount of work by the library staff as must users of ERM reported they were glad to make the switch because it provided them with better control of their electronic resources and the users had only one access point for electronic resources.

As libraries reduce the size of their periodicals collections both in print and electronically it will be important for libraries to include interlibrary loan access. Libraries will need to make sure they can borrow or lend the content users need. Increased pricing will force libraries to look for alternative methods to provide their users with the necessary resources. Open access materials included in the list of licensed electronic resources may increase as one option for libraries. Another option will be requiring users to pay for material they need for research. Free document delivery will become a thing of the past. The services once provided for free by libraries in the near future may have a cost associated with them. With the changes in price structure away from the big deal to a tiered approach and the reduction in budgets for collections and in particular periodicals libraries will need to evolve and make changes to meet the needs of their users.

CONCLUSION

Collection development policies for remote access to library resources require two key components; one is a clear definition in the contract of who is authorized to access the resources in the collection and the second is delivery and access of the materials within the collection. Authorized users can be anyone associated with the institution including visiting scholars and people from the community who are physically in the library to use its resources. The library is responsible for determining only authorized users from using their

electronic resources but they cannot guarantee that unauthorized use will not take place because someone gave the password or their ID to a friend or family member. Delivery and access to the collection is important for two primary reasons. One is to make sure users can access the collection on or off-campus and the second is material can be loaned through interlibrary loan. Most databases provide remote access to collections and it is a rare occasion when users cannot access a resource remotely. If the database cannot be accessed remotely then document delivery needs to be available, especially for distance education students. Document delivery, where the document is downloaded or scanned and then sent to the student as a PDF or some other electronic method. The access to information is an integral part of the core values and beliefs of librarians, however, that belief is often counter to the belief and purpose of the profit making publisher.

Karen Hunter, from Elsevier, in her article works through a list of long held beliefs within the library community that need to be reconsidered by librarians. One of these beliefs is libraries should have the same level of access from one year to the next with their electronic resources without an increase in price from the publisher. While this is nice, alas it will not happen in the immediate future. In fact the cost of journal subscriptions, both print and electronic, have increased every year for the past several years. Now as states reduce funding to state supported public and academic libraries it will force libraries to reduce costs again by reducing their periodical subscriptions, and in turn will lead to new pricing models and different forms of access to periodicals.

Collection development policies and the increase cost of periodical subscriptions have a significant impact on remote access to library resources. Librarians have long held the belief that everyone should have access to information. To that end they provided the resources for users at no charge. With reduced budgets and increased costs for resources the model will change or evolve into one that will meet user needs but with different service options. Users may see more open access periodicals make their way into library collections. To that end some publishers such as *Nature* and Springer are making more content available through open access. Libraries will link to open access collections from ERIC and MEDLINE to provide users with resources in education and medicine while at the same time reducing their cost to pay for the same product through a database publisher. Another option mentioned in the periodical survey report for 2011 was pay-per-view where users will have to pay for material that is not subscribed to by the library (Bosch, Henderson & Klusendorf, 2011). JSTOR and others are already offering this feature by showing users all the content that is available, some of which is not subscribed to by their institution. They can read an abstract of the material and if it is not available in another database the user can purchase a copy of the article. Another possibility is tiered pricing structures, which is used by many publishers, the size of your full-time student population or the types of degrees offered will determine the pricing for databases and journals. The day of big package deals for print and electronic resources is probably on the decline. Providing users with what they need want, and use will be critical to financial health of the library. Libraries will need to develop the statistics and other information to determine what electronic resources are underutilized. Project COUNTER (see Chapter 2) to gather statistics for database use combined with vendor supplied statistics should provide libraries with a fairly accurate indication of the resources being used versus those not used or underutilized.

Increased costs and fewer periodicals will lead to increase demand for interlibrary loan. Contractual agreements will need to include language that allows libraries to lend materials to other institutions. This also brings up issues about copyright and digital rights management for electronic resources. If libraries have less resources will they use Google Scholar as an al-

ternative for students to find scholarly resources at another institution's electronic repository? Google Scholar allows libraries to link their electronic resources through their link resolver or ERM so users can find materials in their own institution. Search results in Google Scholar include articles or papers presented at scholarly conferences and were placed in the institution's electronic repository. Users will find materials from not only their institution but also from a number of institutions both in the United States and around the world. This type of open access expands the base of scholarly research for all library users.

Remote access to library collections cannot take place until the library has a contract for the resources. It is the first step to developing remote access for it is in the contract where the authorized users and access to the collection is defined. Once those definitions are in place then libraries can determine how the collection will be accessed from off-campus. There are different options and the three primary choices are through a virtual private network, EZproxy, and electronic resource management tool. All three provide different means of determining whether or not a user is authorized to access the library's resources. The benefit of a virtual private network is with one password and user ID the user can access the resources they need without having to enter multiple IDs or passwords. EZproxy will require users to enter multiple passwords to get to the resources they need. Electronic resource management tools will provide users with one access point for all the electronic resources available. This eliminates the need for multiple passwords to gain access to the resources. Collection development policies are the driving force and the key to successful remote access to library collections by users.

Digital collections and mobile technologies also have an impact on collection development policies and collection management. As materials move from print to digital format requiring less space to house collections it will require the library to examine the scope and purpose of their collection and how it will meet user needs. One of the key considerations with digital resources is copyright to the material. Copyright was discussed more thoroughly in Chapter 3 but, it does have an impact on collection management policies and remote access to library resources. Copyright determines what constitutes fair use and digital rights management limit the use of digital content. Both copyright and digital rights management control how users can use the digital or electronic resources in a collection. In the last chapter this was an issue mentioned regarding e-books. There are numerous publishers offering e-book collections for use by libraries, however, because of digital rights management laws users are restricted to the amount of material they can download and print from an e-book. They can read them online but are unable to do much else with them. Digital rights management also limits the number of users who can simultaneously use an e-book. One book equals one user at a time. In some ways digital rights management places even further restrictions on copyrighted material making it incredibly difficult to use the material for research purposes.

With the increasing use of mobile technologies, especially tablet devices, libraries and vendors will need to develop the applications or apps for mobile use. Whether it is a tablet device, or a smart phone mobile technology has become prevalent and ubiquitous within our society. Vendors are beginning to offer mobile apps for their digital collections. The concern for libraries is vendors will increase the cost of subscriptions to recover the cost of developing the apps. The apps allow anyone using mobile technology to search the licensed electronic resources of the library. Many libraries have adapted their web sites for mobile devices and in some instances created an app so users can search the catalog and other materials at the library. The devices and their apps will help libraries to evolve to meet the changing needs of users and also connect with users regardless of whether or not they are in the library.

Another issue raised in the literature was perpetual access to journals in collections or no longer subscribed to by the institution. This issue was raised more than once in the literature regarding collection development or collection management policies. If the library has a subscription to a journal in digital format, or a combination of print and digital but, realizes the journal is underutilized or not used at all and cancels the subscription users should be able to access the back issues of the journal for the period in which the library subscribed to the journal.

The same holds true for a journal originally published by one publisher but sold to another, changed names or ceased publication. Once again the library and its users should continue to have access to the journal for the period in which they subscribed to it. As one study of Canadian libraries pointed out libraries do not always follow-up to make sure they still have access to the journal once it is no longer part of their subscription. As the author noted it is important for libraries to check access to journals they have discontinued because most contracts have a perpetual access clause in them. Since the language contained in the contract can be enforced through a dispute with the publisher libraries who lose access to those journals can request the back files be included in their subscription per their contract agreement. If they fail to enforce this section of the contract they in effect are not paying for access to material in reality they are not receiving.

The licensing of materials brought about changes in collection management policies. At one time libraries owned the materials they had in the collection. Printed material, microfilm or microfiche were the formats available to libraries. As technology changed and materials could be converted from print to digital publishers had the opportunity to obtain the rights to publish or distribute journals, magazines and newspapers through their electronic collections. Libraries went from physically owning and knowing what was in their collection to essentially leasing their collection. They are renting the materials users need for their research. Publishers seized the opportunity to gain exclusive rights to specific journals or other publications and bundle them into packages for libraries to subscribe to rather than own.

Another consequence of the growth of digital resources and exclusive rights to distribute or publish specific journals is the cost was controlled by a smaller group of publishers and libraries saw their subscription costs for print and electronic resources increase each year. With reductions in budgets libraries have come to realize this is a problem that needs to be addressed. Contract negotiations are critical to reducing costs but also libraries need to determine what journals they need based on the degree programs offered on their campuses. For the last two or three years libraries have reduced the number of print and electronic journals that were underutilized or were no longer needed by the program.

Unfortunately, most institutions now have to look at subscriptions in print and electronic that are part of their core collection and determine if it is necessary to continue subscribing to it. If an institution is part of a large university system and one of the major research campuses subscribes to the same journal the smaller school will drop their subscription knowing students can obtain access to the journal through interlibrary loan. This philosophy is a double-edged sword because interlibrary loan copyright policies dictate the number of times an institution can loan copies of articles from a particular journal. Once the limit is reached interlibrary loan needs to obtain the article from a different school. This can result in longer waiting times for interlibrary loan requests.

Interlibrary loan is also part of collection management and also another way for students to gain remote access to library collections. Regardless of where a student attends college or where a faculty member works not every institution has all the resources they will need for research. Even major research institutions have begun to cut back on their journal subscriptions. As a result

interlibrary loan becomes even more critical to users needing to gain access to library resources. Ensuring access to resources other libraries do not subscribe to is the primary reason a clause for interlibrary loan needs to be part of the contract with the publisher. Interlibrary loan statistics can be useful for determining gaps in a library's collections. The statistics can be used with books but also periodicals. Information from interlibrary loan can help a library weed their circulating collection and also their underutilized journals. As libraries look to cut costs or determine which journals to subscribe to interlibrary loan can provide information to subject bibliographers. This is just one of the methods that should be used in collection development and management.

Federated search tools are another example of how collection management and development has changed. Federated tools allow users to search across multiple databases at one time based on the search terms they enter. When the federated search is complete it will group the results by database and show the user the number of results from each database. There is one advantage to users and it is the fact they search across multiple databases at one time without having to replicate their search or change search terms for their next search. All the results are in one place and they can go through the results for each database and select the results they want or need for their project. There is a downside to using a federated search tool and it is too many results. In some instances it will be thousands of results making it unwieldy if not next to impossible to narrow the results to a manageable quantity. Some of the search tools do not provide an extensive list of limiters for users to narrow their results leading to thousands instead of a few hundred results. It would be similar to searching Google Scholar without using the advanced search or scholar preferences options.

Google Scholar is another option in the area of collection development policies. Libraries can use their link resolver or electronic resource management tool to link their databases to Google Scholar. The advantage to the institution and the user is the fact they can use Google Scholar as way to identify the resources they want or need for their project and the databases at their institution where they can access the articles. It is a way to start identifying keywords and concepts and identifying possible sources. It also provided users with another means of access to library resources. The electronic management tool or EZproxy can identify authorized users who would then be able to obtain the resources they need from the databases. Institutions can provide a link to Google Scholar from their library homepage or their subject guides as another option for students to look for resources. Librarians are keenly aware students do not start their research at the library. Student research often begins with a search of Google and many times may end with a search of Google. By making them aware and showing them how to find library resources through Google Scholar provides students with better search results and access to library resources instead of the first web site they found in a basic search of the Internet.

Collection development policies now focus on print and electronic resources. Clearly defined collection policies help the library focus their budgets for resources, either in print or digitally, that will be widely used. Negotiating contracts and moving away from large package deals will help libraries improve their collection strategies. Contracts or packages that included resources not needed by users but the institution was required to purchase them because they were part of the package was not a good use of the library's collection development budget. Using database statistics either vendor supplied or through Project COUNTER (see Chapter 2) or both will help libraries determine where to focus their resource dollars and the changes that need to be made to their contracts and subscriptions. Providing the right mix of resources to users is important.

Over the course of the next few years, subscription prices will rise, but libraries will need to work with vendors and users to determine the best mix of materials. The current literature seems to indicate publishers will move away from large package deals and will focus on tiered pricing. Collection development policies will change and the types of resources will become increasing digital and with it will come a greater need for seamless remote access to library resources and also addressing copyright and digital rights management issues to ensure users can not only gain access to the resources but also use the resources once they find them.

Collection development policies developed in the 1980s or 1990s need to be re-examined with the increase in digital materials. The use of electronic resource management tools can help librarians keep better control and access to the digital materials. Digital materials have brought about new concerns and problems for libraries. One is the fact they no longer own the materials but, rather subscribe to them. The second is the cost of digital materials continues to rise every year. As libraries face budget reductions collection development money is shifted from print materials to digital collection subscription fees. Digital materials, especially journals, are the choice of most students because of the portability factor.

Students can access the collections anytime of the day or night from any location on or off-campus. They can print, save or e-mail an article they need. Database vendors are offering mobile access to their collections to meet the growing use of mobile technology. While print materials continue to be included in collection development policies the emphasis seems to be shifting from print to digital and most of the literature focuses on digital collection policies and issues. While there are examples of libraries without books they are few and far between. Someday we might get all of our books from Google but, until then library collection development policies will need to include a mix of print and digital to meet the needs of their users.

REFERENCES

Bosch, S., Henderson, K., & Klusendorf, H. (2011, April 14). Periodicals price survey 2011: Under pressure, times are changing. *Library Journal.* Retrieved fromhttp://www.libraryjournal.com/lj/home/890009 264/periodicalspricesurvey2011under.html.csp

Chisman, J., Matthews, G., & Brady, C. (2007). Electronic resource management. *The Serials Librarian, 52*(3), 297–303. doi:10.1300/J123v52n03_08

Chou, M., a&nd Zhou, O. (2005). The impact of licenses on library collections. *Managing Digital Resources in Libraries, 17*(33), 7–23. doi:doi:10.1300/J101v17n3302

Cotter, G., Carroll, B., Hodge, G., & Japzon, A. (2005). Electronic collection management and electronic information services. *Information Services & Use, 25,* 23–34.

Crawford, A. R. (2008). Licensing and negotiations for electronic content. *Resource Sharing & Information Networks, 19,* 15–38. doi:10.1080/07377790802498523

Croft, J. B. (2005). Interlibrary loan and licensing: Tools for proactive contract management. *Licensing in Libraries: Practical and Ethical Aspects, 42*(3), 41–53. doi:doi:10.1300/J111v42n0303

Dixon, L., Duncan, C., Fagan, J. C., Mandernach, M., & Warlick, S. E. (2010). Finding articles and journals via Google Scholar, journal portals, and link resolvers: Usability study results. *Reference and User Services Quarterly, 50*(2), 170–181.

Emery, J. (2007). Ghosts in the machine. *The Serials Librarian, 51*(3), 201–208. doi:10.1300/J123v51n03_14

Horva, T. (2010). Challenges and possibilities for collection management in a digital age. *Library Resources & Technical Services, 54*(3), 142–152.

Hunter, K. (2005). Access management. *Journal of Library Administration, 42*(2), 57–70. doi:10.1300/J111v42n02_05

Kneivel, J. E., Wicht, H., & Connaway, L. S. (2006). Use of circulation statistics and interlibrary loan data in collection management. *College & Research Libraries, 67*(1), 35–49.

Waller, A., & Bird, G. (2006). We own it. *The Serials Librarian, 50*(1), 179–196. doi:10.1300/J123v50n01_17

Young-Wiles, S., Landesman, B., & Terrill, L. J. (2007). E-resources=e-opportunity. *The Serials Librarian, 52*(3), 253–258. doi:doi:10.1300/J123v52n0301

KEY TERMS AND DEFINITIONS

Collection Development: The policies in place by a library to determine the scope and areas of collection for their library. Collection development policies are guided by the academic programs and research interests of the faculty.

Electronic Resource Management: A system integrated into the library cataloging and acquisitions systems to better manage a library's electronic resources. The system manages the licenses, contracts, payment information, and access rights of a library's electronic resources.

Federated Search: A federated search allows library users to search across multiple electronic resources.

Google Scholar: A search feature within Google allowing users to find scholarly publications. Libraries have the ability to link their resources to Google Scholar and users can set their search preferences within Google Scholar to find articles from their institution's databases or digital repository.

Interlibrary Loan: Also known as ILL is a service offered by all libraries to obtain materials for researchers at another library. Users complete and submit an online form with information about the material they are requesting such as, for example, author, title of book or journal, ISSN or ISBN, publisher and publication date.

Chapter 5
Developing Digital Collections

ABSTRACT

Digital collections are found in most libraries. They include not only databases but also photographs, institutional repositories, manuscript collections, materials from the university archives, or special collections. Designing digital collections and making them available to users expands the resources users can access for a research project.

INTRODUCTION

Remote access technologies for library collections are not limited to library resources such as databases and the catalog. Many colleges and universities have institutional repositories that allow faculty to share research projects and include electronic theses and dissertations. Institutional repositories are used for digital collections created through an institution's archive or special collections. Digital collections expand the scope of a library's collections. Many institutions have digitized their yearbooks, photograph and manuscript collections. Digital collections help preserve collections and make them accessible to everyone.

DOI: 10.4018/978-1-4666-0234-2.ch005

The key to finding materials in online collections is the metadata used to identify the items in the collection. As with any collection or new resource, marketing is important to having the collection used. Digital collections will continue to increase and allow access to more material beyond the library's books and databases.

BACKGROUND

Digital collections provide access to resources beyond the usual books, periodicals and databases. They often provide students, faculty and researchers with access to primary source materials. The Digital Library of Georgia is an excellent example of a digital collection with a wide variety of materials. In 2008, the collection expanded to include a Civil Rights Digital Library with original television video of events from the Civil Rights Movement. Digital collections provide libraries with the opportunity to display their special collections or archives. Digitization does cost money and in today's economy, libraries often seek grant money to support major digitization projects. Digital collections will have specific digitization requirements for materials and the types of materials they will digitize.

Another example of a digital collection is arXiv. org from Cornell University. This institutional repository provides scholarly papers in the sciences especially physics, mathematics, and computer science. An institutional repository is different from a digital collection in the fact it is a collection of scholarly articles or papers written by faculty members at that particular institution. arXiv.org accepts papers from scholars at institutions outside of Cornell University. Cornell and supporting user institutions and the National Science Foundation fund the project. As with any online collection, the ability to search and find the materials you need is crucial to a digital collection.

Metadata for a digital collection allows users to search and find the materials they are looking for. Google is an excellent example of how to use metadata to improve search results. The metadata provides users with better search results through Google. Another important factor in digital libraries is the architecture used to create them. Once they are created if libraries want their collections used, they need to market them and promote them to students, faculty and researchers. Digital collections and remote access to them is crucial to meeting the needs of academic researchers.

Digital library services provide users with access to the catalog, databases, subject guides, interlibrary loan, digital collections, document delivery and reference services. The extent of digital services allows users to browse collections, databases, and the library catalog. It provides researchers with the opportunity to identify the possible resources to use for their project. Users can access these materials on or off-campus with patron authentication through either EZproxy or VPN. Once a patron provides their user, ID and password, they can access the materials they need. User acceptance and student perception of digital libraries or digital library services is important because without them the collections and services will be underutilized. In the digital age, easy access to materials they need and want is an expectation from researchers.

MAIN FOCUS OF THE CHAPTER

The first step to creating access to digital library collections and services is the computer architecture needed to access the resources. EZproxy and virtual private networks (VPN) are two of the more well known methods to authenticate patrons. There are other options and one example is ALADIN created by the Washington Research Library Consortium (Gourley, 2001). The Access to Library and Database Information Network (ALADIN) used by the Washington Research Library Consortium is based on middleware architecture for core services it broker's communication between components (Gourley, 2001). This type of software architecture allows patrons to access different services without having to know how to log into all the library resources. The ALADIN digital library system provides access to content and services for over 500 subscription databases, digital collections and library catalogs for seven medium sized academic libraries in the Washington Research Library Consortium (Gourley, 2001). It also allows access to library digital collections and services through campus portals.

Open access, open source software and digital libraries are linked together in the creation and development of digital libraries. The licensing agreement for open source software allows users to give away or sell any part of the software. The source code for the software must be readily available and users can download it free from the Internet. Users can download the code sell, give away or make modifications without violating the licensing agreement. Open source software is beneficial for digital collections for many of them were created with open source software and as a result is open access collections.

Some of the more widely known open source digital library software are DSpace developed in a joint venture between Hewlett Packard and the Massachusetts Institute of Technology. It allows a university to create a digital repository of faculty research. EPrints is another example of institutional repository software. Like DSpace it can and is used to capture faculty research, conference papers and technical reports just to name a few of the documents that can be saved in EPrints. Greenstone Digital Library software allows archives and special collections to build a digital collection or library and make it available on the Internet. The software allows a library, museum or archive to gather the collection, create descriptions for the items, configure the materials in the collection, build the collection and then upload the collection to a web site to allow it to be viewed and accessed by researchers. (Krishnamurthy, 2008)

New technologies have improved they way digital libraries are created and developed. The Open Digital Library and OpenDLib projects combined with the Open Archives Initiative and the Protocol for Metadata Harvesting provide the framework for interoperability of digital libraries (Eyambe and Suleman, 2004). The authors of the article conducted research with non-technology individuals to create a digital library by selecting from a variety of components made available by the authors. With the use of a graphical user interface (GUI), the users were able to select, drop, and drag the components they selected into their digital library. The results of this research indicated the non-technology users could create a digital library using GUI but a more flexible user interface is needed so new components added

to a digital library can be easily accommodated (Eyambe and Suleman, 2004). Creating the digital library to be user friendly is critical for its long-term survival.

Another factor that is very important when creating a digital library is the URL (Uniform Resource Locator) for links provided within the digital library or digital collection. There are different types of URLS. The first is the absolute URL used to link to a file located on a web site external to the web site where the link will be embedded. The second type of URL is partial or relative and is used when the link points to a file within the linked web site that is within the file directory of the local web site. The last type is an absolute local URL that specifies a path from the root directory of the local site. (Cohen, 2004) Of the three different types of URLs, the relative URL provides better access speed to the web site link and portability because the links can be moved to another server but the links will still work. The main page of the web site is the directory URL and sections of the site will have a slash after the main page pointing to the subsection in the directory. Finally yet importantly is link checking to make sure there are not any dead or broken links on the site (Cohen, 2004). The web consortium group W3C has a link checking application (http://validator.w3.org/checklink) users enter the web address and the link checker provides a list of the links that are no longer working. Link checking, URL creation, and management are very important for access to licensed electronic resources. If links are not properly created or checked on a regular basis users will not be able to access the licensed content from on or off campus locations.

The architecture and programming to create a digital library is important but the metadata is equally important. The most basic definition of metadata is it is data about data. Metadata allows users to find what they are looking for within the digital library. It is the information that describes an item when you are searching a library catalog, a database or digital collection. Without metadata, it would be almost impossible to find materials in online resources. Search results from online resources are generated in one of three ways. The first is full-text searching, the second is searching metadata surrogates or records and the last method is full-text searching of a metadata database.

Full-text searching is used with search engines such as Google or Yahoo. Searching metadata surrogates or records is used to search a library catalog. The last type of search is used in a library catalog search because you can search by title of the book or you can search by keyword over all the metadata (Beall, 2010). Improving search results helps to improve precision, the proportion of relevant documents retrieved compared to the total number of retrieved documents. It also improves recall, the proportion of relevant documents retrieved compared to all the relevant documents in the database. The more options users have to search online resources they will obtain relevant results for their search through the metadata created for the collection.

The key for researchers to find digital collections for their research is the creation of metadata. Metadata provides keywords and subject fields for print and digital collections. Without metadata, one would have a difficult time not only finding but also searching a collection. Metadata is often referred to as data about data, which is true. Without the behind the scenes data or information a researcher would probably not find the information they needed in the format they need it. The type of collection determines the metadata created. For example, if it is a collection of books in a library the metadata will be based on either the Dewey decimal classification or the Library of Congress Subject Headings Classification. Images may require more metadata because of the variety of information that can be obtained from them. For example, there is the image itself which can require more than one subject term or classification. The year or place it was taken may also be part of the metadata. Images are one of the most difficult formats to create metadata

for because of the variety of fields that need to be considered when creating the metadata. The more information provided for the item or the collection the easier it would be for a researcher to find the item or the collection.

D-Lib Magazine (http://www.dlib.org/) an open access journal focusing on issues concerning digital libraries and collections through the years has published several articles about metadata and its importance in the creation of a digital library or collection. An article from the January/February 2010 issue examines the creation of metadata for educational resources in a digital repository. While the focus is on the creation of standards by IEEE (Institute for Electrical and Electronics Engineers) for learning objects the issues raised in the article can be adapted to the creation of metadata for other digital collections. The most widely know metadata hierarchy is Dublin Core. As the article points out without the creation of metadata, it will be difficult to discover resources in an efficient manner. Metadata becomes the means by which materials are found when searching an online collection or the Internet. (Koutsomitropoulos, Alexopoulos, Solomou & Papatheodorou, 2010)

The authors of the article used the IEEE metadata standards for learning objects and mapped them to the Dublin Core hierarchy. For the purposes of the article, the authors defined a learning object as "any entity either digital or non-digital used for education, learning or training." (Koutsomitropoulos, et al.) The authors selected a learning object in DSpace, which uses Dublin Core, then mapped the IEEE learning object metadata to the Dublin Core metadata schema. What the authors found was by using the IEEE learning object metadata standards within an institutional repository made for an effective and efficient method of searching and finding items within the digital repository (Koutsomitropoulos, et al., 2010).

Once a digital library is created, it needs to be accepted by the users. In a 2004 study of an award, winning digital library from the Open University of Hong Kong identified nine characteristics that led to user acceptance of the digital library. The characteristics they identified were interface characteristics, terminology, screen design, navigation, relevance, system accessibility, system visibility, computer self-efficacy, and computer experience and domain knowledge. Terminology and screen design are two elements that are crucial for user acceptance of a digital library. Simple terminology makes it easier for users to find the information they need. Screen design is very important because users will become confused if the buttons or search fields are not properly aligned or not adequately highlighted (Thong, Hong & Tam, 2004).

In an earlier article from 2004 three librarians explored what lead users to accept a digital library by exploring the Electronic Library of the Open University of Hong Kong. This digital library contains over 1,400 electronic resources including full text e-books, e-journals, reference databases and a number of other resources e-formats. It also has links to over 58 distance-learning organizations from around the world (Thong, Hong & Tam, 2004). What the authors discovered in their study of the Electronic Library of the Open University of Hong Kong was three categories of factors that influenced user acceptance of digital libraries. The categories were interface, content of the library and individual characteristics, in other words computer and database search skills. The authors suggest that libraries in creating a digital library need to consider these categories. While libraries do not have control over the users' computer or database search skills, they suggested libraries could play a role in improving a user's search skills through instruction sessions (Thong, Hong & Tam, 2004).

Another factor that will lead to user acceptance of a digital library is usability testing. Once the digital library is created and before it is rolled out to, the entire user population focus groups should be invented to test the digital library interface. Feedback obtained during usability testing can and should be used to improve the interface. Once the changes are made to the interface the focus groups

should be invited back to test the digital library again. How students perceive digital collections can have an impact on how and if the digital collection is used (Thong, Hong & Tam, 2004)

A case study of student perceptions of the Cochin University of Science and Technology in India revealed the majority of the students, 98 percent were aware of the library and almost 28 percent used the digital library two or three times a week and 17 percent of the students surveyed used the digital library daily. The primary reason (62%) given by the students using the digital library was ease of access. For 32 percent of the users they preferred digital formats and 5 percent found it easy to download materials from the digital library (Sheeja, 2010).

The University of Guadalajara (Mexico) conducted a similar study using the voice of the customer (VOC) to determine the areas in need of improvement for their digital library. They posted a survey on the web page of the digital library and received 112 results. They used the Kano Model and Quality Function Deployment to analyze user satisfaction with the digital library. The Quality Function Deployment is listening to the customer and the Kano Model categorizes how the attributes of a product or service meets or exceeds the needs of the customer. This is similar to total quality management in the corporate world. The survey results indicated the users were satisfied with the digital library (Garibay, Gutierrez & Figueroa, 2010)

Digital collections are growing in scope and readily available to anyone with an Internet connection. It allows students at all grade levels to access materials without a password. Google Scholar makes use of the material available through digital collections or electronic institutional repositories. A search of Google Scholar will yield several articles available from a number of colleges and universities. People without access to licensed databases at a university have the opportunity to obtain and gain access to scholarly resources and materials. Faculty members published the articles available in Google Scholar through institutional repositories. Alternatively, they are articles in the process of publication. Open access to materials has been the subject of much discussion for the last five years, especially materials published with federal and state funding and digital collections meet the need of access to scholarly materials to the public.

Digital collections can take many forms and one example is e-book collections. E-books are usually purchased through one of the database vendors and can be subject specific such as, Safari Tech Books or a reference collection such as, Credo Reference or general in nature and include books from a number of subject disciplines. Every library has at least one collection of e-books but their use may not be the highest compared to article databases. Some e-book collections require users to download and install an e-book reader on their computer. Another limitation is the ability to print or save sections of the book. The number of simultaneous users is another barrier to their being widely used and accepted.

In 2008 EDUCAUSE published a report about e-books in higher education. The report highlights two key issues with e-books one is portability and the other is intellectual property rights (Educause, 2008). In order for e-books to widely accepted and used will require a standard technology platform that will work for all e-books rather than requiring multiple technologies, as was the case at the time the report was published (Educause, 2008). It would be cost prohibitive for users to invest in multiple technologies to read books from different publishers (Educause, 2008). Intellectual property rights are necessary to prevent illegal copying and distribution but currently hinder the user from printing or saving pages from an e-book (Educause, 2008). The report goes on to suggest that in order to improve user acceptance and increase use of e-books the publishers of e-books need to develop new business models, technologies and common standards for digital rights management and the protection of intellectual property (Edu-

cause, 2008) The report concludes that within five years students currently in K-12 will be more accepting of and willing to use e-books when they arrive at college and believes there will be a viable e-reader available and, issues of intellectual property will be resolved through technology or business models (Educause, 2008)

In a 2005 an article by Clifford Lynch published in D-Lib Magazine forecasted the future of digital libraries for the next decade. In the article, the author sums up the years of work and funding from several government agencies to create and develop the numerous digital library collections and initiatives. As the author, notes funding for digital library creation is probably ending but future funding will focus on cyber-infrastructure and e-research. Another area for funding will be digital asset management, digital collection creation and management, and institutional repositories. (Lynch, 2010). A major focus in the future for digital libraries will be on digital preservation. The author notes it is becoming of increasing importance as institutions work to preserve materials in their collections. (Lynch, 2010) One of the primary areas benefiting from digital libraries is historical research. Digitizing letters, diaries and photographs provide access to primary sources for researchers. Primary sources of this nature can be beneficial to teaching and learning in history, anthropology and other disciplines in the humanities and social sciences.

Once a digital collection is created it is important to survey the user community to make sure it meets their needs but the collection needs to be maintained. Since most digital collections are created with materials from special collections or archives it is important for an individual in that department check the web site for the collection to make sure the links still work and update the content when new material is available. Digital collections are expensive to develop and once created cannot be abandoned or forgotten. The Digital Library of Georgia was created with sponsorship from the Institute for Museum and Library

Services, Georgia Humanities Council, National Endowment for the Humanities, Georgia Public Library Service, GALILEO (Georgia's Virtual Library) and University of Georgia Libraries. Without sponsorship, it would be difficult to develop and maintain a digital collection of this size and scope.

In 2006 the Institute of Museum and Library Services (IMLS) published their report *Status of Technology and Digitization in the Nation's Museums and Libraries*. One of the questions asked was about funding. Of the museums that responded to the survey 36.9 percent reported they had funding to support digitization projects and of the libraries who responded to the same question regarding funding, only 12 percent reported having enough funding to support their digitization projects. Both museums and libraries reported not having enough skilled staff to accomplish their digitization projects. For museums 65 percent stated they lacked staffing and for libraries 73 percent reported lacking staff for digital projects. The lack of trained staff resulted in the creation of only 1-500 digital images or material by 46 percent of museums and 21.5 percent of libraries. (IMLS Report, 2006).

The Open Collection Program at Harvard University draws materials from the vast resources of the Harvard University Libraries and makes them accessible to all students, faculty and researchers with computer access. This collection, created in 2002 with a grant from the William and Flora Hewlett Foundation, and has since received funding from Arcadia, a charitable organization dedicated to preserving endangered culture and nature. (http://ocp.hul.harvard.edu/). The collections include material on contagious disease, immigration from 1789-1930 and women at work from 1800-1930. Some of the digitized materials include photos, pamphlets and manuscripts. A significant Islamic Heritage collection includes maps, manuscripts and printed texts. The collections provide researchers with information they could incorporate into a research project or use

to find additional materials. The working women collection includes primary sources in the form of handwritten diaries from four different working women.

One of the most important aspects of digital collections is how they are used. Because many of the collections are open access, they can be used for teaching in grades K-12 and college. Once the appropriate grade level collection is find the materials can be incorporated into the class. The National Archives and Records Administration has a section for teachers with lesson plans to instruct students on using primary and historical documents in their research. (http://www.archives.gov/education/) The same type of instruction can be included in college history classes. Most importantly digital collections can be used to support online learning. Digital libraries provide additional sources of information to support distance education and allow students who cannot come to the library to access information that can be used to support their course work. The creation and incorporation of a digital library into online learning will allow students to work collaboratively to share knowledge and skills but most importantly develop partnerships between the library and the online students and faculty. (Sharifabadi, 2006)

The Perry-Castañeda Map (http://www.lib.utexas.edu/maps/) collection at the University of Texas-Austin from the United States, Europe, Asia, Africa, Canada, Mexico, the Middle East and Russia. The collection is significant in scope because many of the historic maps of Europe are prior to World War I. Since the maps are in the public domain researchers are free to download them and incorporate them into any project without copyright permission.

The three examples of digital collections provided do not require a password to access. They are open access digital collections made possible through grant funding. Anyone with access to a computer and the Internet can use the collections. Digital collections of this nature are the norm rather than the exception. The Library of Congress

American Memory Project (http://memory.loc.gov/ammem/index.html) is another very broad and extensive digital collection covering everything from advertising to women's history. The web site does provide information about copyright for the various collections. If researchers have questions about a particular collection or item in a collection, they can contact the U.S. Copyright Office for additional information.

Digital collections open up resources to scholars and provide them with the ability to do preliminary research on their topic or to find materials they may overlook in the course of their research. One of the major problems with digital collections is the lack of an overall index to collections. For researchers to find collections relevant to their research requires them to perform a specific Internet search that includes the phrase "digital collection." Another option is to check the subject guides at colleges and universities. Using the advance search feature in Google or any Internet browser a researcher could limit the domain to .edu and search in a particular subject area (Tibbo, 2002).

Many subject guides contain links to digital collections that are open access. In the early stages of digital collection development, a survey was undertaken to determine how historians searched for primary source materials on the Internet. The conclusion was that 61 percent of the respondents visited a repository's web site but only 46 percent responded their search yielded information they could use for outreach, education or web site design. They did the preliminary search online then contact the repository to request more information or copies of materials from their collections (Tibbo, 2002)

In addition to having monetary resources to develop the digital collection it is also necessary to have the staffing to develop and maintain the collection. Once a digital collection is created, it is important to have qualified people to digitize additional materials and maintain the current collection. In addition to digitizing materials

there needs to quality control to ensure, digitized materials meet the specifications for the collection. Otherwise, it will be difficult for users to read a printed document or see clear images in the collection.

Once the digital library is created marketing of the collection is very important. Making users aware of the new resource is critical to its success. There are several ways digital collections can be marketed. Use your physical space. Place information on bookshelves or in student study areas to promote the electronic collections or resources. Use the web to promote the digital library. This can be accomplished the library's web site and through social network sites. Landing pages are another option for promoting or marketing digital collections. A landing page is a one-page web advertisement you arrive at by clicking on a provided link. Use the campus newspaper or send out flyers, bookmarks or postcards to students living on campus. If the campus has, a radio station promotes the digital library with advertising time on the station. One of the best options is a giveaway that people will use and will remind them to use the collection. Once the marketing campaign is over the library can assess the results and determine the marketing tool that worked the best (Fagan, 2009).

FUTURE TRENDS

Digital collections will continue to grow in size and scope. Because of the growth in digital collections, technology will change and adapt to meet the needs of the institution and the users. Along with the growth of digital collections will be issues of copyright previously discussed in Chapter 3. Currently there are open source and proprietary software available to create digital collections and the number and type of software will continue to grow. Institutions that create digital collections will need to identify the materials within their collections they wish to digitize and create standards to ensure people can access the materials and include copyright information regarding the use of the material from the collection. Database vendors will include more materials in their collections. An example is Alexander Street Press whose collections include videos and graphic novels in addition to music and manuscript collections. Technology will continue to improve to allow for the capture of digital materials. Metadata will continue to be the key to helping researchers find the materials they need. Software such as Archon and DSpace allow institutions to preserve materials and make them available to other researchers or to internal users.

Digital collections and materials have changed the way libraries provide service to their users. No longer do users need to be in the library to work on a research project. Through the years, digital collections have grown in size and scope. Based on current trends digital collections and resources will continue to grow and as a result, libraries will need to re-examine the services offered. Digital collections have moved beyond e-books and e-journals to include learning objects, historical documents and materials, photographs and videos. One area for potential growth is creating an online index or directory of the numerous digital collections. Metadata standards will help users find the resources they need when searching for information and current research indicates the standards will continue to improve to provide users with better search results. Digital collections will not replace the brick and mortar library but digital collections will become an integral part of library collections. An example of adapting to change is the Zell B. Miller Learning Center on the campus of the University of Georgia.

The Miller Learning Center opened on the campus of the University of Georgia in Athens, Georgia in 2003. The building is a multi-use structure with classrooms, areas for studying, group activities, writing and research. It was and is intended to be "one-stop shopping" for students. They can attend a class in the building then stay and study or work on a project with other students. It is an electronic library with no physical collection of books (Barratt and White-Case, 2010). Students have access to over 500 computers, 96 group study rooms, 6 technology service desks; two are dedicated to assisting students with digital and multimedia content creation. The Miller Learning Center does assess the services they offer by counting the number of users of the center's services and resources. They use qualitative surveys to students and faculty to gather information about the services and resources offered. Infrared sensors in the stairs and elevators gather the number of people entering the building (Barratt and White-Case, 2010). This type of learning center is the trend in libraries and continues to be the prevalent design for the next several years. The Miller Learning center is a one-stop shop for students to meet most if not all of their academic and library needs.

The future of digital collections will concentrate on preservation and conservation. Materials in libraries, museums and archives that are in danger of disintegrating because of age will be the focus for most institutions. Preservation of documents or artifacts in danger of disappearing will provide researchers with the opportunity to read the document or see the object. Digital collections are moving beyond and will continue to move beyond collections of photographs or art images. We see more manuscripts, diaries and in the case of higher education materials from their university's archives for example, such as, yearbook collections and other related memorabilia. In the future, more types of materials will appear in digital collections. The long term and future goal will be to develop copyright permissions allowing more people to use the materials in digital collections. An example is images or photographs. Copyright protection usually prevents them from being used for a variety of purposes including research. There are exceptions. Some of the photographic collections in The Library of Congress are in the public domain. One example is the Bain Collection. You can also search Google

Images to find images without restrictions. The future will require the creators of digital collections to provide not only open access but also the copyright permissions to use the material within the collection for research purposes.

There are more materials waiting to be digitized and more collections to be created or expanded. Funding will continue to be an issue but institutions will be able to obtain funding by focusing on the need for preservation for historic or irreplaceable materials and artifacts. The extent of digital projects will probably increase in the future in an effort to preserve materials. Another aspect that needs to be addressed is the creation of an index or the ability for users to find the collections they need when searching the Internet. Right now users search for specific materials or collections, but they may or may not find all the collections pertaining to their research.

CONCLUSION

Improvements in scanning technology and the availability of grant money created the opportunity for libraries, museums and archives to create digital collections. Grant money from organizations such as, the National Endowment for the Humanities and the Institute of Museum and Library Services led to the creation of many new digital library collections. Digital collections provided institutions with the ability and opportunity to bring materials, once relegated to the storeroom, into public view. No longer would someone wanting to view old college yearbooks have to visit the college they could now view them online, page by page.

Digital collections at one time were limited in scope but with new technology and improvements in the ability to digitize materials, they have grown in number and scope. Collections can include anything from photographs to scholarly publications. With the improvement of technology came the databases of publications currently used by every

college and university. Materials have moved from print to electronic and students have the option to print, e-mail or save the articles they find from their searches. More materials will move from print to digital and will probably be born digital. Special collections and archives are able to make their materials readily available to students and researchers. Collections and materials that may have been underused or long forgotten may see an increase in use because they are available in a digital collection.

Some but not all of the software available to create digital collections is open source. Using open source software helps reduce the cost of creating a digital collection but there is still the expense of scanning, creating the metadata, quality control and developing a web site for the collection. Once an institution starts scanning and develops a collection online, they are committed to growing and maintaining the collection. Digitizing materials for an online collection can be expensive and time consuming. Once the initial grant or funding is depleted, the institution will need to seek additional sources to continue with the project. Creating partnerships with other institutions or grant funding agencies is beneficial and often times necessary. Another issue is staffing. Institutions with digital collections will need to staff who is experienced in digitizing materials, creating metadata and developing a web site for the digital collection.

Scanning of materials whether print or images require quality control. Everyone has probably seen the image of the person's thumb in the scanned book in Google Books. The goal is not to have mistakes of this nature appear in your digital collection. If an institution allows other libraries, museums or archives to contribute to the digital collection the standards for scanning need to be clearly defined. This insures and prevents poorly scanned materials being sent to the host institution only to be returned because they were not scanned to the digital collection's standards. The Digital Library of Georgia has specific requirements for materials scanned for the collection. Other libraries, museums and archives can contribute photos, maps or manuscripts to the Digital Library of Georgia providing they are scanned to their specifications. Their web site contains a section about digitizing materials as indicated in the link from the web site: (http://dlg.galileo.usg.edu/ AboutDLG/DigitizationGuide.html). Any institution wanting to contribute to the Digital Library of Georgia needs to follow their guidelines.

The platform or software to create and manage the collection is just as important as the digitizing of the materials. The software available whether proprietary or open source allow users to develop the collection, create the metadata, scan the material, organize the scanned objects then create and upload the digital collection to a web site. Two of the more widely known and used are Archon and the Archivists Toolkit. Both are open source archive software. The use of archive management software allows the institution to create the digital collection from start to finish included the encoded archival description (EAD) and the MARC record.

Encoded archival description creates standards for the information contained in finding aids, inventories, registers and indexes used by archives and museums for their collections. It makes it possible for researchers to use the finding aid or inventory to find the information they need about the collection they are searching. Similar to HTML or XML it contains pre-defined tags that are used for specific pieces of information for the finding aid. The use of EAD is just as important as the creation of metadata for a collection. Without EAD and metadata, it would be difficult to search and find the information with an archival collection. (http://www.archivists.org/saagroups/ead/)

Metadata is data about data but without metadata, it would be impossible to search any collection or catalog. It would be nearly impossible to find a book in an online catalog without the subject headings and keywords. The same would be true for materials in a digital collection. Anyone attempting to search the collection would have a difficult or nearly impossible time finding the material he or she was searching. The metadata supplies the keywords and other pieces of information for each item in the collection. For example, when someone is searching the Digital Library of Georgia and they are looking for photographs of farms they can use the word "farm" to find the specific type of image. Once a collection is created, it is important to market the collection. Another key component to making sure your digital collection is meeting user needs is the creation of the URLs for the collection. If the web site or collection contains broken links it will be difficult to use and find the resources needed for research. Creating relative URLs provide the most stability. Using a link checker will help with maintaining an up to date web site where all the links work. Maintaining and updating the web site is just as important as the other components of the digital collection.

Just because a digital collection was created does not mean researchers will find it. Promotion and marketing of the collection is crucial to its success. Marketing and promotion can be accomplished in a variety of ways and can be used for electronic resource collections at academic libraries. One of the simplest ways to promote your collection is an e-mail to a list. There are several library and archives related lists. Posting to the list will gain attention for your digital collection. Another option is advertisements in college newspapers. If it is, a collection created at a specific university tent cards can be placed in student study areas of the library and around campus. Still another option is post information on the student portal. Promotional material such as a giveaway with the name and web address on it will remind users of the collection. Landing pages or announcements on the library's web site are two additional options.

Understanding how and why people use the collection is important. In early research about how and why historians use digital collections it was determined it was a way for them to identify the institutions they wanted to visit to conduct research. It was a way to weed out the institutions that did not have the materials in their collections for their research project or material that could be used to teach their students about primary sources. In 2012 more primary sources and historical documents are available in digital collections. A good example is the National Archives and Records Administration (NARA) web site. The NARA provides documents that can be used for teaching students about history and it provides teachers with lesson plans to incorporate the documents into their teaching. Most archives and museums have finding aids available online allowing researchers to determine what is contained a collection or collections before they go there to do research. With increased digitization, more material is available online for researchers. Presidential libraries such as the FDR presidential library, one of the first presidential libraries, is beginning to digitize more materials and are available on their web site.

Will digital collections replace the traditional books and journal collections in libraries? Probably not anytime in the near future but, they will become an integral part of the services provided by libraries. Students have come to expect more materials to be available online. Electronic collections of journals and books are just two examples. Students and faculty look for materials that be accessed remotely whether it is a journal, a book or a diary in the archive. Libraries compete with other sources of information especially the Internet. If students cannot find it in the print collection of the library, they will look for materials available electronically. The ability to find what they want and when they want it is crucial to not only the library but also the researcher. Digital collections and meeting the needs of the user are linked. The ability to find the material they need through the library web site is important and linking digital or electronic collections of materials through the library's homepage helps researchers find what they need for their project. It is important for digital collections to be accessible without a password,

so users outside of the institution can gain access them to anytime. Electronic collections of licensed resources must be password protected to prevent unauthorized users from gaining access to them.

Currently e-books may not be widely used or very popular with college students but, it is possible with better technology and improved intellectual property rights they will become more widely used and accepted by students. Current e-book collections use different platforms and technology. Requiring a different reader or technology to download and read the book. Because of copyright laws students can only download and print a limited number of pages from the e-book they need for research. However, for some areas of library collections e-books are better suited to meet user needs. An example is in the area of technology because it changes rapidly and to purchase books for a collection on various types of software, programming or hardware that will be outdated in six months to a year is a waste of collection development funds. Using an e-book collection for technology materials in the long-term allows the library with the means to provide users with up to date materials for their research needs.

Digital collections are now an integral part of many library collections. The incorporation of digital materials into library resources has changed how libraries provide services to their users. It relates to meeting user needs and providing them with remote access to materials when they need it. Many collections are open access. Users need only find the link to the collection to gain access to the materials. Copyright restrictions to materials can be posted on the collection web site. Depending on the collection, users may be able to use the materials from the collection for personal or research purposes. It is the libraries responsibility to post the copyright information just as much as it is the users' responsibility to follow the copyright restrictions for the material they use from the digital collection.

One issue that will continue to plague the creation, maintenance and growth of digital collections will be the lack of funding and adequately trained staff. The report from the Institute of Museum and Library Services was published in 2006, however, if the same museums and libraries were surveyed again in 2011 or 2012 their answers might be the same. In a period of economic downturn as we are currently, experiencing funding is decreasing rather than increasing for libraries and museums. This will provide libraries and museums with the opportunity to collaborate with similar organizations to develop and maintain digital collections or projects. Developing partnerships will allow them to share resources, including, but not limited to, funding, personnel and technology. Another opportunity, depending on the collection, might be to seek corporate sponsorship to complete the project. Digital collections provide researchers with remote access to materials for their projects. With Internet access, a researcher can gain access to a digital collection anywhere in the world.

Digital collections open new opportunities for libraries and researchers. The creation of the digital collection can attract new users to the library's web site and the library can gain recognition for the collection. Marketing the collection will help increase use of any digital or electronic collection. Another key component to the success of any digital collection is making sure it meets the users' needs. The ability to easily search and find the materials within the collection is critical to its success. Meeting user needs regardless of the type of collection, open access digital collection or a licensed electronic resource, is important for the library to obtain feedback on the collection.

In order to preserve materials in danger of deteriorating because of age, digital collections will become more prevalent as libraries attempt to save materials in collections from becoming dust. Digital collections provide library users with additional resources they can use beyond the licensed electronic resources or books available in the library. Digital collections changed and

will continue to change the services offered by libraries to their users.

The library is not dead nor is it in imminent danger of death from digital and electronic resources. Instead digital and electronic collections present new opportunities and avenues of growth for libraries. In a 2008 article by Lyman Ross and Pongracz Sennyey, they highlight the fact that digital collection has no boundaries. Users anywhere and anytime have the same access to materials as someone using the library. While items in print still dominate collections at libraries it is digital collections users make effective use of when they need to complete a research project and the library is closed. (Ross & Sennyey, 2008). Along those same lines is the introduction of Google Books and Scholar.

The Google Books project began as a digitization project to scan the books from major research libraries with the ultimate goal of people everywhere being able to search and have access to all books and all languages and connect people to books they might never have know about and publishers would have new readers. (http://www.google.com/googlebooks/library.html) The project began in 2002 and in 2005; the University of Michigan announced they collaborated with Google to scan their book collection. In the intervening years, publishers have challenged Google Books in court through a lawsuit with the primary issue being the scanning of books still under copyright protection. In March 2011, the settlement agreement reached in the lawsuit was overturned. The project continues along with the legal issue over copyrighted materials.

Google Scholar provides users access to scholarly materials in university electronic repositories and allows universities to link their electronic resources with their link resolver to Google Scholar. When a student searches Google Scholar and sets their preferences to search for materials at their university any times available through their university's databases will be indicated as full text at University. If it is not available in full text, they will be provided with a link to find it in one their university's databases or through the catalog, if it is in print or interlibrary loan. Most university libraries have a link on their library web site to Google Scholar. Librarians and faculty alike know students use Google to search for materials for their research projects. By showing them how to use Google Books or Scholar to find library materials at the university library will make students more familiar with library resources and increase use of the electronic resources available. Instead of finding and using any article from the Internet or a web site students will now have access and know how to access the scholarly resources, they need through a search engine they know how to use.

In the digital wave of the 21st century collaborating with companies such as Google will allow libraries to increase student use of their resources. It helps libraries work with students to make them more information literate and provide them with the scholarly resources they need by showing them how to access them through Google Scholar and Books in addition to the library's web site. Partnerships to develop digital collections will also be critical if library has wanted to increase or maintain their digital collections. Libraries are not dead nor are they in danger of dying but they need to look at alternative ways to connect their users with the resources they need and the ability to connect to them when they want them. The next few years will be one of change for libraries and the practice of librarianship.

REFERENCES

Barratt, C. C., & White, E. (2010). Case study for a large research institution library: The University of Georgia's Miller Learning Center. *Journal of Library Administration*, *50*(2), 135–144. doi:10.1080/01930820903454977

Beall, J. (2010). How Google uses metadata to improve search results. *The Serials Librarian*, *59*(1), 40–53. doi:10.1080/03615260903524222

Cohen, L. (2004). Issues in URL management for digital collections. *Information Technology and Libraries*, *23*(2), 42–49.

EDUCAUSE. (2008). E-books in higher education: Nearing the end of the era of hype? *EDUCAUSE Center for Applied Research Bulletin*, *1*, 2-13. Retrieved from http://www.educause.edu/ECAR/EBooksinHigherEducationNearing/162438

Eyambi, L., & Suleman, H. (2004). A digital library component assembly environment. *Proceedings of the SAICSIT*, *2004*, 15–22.

Fagan, J. C. (2009). Marketing the virtual library. *Computers in Libraries*, *29*(7), 25–30.

Garibay, C. G., & Figueroa, A. (2010). Evaluation of a digital library by means of quality function deployment (QFD) and the Kano model. *Journal of Academic Librarianship*, *36*(2), 125–132. doi:10.1016/j.acalib.2010.01.002

Gorley, D. (2001). *An architecture for the evolving digital library*. Conference Paper, EDUCAUSE Annual Conference 2001. Retrieved from http://net.educause.edu/ir/library/html/edu0122/edu0122.html

Institute of Museum and Library Services. (2006). *Status of technology and digitization in the nation's museums and libraries*. Retrieved from http://www.imls.gov/resources/TechDig05/Technology%2BDigitization.pdf

Koutsomitropoulos, D., Alexopoulos, A. D., Solomou, G. D., & Papatheodorou, T. S. (2010). The use of metadata for educational resources in digital repositories: Practices and perspectives. *D-Lib Magazine*, *16*(1/2). Retrieved from http://www.dlib.org/dlib/january10/kout/01kout.html doi:10.1045/january2010-koutsomitropoulos

Krishnamurthy, M. (2007). Open access, open source and digital libraries: A current trend in university libraries around the world. *Program: Electronic Library and Information Systems*, *42*(1). doi:doi:10.1108/00330330810851582

Lynch, C. (2005). Where do we go from here? *D-Lib Magazine, 11*(7/8). Retrieved from http://www.dlib.org/dlib/july05/lynch/07lynch.html

Ross, L., & Sennyey, P. (2008). The library is dead, long live the library! The practice of academic librarianship and the digital revolution. *Journal of Academic Librarianship, 34*(2), 145–152. doi:10.1016/j.acalib.2007.12.006

Sharifabadi, S. R. (2006). How digital libraries can support e-learning. *The Electronic Library, 24*(3), 389–401. doi:10.1108/02640470610671231

Sheeya, N. K. (2010). Undergraduate students' perceptions of digital library: A case study. *The International Information & Library Review, 42*, 149–153. doi:10.1016/j.iilr.2010.07.003

Thong, J. Y. L., Hong, W., & Tam, K. Y. (2004). What leads to user acceptance of digital libraries? *Communications of the ACM, 47*(11), 79–83. doi:10.1145/1029496.1029498

Tibbo, H. R. (2002). *Primarily history: Historians and the search for primary source materials.* Joint Conference on Digital Libraries. New York, NY: ACM

KEY TERMS AND DEFINITIONS

Digital Collections: Online collections of primary source materials including but not limited to manuscripts, diaries, letters, realia, and photographs.

Institutional Repository: A digital collection hosted by a college or university that stores scholarly research by faculty and students such as, papers published in academic journals and electronic theses and dissertations.

Learning Objects: Materials available for instructors to use in their classes that provide experiential learning for students. Learning objects help students to understand a basic concept or apply a concept to a real world situation.

Metadata: Is data about data. It is the keywords, subject heading and tags to identify and find materials when searching the Internet or a digital collection including a library's online catalog.

Open Access: Scholarly material available on the Internet for free with no copyright restrictions, permissions or licensing requirements. An example is the journals published by the Public Library of Science (PLoS).

Chapter 6
Technology for Remote Access

ABSTRACT

Technology to access materials remotely has gone from document delivery via snail mail to documents received electronically. No longer do users have to come into the library to find articles in scholarly journals, magazines, and newspapers. Books are not always available electronically, but users can search the library's online catalog to find print and e-books without going to the library. The primary technologies used to access materials off-campus are virtual private networks (VPN) and EZproxy. These technologies authenticate users through a password. Once they are authenticated they can access the library collections for their research.

INTRODUCTION

Students are no longer required to access all the materials they need for a research project by coming into the library. The first step was automating the catalog. When libraries moved from the card catalog, which was labor intensive and time consuming to maintain, students could find books for their research from home. The next step was the creation of databases where full text articles were scanned and users could search without the need for a print index. Yes, print indexes still exist but, there are many indexes available from database vendors. With the creation and growth in databases and the improvement in technology users could search for materials from home. They have the option to print, e-mail, or save the article. No longer does a researcher need to physically be in the library to do their research. Articles obtained through interlibrary loan are usually delivered electronically. Some distance education students may still receive some materials via mail but it is usually the exception rather than the rule. Remote access has changed the way library resources are delivered and made the library available 24 hours a day throughout the year.

DOI: 10.4018/978-1-4666-0234-2.ch006

BACKGROUND

EZproxy and virtual private networks (VPN) allow users to access materials, library resources, from off-campus locations. Most libraries connect their databases through EZproxy or a similar technology. This method provides the library with the ability to authenticate the user since databases are only available off-campus to current students, faculty and staff. Security is a major issue associated with remote access to library collections. Another is multiple passwords required by users to gain remote access to the materials they need. This can become a barrier to access because passwords change on a regular basis.

Link resolvers are part of remote access to library collections. Link resolvers are used to determine if a journal article is available in another database, the library's print collection of journals, or through interlibrary loan. Using a link resolver with remote access helps users find the materials they need without having to start a new search in another database. Another method users have to access library material is through their student portal. Most student portals allow students access to e-mail, course management systems and library materials. A big issue with remote access is privacy versus the need to identify authorized users. Another form of remote access is a link resolver such as SFX. A link resolver provides the researcher with the ability to find an article within the other licensed databases or through interlibrary loan. For example, if you are searching in *Academic Search Complete* and the article is not available in full text but there is a link resolver button the researcher can use the link resolver to find the article in either another licensed database or obtain a copy through interlibrary loan. Depending on how the link resolver is set up, the researcher might also be able to determine if the article is only available in print in the library's journal collection.

MAIN FOCUS OF THE CHAPTER

Students cannot always come to the library to study in spite of the fact many academic libraries are open 24 hours a day or have extended hours during the week until one or two in the morning. The other factor is students are not required to go to the library to do research, unless they need to use a book or journal in print. Personal experience from working at the reference desk indicates they would rather use an electronic resource than an item in print that requires them to come to the library. Remote access technology allows users to search the library's catalog and licensed electronic resources. They have all the functionality as if they were physically in the library. Remote access technology makes accessing electronic resources off-campus possible. The two primary technologies in use are proxy servers and virtual private networks (VPN). Both types of technologies allow users, through the use of authentication, gain access to licensed electronic library resources. A third remote access technology is a link resolver. Not every database has the full text of an article and a link resolver helps the user find the article either in another database subscribed to by the library, in print at the library or through interlibrary loan.

There a couple of basic terms related to remote access of library collections. The first is proxy server. A proxy server basically intercepts requests for information. It serves as a firewall to prevent unauthorized users from gaining access to resources that are for internal use only. In order to gain access through the proxy server a user needs a password to gain access. Proxy servers are just one method of security to prevent outside users from gaining remote access to a library's electronic resources (*Webster's New World Computer Dictionary*, 2003). Database licensing agreements prohibit the use of the resource by someone who is not affiliated with the institution.

In the chapter on collection development policies (Chapter 4) access to a licensed resource should be part of the contract between the library and the publisher. This part of the contract stipulates how the resource can be accessed and clearly defines who is considered an authorized user. The proxy server is configured to allow only authorized users to gain access to the licensed resources. A proxy server sends information between the user's home computer and the vendor database that makes it appear as if the person is working at the library rather than from their home (Mikesell, 2004). In essence a proxy server is a filter for requests for information from other servers. When a user tries to access the licensed databases from off-campus the proxy server will filter the request to ensure the person is authorized to use those resources. Once the user is authenticated they can access the resources they need. A proxy server provides access control to resources that should only be used by current employees or students of the institution. A password requirement to gain access to the resources provides a limited amount of anonymity for the user. The proxy server keeps track of the number of users who access it and in some instances the number of times it is accessed by individuals (Lawrence, 2009).

The second term is virtual private networks (VPN). A VPN is another form of security to prevent unauthorized users from obtaining remote access to library resources. A VPN uses encryption to prevent someone from outside the institution from gaining access to their resources (Pfleeger, 2008). Connecting remotely through a VPN allows users access to all the resources as if they were working on campus. They can access library databases without having to enter another password. Your user ID and password to connect to the VPN verify you are allowed access to the network. This is easier for users because they are required to enter multiple user IDs and passwords to gain access to the resources they need.

Student portals used by almost every campus in the United States allow students to use their ID and a password to check e-mail, campus announcements, register for classes, and check their grades and access library resources off-campus. A problem with student portals is the student might need to enter another password to gain remote access to library resources. So instead of one password to gain remote access the student or researcher will need to use a second password. This can be a source of frustration for the library user. Student portals can be configured to authenticate the user then allow them to gain access to licensed library resources. The University of South Florida uses this type of authentication. All students and employees create a "NetID." This ID allows them to sign into the university portal myUSF. With one ID and password students and faculty can access the course management system, library resources and other resources such as e-mail. This type of authentication allows for easier integration of licensed library resources into the course management system. Using EZproxy is the easiest and most effective way for users to remotely access the library's resources from off-campus. EZproxy not only makes it easy for users to gain access to licensed databases it also makes it easy for libraries to configure their databases for remote access.

EZproxy was developed in 1999 by Chris Zagar and in 2008 OCLC acquired the software. At the time of the acquisition over 2,400 institutions in over 60 countries were using EZproxy to authenticate remote user access to licensed databases (OCLC, 2011). The software is customizable and allows the institution to create web pages to allow both on and off-site users to remotely access licensed databases. The institution is responsible for verifying their licensing agreement allows for remote access to its content (OCLC, 2011). Once EZproxy is installed and set up it requires remote users to log in once during their session. Once they are validated as an authorized user during the session they do have to enter the password again to access the library's licensed databases (OCLC, 2011).

OCLC provides the basic configuration for the databases and user authentication. The institution enters the name of the database and the URL for the database. Once the configuration is complete remote users can access the licensed databases off-campus. With the development of EZproxy it became easier to configure and provide remote access to licensed databases. EZproxy ended the need to create browser directed and custom programmed proxy server software (Webster, 2002). When teaching students it is important to show them how to access licensed databases remotely. Students need to know how to find the password to access the library resources and how to connect remotely. Using the example of the University of South Florida there is a link from the library's web site labeled "Log in for full access." Selecting this link takes you to another page where the NetID and password can be entered and the user can then use the licensed resources of the library. In addition to including this information in face to face instruction sessions you can also create a tutorial that can be posted to the library's web site (Ribaric, 2009).

The main advantage to using EZproxy is the user will not have to configure their browser to remotely access licensed databases (Breeding, 2001). Another advantage to using EZproxy is the fact it provides persistent links to licensed databases. Once the link is created it will not change. EZproxy can also be used as a form of assessment by using the logs created each time a user remotely accesses a resource. The logs can be analyzed using log analyzer software. OCLC provides a list of available log analyzer programs some are open source and others are proprietary. Analyzing the logs will show the pages the users accessed, the busiest times of the day and the number of visitors by day. (Lawrence, 2009). In spite of some of the problems with proxy servers it is one of the most effective ways for users to gain access to licensed electronic resources at their institution. EZproxy provides library users with the ability to connect resources as though they were on campus. The EZproxy first alters the links from the web sites of the database vendors.

The next step in the process is the web sites are changed to the EZproxy server and when the user accesses a link to a database from the library's web site while off-campus they are passed through to the EZproxy server each time they access a different database (Mikesell, 2004).

Other proxy server software besides EZproxy is available. Onelog from ITS Ltd. provides access management to licensed library resources in much the same way as EZproxy. Once a user identifies a resource they want to search the software determines if they are on or off campus and requires them to use a password to gain access. Shibboleth is an Internet 2 project and provides single sign-on for users to gain access to licensed resources or course management systems. Once the user signs on through Shibboleth they do not have to enter another ID or password to gain access to the resources they need. Shibboleth allows users to join or create a federation of users to share resources or services. An example would be a consortium of colleges and universities within a university system or within a geographic area. This project uses Security Assertion Markup Language (SAML) for user authentication (Shibboleth, 2011). SAML is an extensible markup language (XML) that authenticates users attempting to access an restricted resource such as, a library database.

A virtual private network or VPN functions differently than a proxy server and has a different configuration. When a user accesses materials through a VPN they are connected through the institutions network. This connection allows a user to access all the resources as if they were on campus or working in their office. There are two types of VPN clients one is remote access and the other is site-to-site. The difference is a remote access VPN is a connection between the users' computer and their office or campus. While a site-to-site VPN is designed for companies with multiple offices and allows each office to have a secure connection over the Internet to the company's network. Each office will have access to the same resources at the different locations. For library collections we will be focus on a remote access VPN since most users will connect from their personal computer to the library's resources (Tyson & Crawford, 2011) .

A remote access VPN requires a network access server and client software. The network access server allows users to connect the secure networks as though they were working in their office or on campus. The software is necessary to create a secure connection to the VPN through the encryption provided by the software (Tyson & Crawford, 2011). Another requirement is a firewall to prevent or restrict certain types of traffic from the Internet passing through the Internet to the network. The greatest benefit of using a VPN connection as opposed to a proxy server is with one sign-on and connection the user has access to all the library's licensed resources without having to pass through the proxy server or needing to enter another user ID and password to gain access to the library's licensed resources. It provides the most secure access to the library's resources and prevents unauthorized users from gaining access to databases or e-reserves. The information is kept secure not only through encryption but also tunneling. Tunneling provides an extra layer of security to the information that is going between the remote location and the main office or in this case the college or university where the user works or attends school (Tyson & Crawford, 2011). Security with VPN requires the computers at both ends of the tunnel to encrypt the data. The aspect of security requires the use of one of two types of protocol. One is Internet protocol security and the other is generic routing security. Internet Security is the most common type of security used to send information over the Internet. Generic routing encapsulation determines the packaging for the passenger protocol for transport over the Internet protocol (Tyson & Crawford, 2011).

VPN provides an added layer of security that is not available with a server proxy. This added layer of security ensures unauthorized users will not gain access to licensed library resources or e-reserves. Proxy servers and the use of EZproxy make it easy for users to gain access to the library's resources while a VPN allows users to gain access to not only library resources but also files they may use on a computer located on campus. There are advantages to each and it depends on the users' needs. If they only need access to library resources then EZproxy will be their best option versus someone who needs access to their files and VPN will be the better option. Two of the major VPN software providers are Cisco and OpenVPN. OpenVPN is open source software using secure socket layer and transport layer security to encrypt information sent between computers (OpenVPN, 2011).

Remote access technology makes it convenient for students to work off-campus. They know library resources will be available 24 hours a day and seven days a week. However, those same technologies can also cause frustration and problems for users. Similar to the frustration they may encounter while searching one of the databases. In an article from 2003 that surveyed 128 library directors of various size academic libraries to determine the costs and problems associated with remote access technologies. The survey had a response rate of 55 percent. The survey results indicated that 94 percent of the institutions, that responded, used a proxy server for users to gain access to library resources. This survey indicated only 30 percent of the responding libraries used or were testing a VPN for users to connect to library resources. Respondents indicated that regardless of the type of remote access technology used, VPN or Proxy server, users reported problems with the technology(Covey, 2003).

Troubleshooting for both types of technology was the primary problem reported by the surveyed libraries. For libraries with proxy servers it was 58 percent and for VPN it was 69 percent. In spite of the problems with troubleshooting most libraries reported they spent less than $5,000.00 per year on maintenance and support for their proxy server or VPN (Covey, 2003). Overall most libraries were

Figure 1. Screen capture of NetID Single Sign-on for University of South Florida. Used with permission.

satisfied with the proxy server they implemented. The author of the study used previous research studies that indicated problems with remote access technologies was just one reason users did not feel libraries were meeting their needs for remote access to library resources. Other factors such as web site navigation and the difficulty of searching resources once they find them on the web site. (Covey, 2003) Remote access technologies might get users to the resources they need but libraries need to provide services to instruct users on how to search the resources.

In order to be in compliance with copyright law for remote access to copyrighted materials it is necessary to have them password protected. A proxy server and EZproxy or a VPN will achieve that requirement. Either type of connection will work for e-reserves or licensed databases. The user will need an ID and password to use the VPN. At many institutions the ID is based on their e-mail address and password. The e-reserve system is often linked from the library's web site and requires students to enter a password created by their instructor. When the library user enters their Net ID and password they will be able to search the library's resources. The University of South Florida uses this type of connection as seen in figure 1.

Once a USF student or employee receives their ID card they can use the number on it to create their NetID and password. The ID and password will allow them to gain access to the course management system and library resources. Once they are signed in they will not have to enter another password to search library resources. Single sign-on and point of access makes it easier for library users. Authentication is performed through this single point of entry. If a person does not have a NetID they cannot log into myUSF. This prevents unauthorized users from gaining access to the university's proprietary resources. Once a user signs in they can start searching the databases but not all databases are full text and they do not have the same journals or magazines. As a result there might be an article they want but it is not available in full text in the database they are searching. So they will need to find the article and the link resolver in the database will direct them to the article or how they can obtain a copy of the article.

It is important to have the technology in place for users to gain remote access to library resources but it is equally important that users know how to connect to the library's resources and to search them once they gain access to them. In a case study by two librarians at the C.W. Post campus of Long Island University of non-traditional students they found students were not always satisfied with their search results through remote access to the library's databases. Through interviews and instruction sessions with follow-up sessions with the students their study indicated students once they gained access to the resources were not sure how to search them and the students who searched did not find what they wanted. What they determined through their study was students liked having remote access but were frustrated by the problems they encountered while searching library resources. The students required assistance by a librarian to help them with their searches. (Boyd-Byrnes & Rosenthal, 2005)

The ability to remotely connect is just one aspect the other is the ability to search the resources once you are connected. The next chapter discusses course management systems and it is through course management systems that librarians can offer synchronous or asynchronous instruction to students on how to use library resources. Teaching them how to search is better through synchronous instruction because it provides users to see in real-time how to construct a search and narrow their results to manageable numbers. Another aspect that is frustrating to users is the ability to find the full-text of an article when the database they are searching only provides an abstract of the article. It is important to show users how to use the link resolver provided within the database. Many companies offer link resolvers for the most part they all work the same way.

Link resolvers such as SFX or LinkSource, just to name two of the available link resolvers, can help users find the resources they need without having to search multiple databases. Here is an example of how a link resolver works. A library user is searching a databases and finds an article they want to use but it is not available in full text. The search result will provide a link to find it within their library's databases. This option will be a button indicating "Find it @". Selecting the link connects to the link resolver which in turn finds the full text of the article in another database, in print within the library's collection or possibly through interlibrary loan. If the article is available full text in another database another window will open with a list of the databases they can find the full text article. Selecting the option "go" will take them to the article. If the article is available in print within the library's collection they will be given a link to the catalog and if it is available only through interlibrary loan there will be a link to the interlibrary loan service used by the library.

If the library uses Illiad for interlibrary loan the user can sign into their account from the database and the citation information needed for the interlibrary loan request will be pulled from the databases into Illiad and the user can submit the request. Once the link resolver is selected it should easily connect researchers with the resources they need. Before selecting a link resolver it should be evaluated for its effectiveness and ease of use. The University of Texas Southwestern Medical Library conducted an evaluation of two different link resolvers before selecting one. Their test focused on the success rate of linking to a full text article within the library's resources. They used selected databases to test the link resolvers and using a sample size of 65 articles their overall success rate was approximately 88% and most users found the full text article with two clicks (Jayaraman & Harker, 2009). Link resolvers make searching easier for researchers but there are problems associated with them. Sometimes they indicate an article is available in full text in another database and it is not. The issues are usually resolved by working with the database vendor and the link resolver.

Most link resolvers work in conjunction with OpenURL. The OpenURL protocol provides the user with a connection between the libraries resources and how to obtain the resource. With OpenURL when the user finds a resource they need this protocol will give the user options on how to obtain a copy of the article. They may be able to select from full text, free e-copies, physical library holdings or interlibrary loan or document delivery. It provides the user with immediate access to the article they found. The OpenURL protocol provides institutions with the ability to determine who is an authorized user and who is not authorized to access licensed library resources. It provides four methods to identify authorized users. OpenURL can identify the IP address of the user or information stored in a cookie, use information from a digital certificate or user attributes from the Shibboleth system. (ExLibris, 2011).

Link resolvers are not perfect. They only return the correct article about ninety percent of the time (Munson, 2006). The library can resolve some of the problems but they cannot always fix the problems with link resolvers. One common issue with link resolvers involves the International Standard Serial Number (ISSN) (Munson, 2006). This is a common problem with newspapers and the reason the errors occur is the method by which they are indexed by the original database or origin where the user found the citation and the target database where the full-text of the article resides. If they are indexed differently by the two databases it will result in the wrong article being selected in the target database (Munson, 2006). There are other problems that can arise with link resolvers including multiple ISSNs in the same record and also the information supplied by the database vendor for the years covered of a particular periodical. If the coverage dates are incorrect the full-text article will not be available even though it indicates in the database it is available in full-text. Another factor impacting the full-text availability of an article is the embargo period. Some periodical publishers impose an embargo on the available dates for full-text such as the current year is not available. In JSTOR there is a five year rolling window for availability. While link resolvers do present problems at times for users and librarians they still provide an effective method to get users from a citation in one database to full-text of an article in another database (Munson, 2006).

A study conducted by three librarians in the California State University System (CSU) students at the Northridge and San Marcos campuses for a two week period in May of 2004 and received 421 responses to their survey. The respondents were primarily undergraduates (54 percent) from a wide variety of disciplines. Survey results indicated that only 50 percent of the students believed SFX met their expectations and 49 percent of the students responded they expected full-text most of or all of the time in their search results. Librarians at the two campuses also participated in the study and the librarians were concerned with the accuracy of results as opposed to full-text results. Both students and librarians agreed that SFX was a better option to conducting numerous searches and while they saw areas for improvement they were for the most part satisfied with the results and the way it works (Wakimoto, Walker & Dabbour, 2006).

Not every institution uses a link resolver and without one remote user will need to use the title of the journal to determine the database the journal is available in full text. This will increase the amount of searching by the user to find full text articles. There are vendor supplied solutions as opposed to using a stand-alone link resolver such SFX. Ovid offers Links@Ovid and SilverLinker allowing users of Ovid databases to link resources to resources within Ovid and resources in other databases. It also provides a link to local holdings, interlibrary loan, document delivery systems and external link resolvers (Grogg, 2006).

Another option is to select the full text option from the database interface. The problem associated with selecting full text is you could exclude articles that might be useful for your research but are available in another database subscribed to by the library. Even though an article or articles is not available full text it might be in the print journal collection at the institution or available through interlibrary loan. Some database vendors provide vendor specific link resolvers. The library can use the vendor link resolver instead of purchasing a stand-alone product such as SFX. The vendor products will search for full text links within multiple databases from the same vendor. Most or all of the stand alone link resolver products offer statistical reports that allow the institution to learn how the link resolver is being used by researchers to find articles they need.

SFX provides libraries with a variety of statistical reports. The value of these reports is they provide the library with an overview of how the electronic resources are being used and what users want but cannot find through their searches. There are a total of 20 statistical reports provided by SFX (Chrzastowski, Norman & Miller, 2009). The options for 19 of the reports have to be selected from four major areas that are query parameters, dates to query, filters and output. The 20 reports range from the number of SFX request and Click-Throughs per Day to Open URLS That Resulted in No Full-Text Services, Selected by Source. The reports provide libraries using SFX with the ability to see what databases are being used, where full text articles are being drawn from, popular journals by target or source and journals requested but not available in full text (Chrzastowski, et al., 2009). The purpose of the statistical reports is to provide libraries with not only with collection management and development information but, also to determine how their resources are being accessed. SFX provides statistical reports but database vendors also provide statistical reports for their products. Libraries can use the information to determine how often databases are being accessed from off-campus but also the number of searches where users do not find full-text articles or the resources they need. The information can be used to provide mediated instruction between librarians and the users either through online classes or through embedded librarian services within online courses.

Another option for users accessing library resources remotely is federated searching. Federated searching allows library users to search multiple databases at once. The two widely used federated search tools is Webfeat from Serials Solution and MetaLib from ExLibris. Once the user connects to library resources from off-campus they have the option to search one database or there will be a link from the library's database page for the federated search tool. Most federated search tools are linked to three or four general databases such as *Academic Search Premier* or *ProQuest Research Library*. There are advantages and disadvantages to federated search tools.

One advantage is by searching across multiple databases at once allows the user to quickly find the resources they need. They can select the results they want and print, e-mail or save the article. The disadvantage is federated search tools can yield too many results and too few options to narrow the search results even further. There are new products in place such as, EBSCO's Discovery Service, ProQuest's Summon Service, and ExLibris's Primo. Federated search tools allow library users to search for information across multiple databases, digital collections and online catalog. The benefit of the search tools from EBSCO, ProQuest, and ExLibris is the fact they are customizable to meet the library's needs and provide more options for users to narrow their search results. Users have the option to select books, articles, subject headings, date range, and if there is more than one library they can limit their search to the materials at a specific library. Yes, they may obtain too many search results but, the possibilities to narrow their results are greater than with federated search tools.

Security is an issue with remote access. There are issues with proxy server security. Some of the issues include hackers finding an open computer to gain access to databases and authenticating users. Since only current employees and students can access vendor databases the proxy server needs to draw from a current list of students or employees that verifies by an e-mail address or student identification number (see also figure 2).

An unprotected proxy server can allow an unauthorized user to download articles from an available database or databases in violation of the agreement with the database vendor. To prevent this type of security breach remote user authentication is necessary (Mikesell, 2004). User authentication requires the library to make sure they have a current list of authorized users the proxy server is authenticating against. Not having a current or accurate list of authorized users can

Figure 2. Schematic representation of a proxy server ©HujiStat/Wikimedia Commons/CC-by-SA-3.0 &GFDL

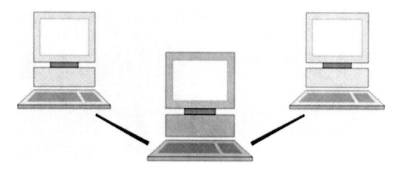

result in people gaining access who are no longer affiliated with the university or users who are authorized being denied access to the resources of the library (Mikesell, 2004). In 2002 this happened to JSTOR.

An unauthorized user gained access to the IP addresses of open proxy servers and began downloading whole issues of journals from JSTOR. While JSTOR took technological steps to prevent this from happening in the future they also suggested libraries who subscribe to JSTOR take a more aggressive approach to authentication and authorization. (JSTOR, 2002) By the time, JSTOR halted the unauthorized access the person had downloaded over 50,000 articles. (Covey, 2003) In an effort to combat unauthorized access to licensed library resources is the use of a firewall.

Firewalls keep out unauthorized users but, they can prevent authorized users from gaining access to library resources. Firewall issues can often be resolved by changing the settings on a user's computer either at work or home. For VPN security a Secure Sockets Layer (SSL) based VPN product provides additional security because it creates a secure connection and controls the servers users can access through their remote connection. An SSL-VPN reduces the threat of access by unauthorized users because they are set up with specific access policies and restrict user access to specific applications. The problem with SSL-VN is they are vulnerable to spyware and virus

infestation. (Beckman, 2010) Patron validation is critical to preventing unauthorized users from gaining access to library resources. Regardless of whether the library uses VPN or a proxy server for remote access the two most important things are linking an updated list of authorized users such as the current list of students, faculty and staff to validate IP user address.

At odds with the need for security are the need for anonymity. Academic libraries do not keep patron records. The code of ethics for librarians includes respecting the right to privacy for patrons and providing equal access to information. The attacks of September 11, 2001 led to the passage of the USA Patriot Act that created the Department of Homeland Security and providing agencies such as the FBI and CIA with the ability to spy on United States citizens suspected of engaging in terrorist activity. Under this law some libraries received requests for patron records from the FBI with a search warrant. The American Library Association is opposed to the section of the law that requires a breach of confidentiality for library records (American Library Association, 2005). The same applies to the use of computer equipment in the library. However, authentication to gain remote access is not the same as requesting patron records. Without some form or method for user authentication unauthorized users will gain access to licensed library resources.

FUTURE TRENDS

Remote access technologies will continue to evolve to include more mobile technologies and applications. Security for remote access will continue to be an issue and will require information technology departments, libraries and database vendors to continue to develop and implement new security measures to prevent unauthorized access to licensed library resources. The JSTOR incident from 2002 is an example of how security can be breached to gain unauthorized access to licensed content. No security is totally fool-proof; however, identifying possible security breaches before they happen will prevent unauthorized access.

EZproxy will continue to be the standard for proxy server connections. It is a proven product with many users. It provides seamless remote access to library resources. The Shibboleth Internet 2 project has the potential to become widely used and accepted. Single sign-on for users will become the standard. Using a single sign-on will eliminate the need for users to keep track of multiple IDs and passwords.

VPN and SSL VPN connections will grow in use. VPN and SSL VPN connections provide additional security to prevent unauthorized access and with SSL VPN the ability to control the applications users can gain access to through their connection. Discovery tools similar to EBSCO's Discovery Service and ExLibris's Primo will become more prevalent as libraries realize and understand how it will improve search results for users. EBSCO and ExLibris will have competition as vendors realize users including librarians are not satisfied with federated search tools. Conversely, the vendors of federated search tools will work to improve the functionality of their products. They will attempt to compete with the discovery search tools by improving the ability of users to narrow their search results. Improvements in product design may lead to increased use.

The demand and need for remote access to library resources will continue to grow. Users will expect to access library resources when and where they want to from off-campus locations. They will also expect to access materials through mobile technologies. As the demand for remote access increases libraries will need to make sure they have the information technology infrastructure in place to meet the needs of their users. They will need to ensure they have the security in place to prevent unauthorized access. Remote access technologies and the necessary security will continue to evolve and play an important role in providing user remote access to library resources.

CONCLUSION

Remote access to library resources has undergone substantial changes in the past 20 years. The earliest form of remote access to library resources for distance education students was document delivery. The user found a citation to an article from a book or article they read and contacted the library who in turn made a copy of the article or requested a copy of the item through interlibrary loan. The user received a paper copy. If they needed books the books were mailed to the person. While books are still delivered by mail the articles arrive to the user electronically. The library scans the article, creates a PDF and e-mail the article to the person. Same holds true for articles requested through interlibrary loan. They are sent electronically to the person who requested them. The earliest database searches, if you were off-campus, required you to call the reference desk and ask the librarian at the desk to search a specific database or resource for the information you needed. They would conduct the search and print a copy of the item you needed and it would be mailed to the patron.

As the Internet grew and database vendors converted articles in print to a digital format the days of asking a librarian to help you search came to an end. With the development of licensed electronic resources users could search databases while on-campus and eventually off-campus. The first remote technology required a dial-up connection. By the late 1980s DSL was being tested and by the 1990s dial-up connections had largely disappeared. As a result of better Internet connectivity the ability to access and search library resources improved. It was also during this period the physical card catalog disappeared. No longer did students have to search through several drawers of cards to find the books they needed for research. Now they could search the catalog on or off-campus. They could the books while working at home and the next time they were on campus find them in the library and check them out. It is the proliferation of licensed library resources that changed the way students search for and find resources for research.

Students on or off-campus have the ability to access the library's resources from any computer. It is the off-campus or distance education students who have the greatest need for remote access to library resources. Therefore it is important students can easily access and connect to library resources. Every library has a link to connect remotely to library resources or instructions on how to connect to library resources when they are off-campus. The two most widely used remote access technologies to connect to library resources are proxy servers and the virtual private networks (VPN). Both work differently but each provides a secure connection to library resources.

A proxy server is an intermediary between the user's computer and the library's resources. The proxy server provides the user with the ability to access library resources as though they were on campus. It acts as a filter to allow only authorized users to gain access to library resources. Once the user selects the resource before they can access it they will be required to enter a password and once the password is entered they can search the resource. A proxy server will determine if the user is authorized based on IP address and the institutions current list of students and employees. This holds true for virtual libraries like the Florida

Electronic Library. For the Florida Electronic Library the user will enter the barcode number from their public library card to gain access to the databases. With copyrighted materials it is necessary they be password protected to prevent unauthorized access to them.

Virtual private networks (VPN) on the other hand provides more security than a proxy server. The data that passes from the network to the user's home computer is encrypted at both ends. Once the user signs into VPN usually with their user ID and password they will have the same functionality they would if they were on campus. If it is a librarian they will be able to access their files in addition to the library's resources without having to enter another password. Virtual private networks are widely used in the corporate world to allow people to work in multiple locations without having to be in the main office. It also allows employees to telecommute. The same is true for students and faculty who connect through VPN. A faculty member can access their files, course management system, and library resources. Students can also access files stored a campus shared drive, course management systems and library resources. It is a single sign-on to access a number of different resources.

Single sign-on is the method used by many academic libraries and universities. The single sign-on allows the user the ability with one ID and password to gain access to the resources they need. Faculty and staff can access services such as e-mail, course management systems in addition to library databases. Students will have the ability to access, e-mail, library resources and course management systems. Single sign-on is similar to a portal because with one sign-on you have the option to access the resources you need without needing to sign-in again. The single sign-on authenticates and authorizes the user to gain access to the resources they need included library databases.

At the University of South Florida once a user signs in through Blackboard there is a link to the library for each of the campuses. The user can select the library for their home campus or the library at the Tampa campus. The authentication through Blackboard means they do not have to enter another password. The Shibboleth project also provides single sign-on for users. You can work at one institution and be teaching or taking a class at another institution but with Shibboleth the attributes are entered that allow users to sign in and gain access to the resources attributed to their sign on. The only resources the user can access are the ones assigned to their ID and password.

Another aspect of remote access technologies are link resolvers and federated searching. Link resolvers use OpenURL to direct users from a citation for an article to the full-text of the article in another database. The user selects the find it @ option in the database and another window will show them if the article is available in another database, in print in the library or interlibrary loan. If it is available in another database the user merely selects the "go" button and will be redirected to the article. If it is available in print they will need to obtain a copy either through document delivery or coming to campus to make a copy. The interlibrary loan option through link resolvers allows users to sign into their interlibrary loan account and the information for the article will be populated into the form and the user will select the submit button without having to re-enter the citation information for the article.

Security is an issue for either VPN or proxy servers. Proxy servers can be identified and hacked into resulting in unauthorized users gaining access to restricted resources. This was the case with JS-TOR in 2002. Libraries using open proxy servers had their IP addresses available on the Internet and they were used to obtain over 50,000 articles. While VPN is still more secure the information passing between the two access points has the potential to be compromised and the connection is susceptible to viruses or spyware. Firewalls prevent unauthorized users from gaining access and regardless of the type of remote access technol-

ogy being used a firewall needs to be in place in order to prevent unauthorized access. While they sometimes can cause authorized users' problems they prevent unauthorized users and limit the amount of spyware, viruses and malware from attacking the system.

The last issue concerning remote access technologies is privacy. Libraries both public and academic do not keep patron records. Remote access technologies require user authentication through their ID and IP address which means the information is retained by the technology and can be used to determine who the user was and the resources they used during their session. With the passage of the USA Patriot Act in 2001 libraries became vulnerable to requests for patron information by the Department of Homeland Security. The information can be used to place someone on a watch list or have a letter of national security sent to them requesting specific information. Librarians would prefer anonymity of a sign-on to gain access to library resources; however, this is not possible. In order to meet compliance with copyright law and also their contract with the database vendor users need to be authenticated and validated as authorized to have access to the resources.

Remote access to library collections starts with the need of distance education students or even students who live on campus and need to access materials after the library is closed. In order to access the materials not only does the technology need to be in place but so does a contract with the database vendor that provides remote access to the resources. The contract will stipulate who is authorized to access the database and how the database can be accessed. Once the contract is signed the library will implement the technology to access the licensed library resources. Most libraries use a proxy server or VPN in combination with a link resolver and possibly a federated search tool to provide remote access to their resources. The combination of different software and applications results in the user having seamless access to library resources from an off-campus location.

This provides library users with the resources they need anytime of the day or night and from any location.

REFERENCES

American Library Association. (2005). *Intellectual freedom issues*. Retrieved from http://www.ala.org/template.cfm?section=ifissues&template=/contentmanagement/contentdisplay.cfm&contentid=21654

Beckman, M. (2010, September). SSL VPN 101. *Windows IT Pro, 71-74.*

Boyd-Barnes, M. K., & Rosenthal, M. (2005). Remote access revisited: Disintermediation and its discontents. *Journal of Academic Librarianship, 31*(3), 216–224. doi:10.1016/j.acalib.2005.03.002

Breeding, M. (2001). Offering remote access to restricted resources. *Information Today, 18*(5), 52–53.

Chrzastowski, T. E., Norman, M., & Miller, S. E. (2009). SFX statistical reports: A primer for collection assessment librarians. *Collection Management, 34*(4), 286–303. doi:10.1080/01462670903177912

Covey, D. T. (2003). The need to improve remote access to online library resources: Filling the gap between commercial vendor and academic user practice. *Portal: Libraries and the Academy, 3*(4), 577–599. doi:10.1353/pla.2003.0082

Grogg, J. (2006). Linking without a stand-alone link resolver. *Library Technology Reports, 42*(1), 31–34.

HujiStat. (2007). *Schematic representation of a proxy server, CC-by-SA-3.0 &GFDL*. Retrieved from http://commons.wikimedia.org/wiki/File:SchematicProxyServer.png

(2003). *In Webster's New World Computer Dictionary* (10th ed.). Proxy Server.

Jayaraman, S., & Harker, K. (2009). Evaluating the quality of a link resolver. *Journal of Electronic Resources in Medical Libraries, 6*(2), 152–162. doi:10.1080/15424060902932250

JSTOR. (2002). Open proxy servers: Gateways to unauthorized use of licensed resources. *JSTOR News, 6(3),* 1-2. Retrieved from http://news.jstor.org/newsPDFs/dec2002.pdf

Lawrence, P. (2009, January). Access, when and where they want it. *Information Today,* 40-43.

Mikesell, B. L. (2004). Anything, anytime, anywhere: Proxy servers, Shibboleth, and the dream of the digital library. *The Eleventh Off-Campus Library Services Conference Proceedings, 41*(1). DOI: 10.1300/J111v41n0122

Munson, D. M. (2006). Link resolvers: An overview for reference librarians. *Internet Reference Services Quarterly, 11*(1), 17–27. doi:10.1300/J136v11n01_02

OCLC. (2011). *EZproxy*. Retrieved from http://www.oclc.org/ezproxy/support/default.htm

Open, U. R. L. (2011). *Website*. Retrieved from http://www.exlibrisgroup.com/category/sfxopenurl

OpenVPN. (2011) *OpenVPN*. Retrieved from http://openvpn.net/

Pfleeger, C. O. (2008). *Computer security in AccessScience*. McGraw-Hill.

Ribaric, T. J. (2009, January). How well do you proxy? *Computers in Libraries,* 19–21.

Shibboleth. (2011). *Website*. Retrieved from http://shibboleth.internet2.edu/

Tyson, J., & Crawford, S. (2011, April 14). How VPNs work. *HowStuffWorks.com*. Retrieved June 7, 2011, from http://www.howstuffworks.com/vpn.htm

University of South Florida. (2011). *Screen capture of NetID single sign-on.*

Wakimoto, J. C., Walker, D. S., & Dabbour, K. S. (2006). The myths and realities of SFX in academic libraries. *Journal of Academic Librarianship,* *32*(2), 127–136. doi:10.1016/j.acalib.2005.12.008

Webster, P. (2002). Remote patron validation: Posting a proxy server at the digital doorway. *Computers in Libraries,* *22*(8), 18–23.

KEY TERMS AND DEFINITIONS

EZproxy: Rewrites the URL provided by the database vendor for their web sites. The URL of the web site is changed to the library's EZproxy server. This results in seamless access to the library's databases for off-campus users.

Federated Searching: Allows a library user to search several databases at once. The federated search tool is configured with the resources to search. The user will enter their search terms and the results are sorted by relevance and database.

Proxy Server: A computer system or software that acts as an intermediary when a user requests information from another server. When a library user attempts to access the licensed databases from an off-campus location they pass through a proxy server that authenticates them as an authorized user.

Secured Sockets Layer: A method to encrypt information between a web server and a browser providing a secure method to transmit private information such as, a credit card number when ordering online.

Virtual Private Network: An encrypted Internet connection allowing employees to access the organizations computers from a remote location.

Chapter 7
Remote Access and Course Management Software

ABSTRACT

In addition to electronic reserves, instructors can link database materials through course management systems (CMS). This type of software allows faculty to link articles from databases into their course materials. This chapter provides an overview of different course management software and explains how instructors or librarians can link course materials into these systems.

INTRODUCTION

There are proprietary course management systems and open source systems. The major proprietary and open source CMS are Angel, Blackboard, WebCT, Moodle, and Sakai. The course management software provides for asynchronous learning and the ability to link articles or other materials into the CMS. Students with their password to the CMS are able to access the material or print it if necessary. There are options to provide links to databases through the CMS, however, students will often need to use a different password to access

DOI: 10.4018/978-1-4666-0234-2.ch007

the library databases if they are not authenticated through the library link provided in the CMS. While this can be tedious and an extra step for students to access the materials they need it also provides them with the opportunity to work on an assignment while using the LMS.

BACKGROUND

There are a number of course management systems available. Institutions can select from proprietary or open source learning management systems. Some examples of open source are Sakai and Moodle and examples of proprietary are Angel, Blackboard and WebCT. Each system allows the instructor to link to library resources. This can include links to the catalog, articles in a database, a specific database or databases and electronic or e-reserves. Another opportunity exists for librarians to work with an instructor and embed themselves into an online class. An embedded librarian program provides the students with library instruction and the chance to work with the librarian to find the sources they need for their research project through remote access. Course management systems provide a myriad of opportunities to link students through remote access to library resources.

MAIN FOCUS OF THE CHAPTER

Course management systems (CMS) provide faculty with the ability to teach classes to students in distance education programs. A CMS allows faculty to incorporate a variety of media and technology into their online class. Through the CMS an instructor can upload Word documents, PowerPoint presentations, links to web sites, videos, and podcasts. Students likewise can upload the same materials into the CMS for assignments or discussions. A face-to-face class can use the CMS for assignments and exams but their primary use is with online programs and classes. There are both open source and proprietary learning management systems. Two of the more widely know open source CMS are Moodle and Sakai. The major proprietary CMS vendor is Blackboard but there are others including CERTPOINT, iversity, eCollege, and Desire2Learn are just a few of the many choices available to colleges and universities. Once the university selects the LMS faculty and students receive training on how the software functions and how to design their course using the features available in the software. Students receive training on accessing course materials, post to discussion boards, submit assignments and take exams. Online courses taught synchronously where the

students and instructor meet at a specific day and time and work in the course management system in real time. The instructor can push web pages, presentations, videos and podcasts to their students and students have the opportunity to interact with the instructor and their fellow-students during the synchronous instruction session. There are many software options for synchronous teaching and some are Elluminate, Adobe Connect, Microsoft Live Meeting and Wimba. All of these options are stand-alone software that a distance-learning program can incorporate into the course management system.

Video tools for synchronous instruction are available through the CMS used by the institution. Blackboard, for example, integrates Elluminate and Wimba into their CMS products. Elluminate and Wimba provide instructors with the ability to use a web camera while teaching a synchronous instruction. The session can be recorded and the instructor can embed the link into the course material. Connecting distance education students with library instruction is a necessity in the 21st century. A study of library instruction to distance education students by the University of the West Indies and the University of Iowa revealed the importance of technology in reaching students taught off-campus (McLean and Dew, 2006). Both universities have different off-campus programs. The University of the West Indies used videoconferencing to instruct their distance education students on locating, evaluating and using information from library resources. The video conferencing instruction session introduced students to library resources and services (McLean and Dew, 2006). The University of Iowa used videoconferencing to provide an online class to distance education students that instructed them on using the library's resources and services. The course was created for their distance education MBA program and the success of this initial class led the library to explore expanding their online instruction to distance education students (McLean and Dew, 2006).

Libraries offer virtual reference through chat, e-mail, or text but, another alternative is video reference. Video reference is real-time interaction between the librarian and the patron. A video reference transaction requires the people involved to communicate with audio, video, chat and co-browsing (Hillyer and Parker, 2007). The video reference service was started at the University of Nebraska Omaha(UNO) using off the shelf web cameras and microphones. They used Polycom PVK software to create the interface that provided video and audio streaming between the library and the patron. After initial set up issues were resolved by the systems office at UNO the library marketed the service to their users (Hillyer and Parker, 2007). The library used a variety of resources including bookmarks, brochures and flyers. Plus it was promoted in library instruction sessions and outreach events. Unfortunately, the service had limited hours and as a result the video reference service was underutilized and the new Dean of the University Library discontinued the service based on the low usage statistics (Hillyer and Parker, 2007).

Video conferencing technology can be used for library instruction sessions for distance education students or reference services. Instruction sessions using video conferencing will simulate face-to-face instruction. Students will have an opportunity to learn how to use and access library resources and services. Most CMS have web or video conferencing included and once the instructor adds the librarian to their class they can use the video conferencing tools to teach students synchronously. An added benefit is the session is recorded and students can refer back to it throughout the semester. Video reference services provide libraries with the opportunity to work with their users in real time. This would be very beneficial to distance education students. Especially those students who live too far from campus. The real time interaction allows the student to receive individual research help for their project.

An asynchronous instruction session allows the students to review the course materials on their own. Some asynchronous classes are work at your own pace while others require students to submit assignments and post to discussion board by a specific due date. A course management system regardless of whether the university selects an open source CMS or proprietary one requires faculty to create an online presence especially when teaching a completely online course. Working with students in online courses requires follow-up by the instructor especially if students fall behind in the coursework. Students who are struggling with the coursework or using the learning management system should contact the instructor or the distance education department for additional help.

Course management systems are not always intuitive and can frustrate instructors and students. Most students and instructors are technologically perceptive but often have problems using course management systems. Every CMS allows instructors to upload written documents, for example a syllabus, an exam, quiz, or lecture notes. Instructors can also upload videos and podcasts or links to web sites. They can provide links to articles from a library database or a link to one of the databases at the library. Course management systems provide instructors with the ability to develop their own course content within the course management system. They also use the options within the course management system to create quizzes or exams. The many options available with the CMS are one reason why most colleges and universities have a faculty development center or center for teaching and learning. This type of resource allows faculty to learn how to use the software and develop course materials that will be effective in the online environment. Materials used in an online class should be engaging and help students learn key concepts for the course.

Screen capture software allows an instructor to create a video or tutorial for students showing them how to search for information, use a specific database, or find information on the Internet. The software will capture their computer screen and record their voice as they walk the student through the process. Screen capture videos of this nature should only be about two minutes. Anything longer and students will lose interest. A large video of this nature will also take a long time to load and if the student has a slow Internet connection, they will close it without even watching it. A better solution is to make a series of smaller videos to explain the topic. The same holds true for podcasts. Shorter is better but can also be used to record an instructor's lecture. For the most part course management systems work well but they are not always the easiest software for students to navigate and become a source of frustration for students and sometimes instructors. The 2010 Educause Center for Applied Research(ECAR) Study of Undergraduate Students and Information Technology indicated students did not like using learning management systems for their online courses.

Since 2004 Educause has surveyed undergraduate students at colleges and universities around the country to get an overview and better understanding of student's adaptation and use of technology in their courses and personal lives. The study examines a variety of technology related issues including how instructors use technology in their courses. Each year the study reveals new areas for future research and new ways in which students are using technology in college. The 2010 study provides additional insight into how undergraduates really feel about course management systems and other campus technologies instructors' use while teaching. The study found that students who were satisfied with their institutions course management system were also satisfied with the availability of information technology services for their coursework. Students were neutral when it came to the use of technology in their classes by instructors (ECAR, 2010).

Of the students surveyed only 47 percent felt their instructors used technology effectively. Other survey results indicated 49 percent of students felt their instructors had adequate technology skills to use technology in their classes. While 38 percent felt their instructors provided adequate training to use technology in their classes (ECAR, 2010). This survey's results over the past seven years indicate that between 55 and 60 percent of the students prefer a moderate amount of technology in their courses (ECAR, 2010). Since the 2005 study, the use of learning management systems has grown from 72 percent to slightly over 90 percent in 2010. The students surveyed indicated that almost 80 percent of them use it weekly and sometimes more often and slightly more than one-third of the students reported they use the course management system daily (ECAR, 2010).

While 90 percent of the students reported using a course management system, a little over half of the students surveyed said they were satisfied with their overall experience with them. The percentage of student satisfaction with course management systems has dropped 25 points from 76.5 percent in 2005 to 50.6 percent in 2010. Students response to the open ended question about online courses indicated the course management system was not easy to use, they were difficult to navigate and attach documents and little training was provided on how to use the course management software. Even students who had positive experiences using a course management system reported they would more training on how to use the software (ECAR, 2010). This annual study from Educause provides colleges and universities with an idea of the types of technologies used by students in their daily lives.

The study also indicates students perceive the technology supplied by the university in the form of course management systems. The overall impression of course management systems is not entirely favorable, however, they probably will not cease being used on campuses anytime soon especially for distance education courses (ECAR, 2010). The advantage to course management systems is the fact the material is password protected. You cannot gain access to the system without a user ID and password. In spite of the user ID and password requirements unauthorized access and cheating can take place. Students can log into the course management system and have their friends or another student in the class take their exam. They can also allow their friends or a student in a different class the ability to access course materials, including copyrighted materials, by signing in and allowing them to use the materials. Does this violate fair use? It probably does because a student not enrolled in the course is using the materials, as results they are not an authorized user. However, this would be difficult to prove.

Synchronous teaching and embedded librarians help the library create a presence in the online class environment. It provides the library with the ability to incorporate their resources into online and distance education programs. In a 2004 survey of the Association of Research Libraries (ARL) of the 103 libraries in the survey only 36.9% did not offer library services to distance education students (Yang, 2005). Being a distance education librarian is not without its challenges. Without faculty support, it becomes difficult for the librarian to encourage students to use library resources. Faculty support is critical to improve student use of library resources through remote access. Another issue raised by distance education librarians is their lack of knowledge about copyright and electronic reserve issues and policies (Yang, 2005). There are other challenges related to remote access of library resources as the University of Wisconsin-Eau Claire librarians discovered when working with an online class in marketing.

A marketing class allowed students from four different state campuses to register for the course. The students from UW-Eau Claire had access to the resources of their campus library and the students from the other campuses were limited to the resources of their respective campuses. In order to provide equitable access to resources the librarians

at UW-Eau Claire decided students, regardless of the campus where they enrolled for the class, would have access to the UW-Eau Claire Library's resources. This would require students to have a user ID and password to log into the proxy server (Markgraf and Erffmeyer, 2002). Students when required to remotely access a licensed database from off-campus they had questions about setting up and using the proxy server.

When students are required to access materials off-campus, they should receive instructions on remotely accessing the library's resources. Systematic instructions are often necessary and should include how to obtain the password and what is the required username or student ID they need to use. Embedded librarians in an online course provide students with the opportunity to ask the same person for help and the librarian will get to work with students throughout the semester instead of for just one instruction session.

An embedded librarian program goes beyond the usual chat reference or ask-a-librarian service. An embedded librarian works with an online class either for the entire semester or for part of the semester to help students develop and find resources for their research project. This can require a great deal of time by the librarian in order to achieve the expected results which for most faculty members and the librarian is students will find better sources and not wait until the assignment is almost due to start working on it. With a librarian, working with the students in an online class makes the students aware of not only the available library resources and how to access them remotely but also the ability to work with a librarian to help them identify the sources appropriate for their research topic. Duke University in the fall of 2007 started an embedded librarian program with four librarians working with a dozen faculty members.

The librarians had course builder access to the faculty member's course in Blackboard. With course builder access, the librarians were able to include their contact information and links to general library and subject-specific resources (Daly,

2010). They also included information on citing information and short animated tutorials. When Duke University began using LibGuides for their subject guides, they were able to embed the course subject guides into the Blackboard course. To assess the use of the course specific LibGuides the task force that developed the embedded librarian program determined the subject guides embedded in the online courses did not receive the same level of use as the ones created for a face-to-face instruction session. (Daly, 2010).

While the subject guides may not receive the same use, it is an opportunity to work with students in the online class and provide them with the links they need to library resources. There are variations of embedded librarian programs but the overall goal is to provide distance education or online learning students with library services to meet their research needs. In its most basic form a librarian provides their contact information in the course management system so students can contact them if they need research help. Other variations include the librarian working with students to help them develop their research strategies and identify sources to find materials for their research project. An embedded librarian program can include research assistance and reference services. An example of a well-designed embedded librarian program is on that involves faculty and librarian collaborations. The Community College of Vermont used this type of collaboration for their embedded librarian program.

Victoria Matthews a psychology instructor collaborated with librarian Ann Schroeder to develop an embedded librarian program for her Introduction to Psychology class. As a teaching assistant in Matthew's class Ann Schroeder participated in the mid-term and end of semester student discussions of their research paper (Matthew & Schroeder, 2006). She also used the discussion forum to provide students with information on how to cite sources uses APA style (Matthew & Schroeder, 2006). By the spring of 2006, the program was expanded to 43 classes (Matthew &

Schroeder, 2006). As the program expanded so did the types of services offered to the students. Librarians worked with students on small group projects, and answered weekly questions in an "Ask the Librarian" discussion board (Matthew & Schroeder, 2006). They also assisted students with Internet research and helped students in a family law class find Vermont Statutes for their class (Matthew & Schroeder, 2006). While some services were more effective than others were, the program and services offered provided students with the ability to work with a librarian even though they were not on campus (Matthew & Schroeder, 2006). The initial work of Matthew and Schroeder has expanded to include a support course for the social sciences and videoconferencing (Matthew & Schroeder, 2006).

Libraries can choose one of two ways to embed library resources. The first is to create a macro-level courseware integration of library resources (Shank & DeWald, 2003). This method of embedding library resources requires librarians to work with courseware developers and programmers to include a library presence in the course management system (Shank & DeWald, 2003). The other option is micro-level courseware integration where the librarian works one-on-one with faculty to create a library presence in their online course that will meet the specific needs of the students. It provides customized library resources for example, links to specific databases, e-book collections, tutorials or subject guides. With the growth of online courses, it will be important for libraries and librarians to have a presence in online courses. Without a presence in an online course, the library will not be the first choice students will make when they search for resources for their course work. (Shank & DeWald, 2003)

Meeting distance education students needs is critical to the students and librarians working with specific departments or programs. In the spring of 2004, Ellysa Stern Cahoy and Lesley Mutinta Moyo conducted a 15question web based survey of 250 randomly selected Penn State World Campus faculty members and received 57 complete responses. The purpose of the survey was to determine how faculty members within the Penn State World Campus promote library resources and services to their students in online courses. Some of the major findings from the survey indicated that 77 percent of the faculty who responded felt the library's role in distance education classes was to provide access to library resources and another key finding was the fact that 62 percent of the faculty who responded did not require their students to use their library for their coursework (Cahoy & Muntinta, 2005). The faculty members in the distance education program at Penn State World Campus were unaware of the library's resources and support services available to their online students. This type of study indicates librarians need to work with faculty teaching online courses to increase their awareness of library resources and services available to online students. Promotion of resources and services will require an active outreach program including collaborative work between librarians and faculty members to increase their students' use of library resources and services available to them as distance education students(Cahoy & Muntinta, 2005).

Auburn University Montgomery library conducted a survey, similar to Penn State, of their distance education faculty to determine how to meet the needs of their distance education students. In the fall of 2005, library sent a survey to the 102 faculty members who had a WebCT course on the campus server (Hightower, Rawl & Schutt, 2005). Out of the 102 surveys sent, they received 29 completed surveys for a response rate of 29 percent. The faculty taught in business, nursing, liberal arts, education and the sciences. The purpose of the survey was to determine how and if faculty linked library resources to their online classes through WebCT, determine why faculty do not link the library resources to their classes and determine the extent of the interest by faculty to include library resources in their online classes (Hightower, Rawl & Schutt, 2005).

Of the 29 responses received, only seven stated they linked library resources and services in their online classes (Hightower, Rawl & Schutt, 2005). The remaining respondents indicated they would be willing to link library resources and services in their online classes. After the survey was completed, the Library Instruction Coordinator used follow-up interviews as a method to promote library instruction classes for their students. One major outcome was an increase in requests for library resources and services and the development of additional opportunities for working with faculty in their online classes (Hightower, Rawl & Schutt, 2005).

The Ohio State University created the Carmen Library Link to connect students in online classes to library resources. This library embeds the link in every course page in their course management system. The student clicks on the link and it takes them to a library resource, which could be a link to a database with a description of the database, or it could be a link to the library's catalog. To create this link the librarians used a series of widgets, one widget could be for the library catalog and another could be for a database. In order to make changes to all the pages in the course management system they make a change to the widget and the change flows to the course pages (Black & Blakenship, 2010).

The creation of the link provided an opportunity for the libraries to work with teaching faculty and the learning technology departments. Collaborating with the teaching faculty determined the resources that needed to be included on a link for the course page in the course management system. By the spring of 2009, the link was functional and as a result the library was able to reach more students in more classes than they would teaching an in-person instruction session. Faculty input regarding the resources for the link provided students with access to resources including web sites, databases and citation information they would need for their course. The feedback from students was overwhelmingly positive because they had quick and easy access to the library resources they needed for their courses (Black & Blakenship, 2005).

Early editions of course management systems did not provide the ability to link library resources through the course management system. The linking of articles was a cumbersome process and persistent links for the article from the database were not prevalent. Another issue with early versions of course management systems was the use of copyrighted material in the course management system. For e-reserves, the library will obtain copyright clearance from the Copyright Clearance Center but with course management systems if the instructor posts copyrighted material they would be responsible for obtaining copyright clearance to use the material in their online course (Gibbons, 2005).

Libraries can provide links to their resources and services such as, course reserves through a course management system. Sakai is an open source, course management system developed by the University of Michigan, Indiana University, Massachusetts Institute of Technology and Stanford (http://sakaiproject.org/). As of this, writing over 350 institutions are using Sakai for their course management system. Earlier in the chapter, the study from Educause indicated students do not find proprietary course management systems easy to use but Sakai is more user friendly than the proprietary course management systems. Proprietary course management systems can be difficult for both students and faculty to navigate. Moodle and Sakai on the other hand are more intuitive and user friendly. It is easy to upload information, post to the discussion board, and create course content just to name a few of the positives aspects of these open source software products (Young, 2008, Beatty & Ulasewicz, 2006, Chester, 2010).

Moodle is also open source, course management software and is developed and maintained by a group of developers from around the world (http://moodle.org/). Moodle and Sakai are excel-lent alternatives to proprietary course management systems. They provide the same features as proprietary course management systems. The University of Dayton in 2007 transitioned from WebCT to Sakai and in 2008, the switch to Sakai was complete. In 2009, the library at the University of Dayton began to explore the possibility of moving their e-reserves to Sakai from the system they were currently using. It would save the library money and provide students in online courses the ability to connect with the reserves while in the online class. Instead of using two systems, they would only need one (Escobar, 2010).

By the fall of 2009, the library began the migration of their e-reserves to Sakai and ran their old e-reserve system in parallel with Sakai until the migration and transition was complete. There were some initial set up problems with e-reserves and Sakai but the library worked with their campus information technology department to create e-reserves folders in each of the online course pages. This allowed the library to upload e-reserve documents into the course management system. While there were some initial problems the library worked in collaboration with information technology and the teaching faculty to resolve the problems with the result being they successfully completed the transition of e-reserves from their proprietary system to Sakai (Escobar, 2010). The only negative impact was the library was no longer able to gather usage statistics on their e-reserves but they were able to correct the problem by installing Site Stats that allowed the library to obtain the necessary information (Escobar, 2010). By eliminating their proprietary course management and e-reserves systems, the library was able to save money by combining both functions in Sakai. This switch made it easier for students to access the e-reserves for their online course because they were in the course management system and did not have to sign out and use another password to gain access to the materials they needed (Escobar, 2010).

Working with students in an online course can also be an opportunity to help students develop their research skills. Some courses use a blended or hybrid method of instruction. The students will attend a lecture at different times during the semester and when they are not meeting face-to-face, the class meets online and will submit assignments, take tests and quizzes online. The online portion of the class can include additional materials such as podcasts; tutorials or web sites students can use to supplement the information from the textbook or in class lectures (DaCosta & Jones, 2007). Faculty members will often post their lectures or PowerPoint slides in the course management system. De Monfort University in Leicester, England used a hybrid class to help students develop research skills. The librarians provided links to the electronic resources of the library through the course page for each of the online instruction sessions. By providing links to library resources through the course page for an online course librarians are able to meet students where they are working at their point of need (DaCosta & Jones, 2007).

Why use a course management system instead of a web site, blog or wiki? One primary reason is a course management system only allows current students and faculty or staff to sign into them. User ID and password protect them. Because they require a password libraries and faculty can provide links to licensed library resources and copyrighted materials. Conversely, blogs, web sites and wikis do not require passwords to gain access to them. Once a person creates them, anyone can access them. If you provide links to an article from a database, it will result in anyone who visits the web site, blog or wiki with the ability to read and download the article. This would no longer constitute fair use and the university would be in violation of copyright law. However, faculty members do use wikis for students to submit assignments or work in groups.

Wikis are gaining use as a method to develop materials for the course before an instructor uploads them to the course management system. This allows the instructor with the ability to make changes quickly and upload them. Course management systems are not always user friendly and do require a lot of time to create and upload materials even with training. They can be a frustrating experience for both students and faculty alike. Course management systems allow you to use a template, create a course from scratch or copy a course from a previous semester. Depending on the course most of the time the instructor can copy the information from another course. They will need to remove any copyrighted materials before copying the course content. If they want to use the same copyrighted materials, they will need to obtain copyright permission before they can include it in their course content.

FUTURE DIRECTIONS

Course management systems are here to stay. Based on surveys of students and faculty it appears they will probably become more user friendly. The ECAR study result of undergraduate use of technology indicates student use the course management system but become frustrated by it when they cannot upload files or send e-mails through the system. In the first chapter on distance education, the most recent statistics indicate distance education will continue to grow over the next several years. As a result there will be more online classes which means, libraries and librarians will need to find a way to reach those students in online classes. Technology to work synchronously with students is already available and libraries will need to invest in the technology and training to ensure librarians have the skills to work in the online environment with students and faculty. It will also be critical for librarians to work with faculty to develop a library presence for a course.

This improved collaboration between librarians and faculty will provide students with links to library services and resources at their point of need. Librarians will need to receive ongoing training to know how to develop and upload materials and resources into a course management system. As budget cuts continue, they will need to examine combining services into course management systems. Combine e-reserves into the course management system if possible. Most importantly, libraries and librarians need to develop and maintain a presence in online courses. Another future trend will be course management systems will become more robust. They will provide the instructor and the students with the ability to incorporate multi-media materials within the course management system. The single sign-on provides students and instructors alike with the ability to access library materials remotely from the course management system. A colleges and universities look to reduce costs they may look to an open source CMS rather than a proprietary system. A 2008 article from the *Chronicle of Higher Education* focused on colleges and universities moving from Blackboard or other proprietary CMS to an open source CMS to save money over the long term. At the time of the article, Blackboard had 66 percent of the market versus Moodle with only 10 percent of the market. Clearly, Blackboard is the leader in market share but students find it frustrating to use (Young, 2008).

CONCLUSION

Course management systems are an alternative method to remote access to library resources. They provide students and instructors with the ability to have links to library resources they need for their course work. In addition to links to library resources instructors will be able to incorporate a number of different media into the course management system. A CMS is used primarily with students enrolled in an online class but they are also used for face-to-face and hybrid classes. Instructors teaching a classroom will often use the CMS for students to access and submit assignments, review lecture notes or presentations, take exams or quizzes and access library resources including articles from databases or e-reserves. With one sign-on, students will be able to access the materials they need for their classes and to library resources.

As with most technology, there are advantages and disadvantages to using a CMS. One of the major advantages is the fact students will have access to the resources they need 24 hours a day and depending how the library resources are linked to the CMS with one sign-on a student should be able to access the licensed electronic resources of the library without having to enter another password or user ID and password. Depending on the CMS in use by the institution, it might be possible to incorporate e-reserves into the CMS.

Merging the e-reserves into the CMS will result in a cost saving to the library because they will not have to use a separate system for their e-reserves. Students will not need another password to gain access to the course reserve system. The other option is faculty within the CMS can provide links to articles from databases or PDF copies of the articles into the course content. However, in order to do this the library or instructor will need to obtain copyright permission before including the article in their course. Once the course ends, the instructor needs to remove the material from the CMS and if the instructor plans to use the same material the following semester, they will need to obtain a new copyright permission. Another advantage is the CMS is password protected allowing instructors and librarians to upload copyrighted materials without being in violation of copyright law. Database licensing agreements stipulate who has access to the materials and how to access them through course management systems. Course management systems provide an alternative form of remote access technology. They accomplish the same thing as a proxy server or a VPN. There are disadvantages to using a CMS especially a proprietary CMS.

Most freshman and sophomore college students are digital natives. They are comfortable and can use most types of technology available. They are technology savvy. A CMS, however, is not intuitive to use. Many run on a Java platform and as a result, students often have a difficult time navigating the software, which includes uploading assignments, opening assignments, taking a quiz or exam and posting to the discussion forum. Faculty members also encounter problems with the CMS. Changes are not quickly made and it can be time consuming to make changes or to set-up a new course. A work around to the problem is to create a wiki where the instructor can outline the course and make changes quickly. A link to the wiki can be included in the CMS so students can refer to it when they need to know a due date or find information on the syllabus. Instructors can also include a link to a wiki for students to create or post assignments. Once the course is created in the CMS the instructor can copy the class layout for the next semester. This option provides the easiest and quickest means for the instructor to set-up their course in the CMS.

The Educause survey of undergraduate use of technology indicates the use of course management systems has increased significantly since the first Educause survey in 2004. While the use of course management system has increased over the past six years students indicated they used them but found them difficult to use because of lack of training. Students indicate in the survey that they receive little training on how to use the technology. They also indicated faculty could not teach on how to use the software and felt the faculty themselves did not know how to the use the software. Many colleges and universities have a faculty training and development center along with a distance education department. The primary purpose of these departments is to provide students and faculty with training on various technologies including course management systems.

However, just because training is offered does not mean faculty or students will take advantage of the training opportunities available to them. As a result, students will have a difficult time using the course management system and the instructor will also have a difficult not only using the software but also helping students when they have a difficult time navigating the course management system. In order to make an online class successful an instructor needs to have a presence in the online class. If they are unable to navigate the software, it will be difficult for them to have a presence in the online and engage students in the class. Without a presence within the online class students will lose interest and will fall behind. An embedded librarian program in an online class helps connect students to library resources.

A successful embedded librarian program created in conjunction with teaching faculty and the information technology department. In its most basic form an embedded librarian program will provide a link or contact information to the librarian who is works with that specific academic department. There are other variations of the embedded librarian program. The Ohio State University created the Carmen Library Link to connect students in online classes to library resources. The link was created in conjunction with the information technology department and teaching faculty. This link connects students to the librarian for the academic department or the specific course and library resources. When the student clicks, on the link it will take them to a library resource, which could be a database or the online catalog depending on their need. The librarian can interact with the students through the discussion board and work with students to identify appropriate library resources for their research project. Most of the libraries with an embedded librarian program are using a combination of a link to library resources in addition to having a librarian answer student questions regarding their research project through the discussion board.

By linking library resources through a CMS provides students with another means of remote access to library resources. The University of

South Florida provides a link to all of their campus libraries through Blackboard. Once the student signs into Blackboard, they will be able to select the link to their campus library and search for resources. Because it is a single sign and it validates them as an authorized user through the CMS, they will not enter another password or ID to search the library databases. Single sign-on for remote access to library resources provides authorized users with a simplified way to use the library's resources. The single sign-on validates the person as an authorized user and they are able to search any and all of the library's electronic resources without entering another ID or password. With one sign-on a user could gain access to the CMS, library resources and e-reserves. This method provides less frustration for the users and easier means of access control for the information technology department.

In order to determine the types of resources students in distance education courses need librarians have to work with the faculty to determine how and if they are promoting library services and resources to their distance education students. Surveying faculty at Auburn University in Montgomery and Penn State World Campus provided the librarians with the information they needed to develop a program to meet the needs of the distance education students at the two campuses. Without the survey information, the librarians at either school could not develop programs to address the needs of their students and to make distance education teaching faculty aware of the library resources available to their students.

An embedded librarian program can also include instruction for students. Instruction through the CMS and with an embedded librarian program can be synchronous or asynchronous. The type of instruction depends upon the needs of the instructor and the students. Asynchronous instruction, in the case of an embedded librarian program, would be answering questions on the discussion board and posting tutorials or other instructional materials on the course page. Students can then review

the materials or respond to the discussion board post anytime they are in the course. Synchronous instruction allows the librarian to work with the students in real time.

In a synchronous instruction session the librarian can use for example, Wimba, Elluminate, Adobe Connect, Go ToMeeting or Microsoft Live to show students how to search a database, properly format a citation, use a bibliographic management software such as Ref Works, End Note or Zotero. This type of instruction session in the CMS provides the students with the opportunity to search on their own while in the instruction session. Most course management systems allow students to work in break out or discussion rooms. While in working in groups the librarian can provide them with a link to the library's resources and provide them with the opportunity to learn how to access the resources from off-campus in addition to learning how to search.

Colleges and universities have many choices for a CMS. There are several proprietary systems available in addition to open source systems. Blackboard has the largest percentage of market share of the proprietary course management systems. The two widely known open source, course management systems are Moodle and Sakai. The proprietary systems can be frustrating for both students and faculty. Students and even faculty who are technology savvy do not find a proprietary course management system to be intuitive. As a result, faculty may have a difficult time creating their course and working with their students in the CMS environment. Students, on the other hand, may also have a difficult time opening course materials, assignments, taking tests or uploading assignments to the CMS. While many distance education programs offer training or support services an online tutorial in addition to classroom training may help students and faculty master the software.

Moodle and Sakai allow the institution to customize the software to meet their needs. Both Moodle and Sakai have the same features as a proprietary course management system but they are not as difficult to navigate as some proprietary course management systems. The University of Dayton was able to integrate their e-reserves into Sakai and eliminate their separate e-reserve system, which in turn led to a cost savings for the library. It also provided students with the ability to access the course reserves at their point of need. Instead of having to sign into the e-reserve system, the students can just use the link with the course page to access the article or material they need. Linking library resources through a course management system provides the library and librarians to meet students at their point of need for information. Embedding library resources and the librarian into an online class provides students with seamless access to the resources they need. As the number of distance education courses increase embedded librarian programs and remote access to library resources through course management systems will continue to grow.

REFERENCES

Black, E. L., & Blankenship, B. (2010). Linking students to library resources through the learning management system. *Journal of Library Administration, 50*(4).

Cahoy, E. S., & Moyo, L. M. (2005). Faculty perspective on e-learner research needs. *Journal of Library & Information Services in Distance Learning, 2*(4). doi:doi:10.1300/J192v02n0401

DaCosta, J. W., & Jones, B. (2007). Developing students' information and research skills via blackboard. Communications in Information Literacy, 1(1).

Daly, E. (2010). Embedding library resources into learning management systems: A way to reach Duke undergrads at their points of need. C&RL News, April.

EDUCAUSE Center for Applied Research. (2010). ECAR study of undergraduate Students and Information Technology 2010. Retrieved from http://www.educause.edu/Resources/ECARStudyofUndergraduateStuden/217333

Escobar, H. Jr. (2010). Reserves through Sakai: University of Dayton's primary tool for electronic reserves. Journal of Interlibrary Loan. *Document Delivery & Electronic Reserve, 20*(4). doi:doi:10.1080/1072303X.2010.507457

Gibbons, S. (2005). Integration of libraries and course-management systems. *Library Technology Reports, 41*(3).

Hightower, B., Rawl, C., & Schutt, M. (2007). Collaborations for delivering the library to students through WebCT. *RSR. Reference Services Review, 35*(4).

Hillyer, N., & Parker, L. (2007). Video reference--It's not your typical virtual reference. Internet Reference Services Quarterly, 11(4), 41-54. DOI: 10-1300/J136v11n0403

Markgraf, J. S., & Erffmeyer, R. C. (2002). Providing library service to off-campus business students: Access, resources and instruction. Library Services for Business Students in Distance Education: Issues and Trends, 7(2/3).

Matthew, V., & Schroeder, A. (2006). The embedded librarian program: Faculty and librarians partner to embed personalized library assistance into online courses. *EDUCAUSE Quarterly, 4*.

McLean, E., & Dew, S. H. (2006). Providing library instruction to distance learning students in the 21st century. *Journal of Library Administration, 45*(3-4), 315–337. doi:10.1300/J111v45n03_01

Shank, J. D., & Dewald, N. H. (2003). Establishing our presence in courseware: Adding library services to the virtual classroom. Information Technology and Libraries, 22(1).

Young, J. (2008). Blackboard customers consider alternatives. *The Chronicle of Higher Education, 55*(3).

KEY TERMS AND DEFINITIONS

Asynchronous Instruction: Instruction that is recorded and posted to the course management system. Students can review the material at their own pace.

Course Management Systems: Used by colleges and universities to provide students with the ability to take classes online. The course management system allows instructors to upload assignments, exams, course content, such as, videos, web sites, and links to articles. Students in turn can submit assignments, take exams, e-mail the instructor, or post to discussion boards.

Distance Education: Courses taught off-campus through a course management system. Distance education classes can be hybrid, requiring the students to attend a set number of classes on campus or completely online.

Embedded Librarian: A librarian assigned to an online class who provides library instruction and research assistance to students in the online class.

Synchronous Instruction: Instruction in an online class that takes place in real-time. The instructor has the ability to provide hands-on instruction to students through the course management system.

Chapter 8
Social Networks and Web 2.0 Tools

ABSTRACT

Social network sites such as Facebook and Twitter can provide another opportunity for users to remotely access library resources. The creation of a library Facebook page provides the library with the ability to promote licensed databases and the information users need to remotely accesses those resources and course or electronic reserve materials. Twitter accounts provide libraries with the opportunity to keep users informed about changes to licensed databases, in other words, anytime they add or discontinue resources or there is a problem accessing them remotely. Another option is foursquare. Foursquare allows you to find your friends and discover your city or library. Libraries can use foursquare to introduce students to it resources and services. The library could develop a contest for users to earn points and badges by discovering information about the library such as, new books, databases or services. Social networks provide libraries and users with new ways to promote and provide remote access to licensed databases.

INTRODUCTION

In 2004 Mark Zuckerberg started Facebook from his dorm room at Harvard University. This social network has over 500 million members and growing (Fletcher, 2010). It has members from around

DOI: 10.4018/978-1-4666-0234-2.ch008

the world and its members range from a variety of ages. It has extended beyond college students although they are still the core members. Because Facebook is still widely used by college students, it provides libraries with the opportunity to promote their resources and provide remote access to materials through social networks. By creating a Facebook page libraries can include a link to their web site allowing students to access library resources. Libraries can also use it to promote new resources and include links to tutorials on how to use library materials and remotely access licensed databases. Wikis and blogs are also part of social networks. They provide people with alternative sources of information and often have an RSS feed that allow users to read the most recent changes to the wiki or blog.

BACKGROUND

Facebook and Twitter are the two most popular social networks available to libraries to connect and stay connected with the students. It is an opportunity to build relationships with students and faculty. Facebook provides the library with the ability to market their services to a broader group of researchers. It presents the library with the ability to market not only their services such as, reference and instruction but also programs such as, outside speakers, poetry readings, book signings and research consultations. Since students have, a wide variety of Internet resources to select from it is important for libraries to connect with students where they collaborate and meet. Social networks become an extension of outreach to students and faculty. Web 2.0 tools encompass not only social networks but also blogs, wikis, RSS feeds, instant messaging, podcasting, and virtual communities. A review of 81 academic library web sites in New York State examined their use of specific Web 2.0 tools. These tools when combined with a traditional library web site enhance the services offered to students and faculty. The tools become an additional way to provide remote access to library resources.

MAIN FOCUS OF THE CHAPTER

Danah Boyd and Nicole Ellison in their 2007 article about social network sites provide an in-depth definition of social network sites. According to Boyd and Ellison social network sites; "construct a public or semi-public profile within a bounded system, articulate a list of other users with whom they share a connection and view and traverse their list of connections and those made by others within the system." (Boyd & Ellison, 2007, p.1). Boyd and Ellison clearly and concisely convey the primary reason people join a social network. The connection they make with friends and colleagues who share similar likes and interests, or belong to or work for the same organization. It creates a common bond and can lead to collaboration and sharing of information.

Social networks connect people through common interests and through the social network develop relationships that can help them solve problems or achieve a common goal. Social network services like Facebook, Myspace, Twitter, Flickr, YouTube, Delicious, LinkedIn and foursquare help bring people together into a social network. Through a social network, people can find old friends, family members former co-workers or current business associates. They can also tag information found on the web. Through the social network, people can develop connections and form relationships allowing them to share information or work together on a group project. While libraries may not post links to licensed resources through a social network service they can provide information about accessing the licensed resources or new resources available to library users. What is the purpose of social network sites?

Facebook and Myspace are social network sites that allow users to create a profile page. Once the person creates a profile page, they can post photos, links to web sites, videos, information about what they are thinking or doing at a given moment. At one time, Myspace was the leader in social networking sites but Facebook quickly overtook them and as result Myspace lost half of their traffic to Facebook. In November of 2010, MySpace announced their users could connect their Facebook profile to Myspace. Myspace once dominated the online social networking sites they now revamped themselves as an entertainment site and can use pull their likes and interests from Facebook into Myspace (Raphael, 2010).

Facebook in early 2011 had almost 500 million users. While social networks cannot replace face-to-face contact, they do allow people to reconnect with old friends and stay in contact with family who live out of state. Facebook no longer is just for individuals as it grew so did its user base. Many businesses and libraries, just to name two examples, have a presence on Facebook. Academic libraries with a Facebook page use it primarily to promote library events, such as exhibits, displays or lectures, and highlight new resources added to the collection. Even though the library cannot provide a link to the licensed resource, they can provide a link to the library's web site so users can access the materials. The library Facebook page might not receive many visits if updates do not take place on a regular basis, but if the updates take place in a timely manner users will turn to it when they want information about the library. Students who are collaborating on group projects can use Facebook as a place to meet. Since almost every student has, a Facebook account students working on a group project can create a profile page for their project and use it to share information and ideas. It is a form of social networking meets cloud computing.

Twitter allows users to provide and receive instant updates from their followers. It is a combination of instant messaging and micro-blogging. The tweets, the name for Twitter posts, are read on the users profile page and are limited to 140 characters. At conferences there are often people posting to Twitter during a session. This allows individuals who are attending another meeting at the conference to follow the discussion in another session. As with Facebook once the user creates a profile page, they can begin sending tweets. The Library of Congress announced in 2010 they were going to archive the messages posted on Twitter (Library of Congress, 2010). So why

would a library want a Twitter account? Academic libraries can use the account to post announcements. For example, a lecture is taking place in the library and students can receive extra credit for it a tweet will alert students to the event. It is another method to announce new resources or a change in hours. Once again, you cannot post links to licensed library resources to Twitter, but users can receive a link to the library's page and with the link gain access to the licensed resources of the library.

LinkedIn is for business contacts and associates. Creating a LinkedIn profile allows you to enter your current work information, post your resume and connect with people you currently work with or may have worked with in another organization or professional association. This social network site usually attracts people who are older as opposed to Facebook or Twitter where the users can be as young as 16. LinkedIn is the Facebook for the business or professional world. People can search profiles and contact you with a job opening or post information related to your profession. It is the type of social network where the users' connections are their professional affiliations.

Flickr allows users to create an account and post photographs. The photographs can be organized and shared with family and friends. While this social network site is a different from the previous ones it still provides libraries with the opportunity to show users through photos of the events that have taken place in the library. In addition to uploading, the photos to the Flickr account libraries can use the photos to create postcards, scrapbooks or posters. They can use the photos to promote a future event. This type of social network promotes the library and its resources through photographs.

Delicious, now owned by Yahoo, is a place to store links to web sites or other Internet resources you use for work or school. Creating the account allows you to share those resources with other Delicious users. Once you post your links to your account, you can tag them so other can find them. It allows users to organize them into groups by tag name. Other account users looking for similar resources can use any of the links they find through their search. It is a simpler way to search for resources than using a search engine and getting more results than you need or want. Libraries can use a Delicious account to post links to tutorials or subject guides. Once again, it becomes a method for libraries to promote their resources and a way to connect users with the library's web site and other resources.

Foursquare allows users to check out the city or any location they are visiting. Users only need a cell phone with Internet access. Once the user downloads the foursquare application they can link the foursquare app to Twitter or Facebook's accounts. They can also use foursquare with text messaging. Foursquare provides users with tips and recommendations and users can add places not listed. When you check into a place, you can use foursquare to update your location and your friends can meet you there.

Many web sites especially sites such as You-Tube provide people with the option to share a video on Facebook, Twitter, Blogger and Myspace and other social network sites. Many of the news web sites also offer the same options. Sharing information becomes easier. It allows for collaboration on projects and sharing information through a social network means you do not have to meet in the library to work as a group. At some point you may need to meet as a group to complete the project but the initial research and sharing of the information is through social networks. Students use Facebook, as a way to connect with friends and the library's presence on Facebook may cause students to interpret their presence as an intrusion in their personal space. The question is why would libraries want to create a presence on social networking sites and do students want them there?

Part of the reason is libraries use social network sites as a way to connect with their students online. It provides libraries with the opportunity to meet students at their point of need. Students can find the library on Facebook and learn about the new resources available, the library's hours, or research help. In order for the Facebook page to be, an effective form of communication updates should take place on a regular basis. Creating a Facebook page and then never updating it serves no purpose. Students will stop looking at the page if they do not and cannot find the information they need. While the library cannot post links to their databases they can use Facebook and other social network sites as a way to communicate to students new databases or the information on to connect to resources when they are off-campus. Social network sites become self-promotion for the library.

Valparaiso University in Indiana conducted a survey of the students enrolled in Valpo Core and first-year honor students. The purpose of the survey was to determine student use of Facebook and MySpace and the library's presence in those social networks (Connell, 2009). The response rate for the survey was 50.8 percent (Connell, 2009). When asked, only 17 percent of the students responded they would friend the library in Facebook percent while almost 58 percent said they would not be proactive and friend the library in Facebook (Connell, 2009). The majority of the students also said they would be receptive to the library communicating to them through Facebook (Connell, 2009). The comments from students regarding the creation of a Facebook profile by the library were overwhelmingly positive. Because students check their Facebook profile before looking at their campus e-mail or messages in the course management system they would read announcements posted by the library on their Facebook profile. Once the library creates a profile it is important for the library to promote their presence to students. This can be done through word of mouth during an instruction session, blogs, freshman orientation and the library's web site (Connell, 2009).

Some other uses of Facebook are outreach to students but libraries need to determine if students want the library or librarians to be their friends on Facebook. When libraries decide to use social networks as a way to communicate with students they need to consider how they will market this to students. Mississippi State University created groups in Facebook to communicate with student employees. The groups were a success and the university eventually created an open group, advertising it to students and at the end of four months had over 180 members in their group. The library advertises upcoming events to this group. The library also created a Facebook app for students to add to their profile on Facebook (Powers, Schmidt & Hill, 2008).

The librarians at Mississippi State University formed a Library 2.0 Committee in the summer of 2006 (Powers, Schmidt & Hill, 2008). The committee focused on the various Web 2.0 tools available and began offering training to the librarians in the spring of 2007 on blogs, wikis, instant messaging, podcasting and Facebook (Powers, Schmidt & Hill, 2008). In August of 2007, they created their Facebook group and by December over 180 Mississippi State University students, faculty and staff had joined the group (Powers, Schmidt & Hill, 2008). They used their wall to post news, library hours and services, and information about upcoming workshops. With the success of this group three of the library's departments, Instructional Media Center, Access Services and Reference created closed groups for their student workers. The creation of these closed groups improved communication and collaboration between the student workers. Mississippi State University in November of 2007 created a Facebook app that allowed users to search library resources from the user's Facebook page (Powers, Schmidt & Hill, 2008). The user has the ability to search for library resources at their point of need. The app also connects users to the Ask-A-Librarian service. If they have a question, they can connect to this reference service and a librarian will answer their question.

The ability to link students to library resources through their Facebook page provides a further extension of remote access to library resources. Users can connect through Facebook and through a proxy server would be able to search the library's resources. While Facebook has its limitations for the librarians at Mississippi State University, it provided them with the ability to connect with their students at their point of need. It provided the library with the opportunity for outreach through Facebook (Powers, Schmidt & Hill, 2008).

Four librarians at the University at Buffalo Health Sciences Library examined how health sciences libraries use Facebook. They sent a survey to 144 health sciences libraries and 50 percent responded. Only 12.5 percent of the libraries indicated they had a Facebook page for their library. The way in which the libraries used their Facebook page ranged from sending library announcements to providing a means for communication for library employees (Hendrix, et al., 2009). One, of the primary reasons given for not creating a Facebook page by health sciences libraries was the belief that Facebook was not appropriate for an academic setting. This small but initial study of Facebook use by health science libraries indicates that a follow-up study should is necessary to determine if use of Facebook is growing among health sciences libraries.

A recently published follow-up study, to the one conducted by the University at Buffalo, focused on 12 academic libraries and the perceived versus actual use of their Facebook pages. While the study used a small sample of academic libraries, the results indicated the actual use of the library's Facebook page was less than the perceived use of the page. One outcome of this small study was librarians claimed they were doing more with their Facebook pages, but examining the pages, the content was not on the page (Jacobson, 2011). The primary conclusion of this study of 12 library Facebook pages indicates if libraries are to use Facebook as a means of outreach to students they need to realize it is time consuming. Facebook pages for academic libraries might be better utilized by libraries who host a variety of events or exhibits since libraries seem to use it primarily for marketing and communication (Jacobson, 2011). Essentially this was a follow-up study to the one conducted by Hendrix, et al. and came to a similar conclusion as the study conducted by Hendrix that libraries are using Facebook as a marketing tool for their services and resources but unfortunately users are not always using them to extent libraries perceive. As a result, libraries need to determine why they want to create a Facebook page and how much they will actually do with the page. Both the Hendrix and Jacobson studies indicate once libraries create Facebook pages, the updates do not take place on a regular basis. However, other examples seem to indicate libraries can and do have an active presence in social networks.

A study published in 2009 of 81 New York state academic libraries examines the library web sites for links to any of the Web 2.0 tools. If one or more of the Web 2.0 tools were adopted the sites under went further examination to determine how they were being used by the library. Out of the 81 libraries only 34 implemented Web 2.0 tools. The two most popular Web 2.0 tools adopted were IM (instant messaging) and blogs. This other Web 2.0 tools found on the web sites were RSS feeds, tagging and wikis.(Xu, et al., 2009). As noted by the authors of this study Web 2.0 tools can lead to a more collaborative and participatory interactions between librarians and users (Xu, et al., 2009). One of the least adopted Web 2.0 tools by the 81 libraries in this study was podcasting. Out of the 81 libraries, only two used podcasts. Adoption of Web 2.0 tools creates a participative and collaborative environment for librarians and their users. It becomes a two-way flow of information (Xu, et al., 2009).

A 2006 article in Educause Quarterly examines library culture, the millennial generation and the disconnection between the two. One reason for this disconnect was the fact libraries do not embed themselves in the places where students collaborate and search for information. The article identifies three categories for millennial students and the library that leads to a disconnection between the two groups. One is technology, the second is policy and the last is opportunity (McDonald & Thomas, 2006). In the area of technology the articles notes libraries are unable to provide the resources for students to create digital scholarship (McDonald & Thomas, 2006). Some policy concerns are the lack of library presence in social networks and the library's concerns over the privacy of their patrons. Some of the missed opportunities to connect with millennial students are not providing self-paced independent methods of student learning and the lack of packaging information so it looks similar to information in online web sites (McDonald & Thomas, 2006). Another missed opportunity is not providing information literacy instruction to users in the online environment (McDonald & Thomas, 2006).

The use of social media and networks has transformed libraries from a one-way flow of information to a two-way flow of information between librarians and users. Libraries traditionally have been early adopters of new technology and in this case, Web 2.0 tools provide libraries with additional avenues for outreach, marketing and providing user services. As libraries decrease the size of their print collections and increase their digital resources Web 2.0 will play an even larger role in meeting the needs of library users. Blogs, wikis, Facebook pages, Twitter feeds and other social media will help to meet the user at their point of need. Blogs and wikis can provide updates about library services and resources. Facebook can provide the library with the opportunity to create and implement an app that will allow users to connect with library resources through their Facebook page.

Twitter can provide users with updates about the library by providing a feed to a newsletter or a link to the library's web site or blog. The California Digital Library uses Twitter to provide updates about the digital library to a wider audience. In order to ensure the comments posted were about the California Digital library the library provided guidelines for both group and individual accounts, which clearly stated any tweets, would reflect on the library and to make sure the tweets were professional (Starr, 2010). Social media and social networks have the capability of developing collaborative learning communities not only for librarians but also for library users (Starr, 2010). Social networks bring together people with common interests and provide them with a forum to exchange ideas and to share their knowledge with others thereby creating a two-way flow of information. (Starr, 2010)

When libraries only had print collections and social media was non-existent or in its infancy, the flow of information was one-way from the library to its users. Now users can participate and provide information allowing the library to share information obtained from users or other social media forums. Social media and networks open up new opportunities for libraries to share knowledge and continue to make libraries relevant in an ever-increasing digital society. There are some issues concerning social networks and library use and the primary one is privacy.

The American Library Association Code of Ethics (http://www.ala.org/ala/issuesadvocacy/proethics/codeofethics/codeethics.cfm) requires library patron information be kept confidential. As libraries moved into social networks there was concern patron information would be public knowledge. In social networks, the patron is making their information known to others often using a library computer. The library has no control over who accesses the user's information especially when the user freely provides their personal information to others. Originally, because of privacy issues, there were concerns about organizations like libraries having a presence in social networks. The library's presence on social networks provides users with another method of communication with the library.

An ongoing issue with Facebook is their privacy settings. In the fall of 2011, Facebook made changes providing users' with better control over the information they share and who they share it with. Information is available about an individual from their Facebook page. Recent news articles report user information is available through various Facebook apps. As with any Internet site users need to protect their personal information as best they can. Be careful with the type of information you provide and the applications you use.

Just as course management systems provide opportunities for libraries and librarians to participate in an online class, social networks provide similar opportunities to connect with users where they meet and collaborate. Since Facebook provides users with the ability to create, an app or application for their software libraries can create an app that will allow users to access their resources. In an upcoming chapter, I will discuss mobile applications but Facebook has a mobile application for every smart phone and libraries realize the importance of having a mobile web presence. If the library web site is not accessible with a mobile device, it will be difficult for users to find the information they need when they are not in the library or at a computer. An example would be a student who needs to find a book and uses their mobile device to search the catalog.

If the library creates a Facebook app that allows students to search library resources while in Facebook it provides users with the ability to stay in Facebook yet at the same time, work on their project. This provides users with the ability to collaborate on a project through Facebook. Rather than using the course management system users can use Facebook to collaborate and develop their project. A library app in Facebook meets students at their point of need. If the app links to reference services, users will have the ability to work with a librarian in real time to obtain help for their research. Social networks expand the library's ability to connect with more users by working where they meet and collaborate.

A 2006 survey conducted by two librarians at Jacksonville State University about Facebook, they mailed 244 surveys to reference and public service librarians and received 126 completed responses (Charnigo & Barnett-Ellis, 2007). The purpose of the survey was to obtain feedback about librarians' perception and understanding of Facebook. What this early study indicated, the study took place about a year after the launch of Facebook and 54 percent of the librarians surveyed did not see a connection between Facebook and academics. Others saw the potential for Facebook to help distance education students connect with other students and for libraries to promote their services (Charnigo & Barnett-Ellis, 2007).

One particular area the study focused on concerned library's who blocked student access to the site. While a few respondents suggested blocking or regulating the site but the majority, saw no reason to block access to the site (Charnigo & Barnett-Ellis, 2007). Jacksonville State University at the time of the survey and with the publication of the article in 2007 blocked access to Facebook in all their computer labs (Charnigo & Barnett-Ellis, 2007) This early study had its limitations because many librarians did not know about Facebook, but it does provide early perspectives on the social network site. While some librarians saw the potential academic use of Facebook, others did not. The survey concludes libraries need to embrace new Internet services as a means to connect and communicate with their users (Charnigo & Barnett-Ellis, 2007).

Blogs and wikis are still used as a form of social networking. Both types of sites allow users to post articles, links and usually have an RSS feed that allow a follower of the blog or wiki to receive updates. Blogs are web logs where users create a page and then post their thoughts or share information including videos or PowerPoint presentations. Anyone who follows the blog can post comments about the information contained on the page. Wiki is the Hawaiian word for quick and wikis allow users to quickly change, add or delete information to their page. Instructors can use them to post updates to course information or use them for student assignments. Since they require little time to create or change, they are an alternative to creating a web site or a blog. An RSS (Real Simple Syndication) feed is another way for users to receive updates from a blog, wiki, or web site. Subscribers to the RSS feed can receive updates through an RSS feed aggregator or reader that will group all the updates into one location. This prevents the user from receiving multiple messages to their e-mail account. They can use the RSS feed reader and find all the updates in one place. One thing to keep in mind is with the growth of Facebook and more groups, organizations and companies having a presence on the social network where the information can be quickly updated it is possible RSS feeds will become a thing of the past.

In February of 2010 Pew Research Center published updated statistics on their 2006 "Social Media and Mobile Internet Use Among Teens and Young Adults" report. Only 14 percent of teens reported blogging, which is half the amount who reported blogging in 2006. By comparison, 1 in 10 adults maintain a blog and this number have remained consistent since 2005(Lenhart, Purcell, Smith, & Zickuhr, 2010). Another increase was in the number of teens who use a social network site increased to 73 percent from the 55 percent reported in 2006. The number of adults who have a profile on a social network site rose to 47 percent from 37 percent and 73 percent of the adults reported having a profile on Facebook, 48 percent have a profile on Myspace and 14 percent reported having a profile on LinkedIn. According to the survey, update 37 percent of young adults in the age group of 18-24 use Twitter and 19 percent of adults use Twitter (Lenhart, Purcell, Smith, & Zickuhr, 2010).

The statistics from Pew confirm the growing use of social network sites and not just by young adults but by older Americans. It is a way to stay connected with family and friends and organizations or groups; people have an interest in or belong to. Libraries by using social network sites are able to reach their users with timely information. The information can be anything from the library closing due to inclement weather or to an event-taking place at the library. It improves communication between the library and its users.

The major point conveyed in the literature and case studies is twofold. The first is social networks provide libraries with the opportunity to provide links to library resources to students where they meet and work with their friends. The second is social networks provide libraries with the ability to communicate with a wider audience of students. Social networks allow libraries to get their message out to users faster and in a forum where users will read them. A good example of this is the work done by Mississippi State University library where the librarians developed a Facebook page and then created Facebook groups for their student workers. Adopting the technology and finding ways to reach out to students is critical and Mississippi State was able to do just that adopt and use the technology in a way that had meaning and purpose.

FUTURE TRENDS

Social network sites such as, Facebook and Twitter will continue to grow in use and acceptance as a way to communicate with students. Effective use of the sites libraries will require libraries to develop a target group of students and determine the types of information they want to send to students through such sites. The key to the library successfully using such sites is how they market the site to students. While not every student will friend you or like you on Facebook, the students who do are the ones who probably frequently use the library and will more than likely tell their friends about library events of interest to them. Libraries will continue to adopt new sites to market and promote their services to students.

They will also find opportunities to connect library resources at the point of user need. Development of library Facebook apps will continue to grow to provide students with the ability to search library resources through their Facebook page. If libraries are going to continue to be relevant to user needs and provide the services they want when they want them it will require libraries to keep up with current technology and adopt and adapt it to their own use.

Social network sites will continue to grow and with the success of Facebook, it is likely new social network sites will target specific groups of people or interests. Internet usage and in particular the use of online social networks by teens, young adults and adults will continue to grow. The growth of social networks will lead to new opportunities for libraries to connect with users. One aspect of social network sites that needs to be explored is who will archive the information from deleted accounts or if the site ceases to exist. The Library of Congress has agreed to archive all the tweets from Twitter. The question to ask is who will archive the information from other social network sites? Where the information will go if the site disappears? Privacy on social network sites is spotty at best and is an issue social network sites will need to address in the near future.

CONCLUSION

Libraries in the 21st century compete with a number of sources of information. At one time, the library was the only source for information for a research project with the growth of the Internet and digital materials and collections users were no longer required to use the physical library. Libraries must compete for their users' attention and meet users at their point of need. Embedding library resources in an online class is one way but working with students through a social network site is another possibility. When Facebook came into existence libraries did not see a connection between social networks and academic libraries. In the intervening years and with the growth of social networks and social media the connection is more readily apparent.

Social network sites provide more than an on-line site for people to meet with their friends from high school or college. They are a place where people can collaborate and share information. It is a place where groups can send information about their organization. It is a place where people share news and other information. Libraries are usually early adopters of new technology and the literature indicates many librarians recognized the opportunity for them to promote their resources and services. For distance education students it can be a way for them to connect with other students on the campus and learn how to search library resources when are off-campus. It is a way for libraries to push links to their resources including the catalog.

Social network sites provide students, especially distance education students with the ability to connect with their classmates and collaborate on projects. Even though course management systems provide a forum for discussion and the ability to work in groups, collaborating through the social network site is easier. Based on the Pew Research Study most young adults and adults have an account on one or more social network sites. If the library creates, a presence in a social network site, students will have the capability of searching for library resources while collaborating with their fellow students in the social network site. Even if they are not working with other students and need to find information for a project, they could use the library page to find resources without having to leave the social network site. It becomes convenient for students while at the same time libraries will meet their students at their point of need.

The use of social network sites provides libraries with the opportunity to use Library and Web 2.0 tools. Before libraries adopt any of the technologies they need to determine how they will use them and how they fit with the library's strategic plan. One concern of libraries that repeats throughout the literature was privacy. The American Library Association's Code of Ethics states libraries are to protect the privacy of their patrons' records. Librarians are concerned the lack of privacy controls on social network sites will erode the privacy of their patrons. As one article noted (McDonald & Thomas, 2006) patrons, using social networks are freely submitting their information for people to read.

Most social networking sites have privacy controls and while they are not perfect, they can and do prevent people who are not part of the user's friends list from reading the information on their profile. While privacy should concern librarians, they need to recognize the opportunity social network sites have to reach a large percentage of their students. Another advantage of providing links to library resources is the fact social network sites offer mobile access to their sites. If the library posts links to their resources through Facebook users will have the ability to connect through their mobile device to library resources.

Blogs and wikis were two of the earliest Web 2.0 tools and a forerunner of social networks. People could share information with people who had common interests. Both blogs and wikis allow users to post links, photos and text. While both of these tools still exist, they are used to a lesser extent than social network sites. RSS (Real Simple Syndication) feeds were also an early Web 2.0 tool. When a user subscribed to an RSS, feed they received updates through a feed reader. RSS feeds commonly found on blogs, wikis, web sites or anything that updates on a regular basis. The feed reader consolidates all the updates in one place and the user can scroll through to read the updates. It is possible with the advent of social network sites and the fact many organizations have a page in one if not more of the social network sites RSS feeds may become a thing of the past. If the organization updates their social network site then users can obtain the updates through the social network site rather than through an RSS feed.

Facebook is no longer the only social network available to users. Foursquare is another option for libraries and its users. Foursquare allows users to check into a location then explore the location they are at and provide reviews about it. Foursquare gets users to explore the library through tags. The tags tell users about resources available at the library for example, free Wi-Fi. With Foursquare, the library can also provide tips to users about themselves. The tips can be about the collection, new materials added to the collection or resources that can be borrowed from the library besides books, for example, a video camera or a laptop. A library can use Foursquare to connect users to the library by creating small contests that attract users to events in the library. Through the contest, users will obtain information about library resources and services. Twitter has the capability of providing users with instant updates taking place. Most conferences ask individuals to provide tweets during the conference to keep attendees up to date. During the conference, tweets provide information about the discussions taking place in the sessions. This ongoing dialog allows users to attend one session while following another.

Privacy concerns aside social networks are creating and will continue to create new opportunities for libraries to connect with their students. If the library creates a Facebook page, will students like it? Chances are the answer will be yes. While the library may not have significant numbers of students like their page, the ones who do will be able to connect with the library and learn more about its resources and services. If the library creates an app that allows users to link to their resources while the user is in Facebook then the library has connected with the student at their point of need. Social networks have improved the connection between users and the library. They provide a venue for the library to not only post information about events or links to library resources but,

also to post photos about events in the library. In order for blogs, wikis, and Facebook pages to be an effective form of social media need to be regularly updated. Facebook pages also require maintenance. At least two of the studies mentioned libraries did not maintain their Facebook pages on a regular basis and as a result, they did not receive a great deal of use by users.

If the library wants to increase the use of their resources and keep their users informed about new resources or events then someone within the library needs to maintain the page. Blogs and wikis are still in use. Many libraries still have a blog or wiki associated with their library web site but Facebook seems to be the dominate method of communicating information about the library to users. Twitter is another way to communicate information about the library. Tweets will require the library to appoint someone to administer the account and post tweets. Twitter is a quick way to get information to users, for example, if an event is taking place in the library that students should attend the group or department sponsoring the event sends a tweet to notify students when and where the event is taking place.

Social networks connect people with common interests. They also provide a faster method of communication with people. While social networks may have their limitations, their exponential growth over the last six years indicates they will be around for many more years. Social networks are all about connecting with others and provide libraries with the capability to meet users at their point of need and to connect with users where they meet and work with their fellow students. Libraries will continue to use and adapt social networks to connect with their users and for users to gain access to the resources they need when they need them. While some users may think the library is spying on them, the library is providing them with the opportunity to work and socialize without having to leave the social network site. Libraries now see the benefits of meeting and collaborating in the social network site.

REFERENCES

Boyd, D. M., & Ellison, N. B. (2007). Social network sites: Definition, history, and scholarship. *Journal of Computer-Mediated Communication, 13*(1). doi:10.1111/j.1083-6101.2007.00393.x

Charnigo, L., & Barnett-Ellis, P. (2007). Checking out Facebook.com: The impact of a digital trend on academic libraries. *Information Technology and Libraries, 26*(1), 23–34.

Connell, R. S. (2009). Academic libraries, Facebook and MySpace, and student outreach: A survey of student opinion. *Portal: Libraries and the Academy, 9*(1), 25–36. doi:10.1353/pla.0.0036

Fletcher, D. (2010). Facebook: Friends without borders. *Time, 175*(21), 32–38.

Grossman, L. (2011). 2010 person of the year Mark Zuckerberg. *Time, 176*(26), 46–75.

Hendrix, D., Chiarella, D., Hasman, L., Murphy, S., & Zafron, M. (2009). Use of Facebook in academic health sciences libraries. *Journal of the Medical Library Association, 97*(1), 44–47. doi:10.3163/1536-5050.97.1.008

Lenhart, A., Purcell, K., Smith, A., & Zickuhr, K. (2010). *Social media & mobile Internet use among teens and young adults.* Pew Internet, Pew Internet & American Life Project. Retrieved from http://www.pewinternet.org/Reports/2010/Social-Media-and-Young-Adults.aspx

Library of Congress. (2010). *Twitter donates entire tweet archive to Library of Congress.* Retrieved from http://www.loc.gov/today/pr/2010/10-081.html

McDonald, R. H., & Thomas, C. (2006). Disconnects between library culture and millennial generation values. *EDUCAUSE Quarterly, 29*(4), 4–6.

Powers, A. C., Schmidt, J., & Hill, C. (2008). Why can't we be friends? The MSU libraries find friends on Facebook. *Mississippi Libraries, 72*(1), 3–5.

Rainie, L., Purcell, K., & Smith, A. (2011). *The social side of the Internet.* Pew Internet, Pew Internet & American Life Project. Retrieved from http://www.pewinternet.org/Reports/2011/The-Social-Side-of-the-Internet.aspx

Raphael, J. R. (2010). Myspace's Facebook 'mashup'--Why bother? *PC World.* Retrieved from http://www.pcworld.com/article/211127/myspacesfacebookmashupwhybother.html

Starr, J. (2010). California digital library in Twitterland. *Computers in Libraries, 30*(7), 23–27.

Xu, C., Ouyang, F., & Chu, H. (2009). The academic library meets Web 2.0: Applications and implications. *Journal of Academic Librarianship, 35*(4), 324–331. doi:10.1016/j.acalib.2009.04.003

KEY TERMS AND DEFINITIONS

Blog: A web log created by an individual or organization to provide information of interests to the blog's followers. Most blogs have an RSS feed that will provide the follower with updates.

Social Networks: Online websites that allow members to connect through common interests. Social network websites allow users to share information about themselves with others. Groups and businesses such as libraries can create profile pages. Students can choose to like the page and follow the updates provided by the library.

Web 2.0: Web applications that allow users to share and create information.

Wiki: The Hawaiian word for quick. Wikis like blogs are Web based and can be updated by anyone. An example is Wikipedia. They support a variety of content including links to web sites, videos and images.

Chapter 9
Mobile Technologies

ABSTRACT

Millions of people have a smartphone, and with smartphone technology comes the ability for Internet connectivity and with that the ability to access library resources. EBSCO, Elsevier, ProQuest, Gale/ Cengage, and other database vendors have capitalized on the increased use of smartphones by developing the capability for library users to access EBSCO databases from their smartphones. Mobile technology extends beyond smartphones and includes technology gadgets such as e-book readers, the iPad, netbooks, and laptops. As technology that is more mobile becomes available, the ability and need to connect remotely will increase. Mobile technology has grown beyond cell phones and personal digital assistants to other types of devices most recently Apple's iPad. Gone are the days when the only computer available was the one on your desk. With better technology came laptops, and now netbooks and e-book readers. To access the Internet, campuses have wireless technology in most classrooms and libraries. The proliferation of mobile technology and the ability to gain access to the Internet from almost any place means libraries and database vendors need to make sure their websites and resources are compatible with mobile devices.

INTRODUCTION

Technology has advanced significantly from the first computers and cell phones. As processors and computer chips became smaller with increased speed the cost, size and weight of mobile technolo-

DOI: 10.4018/978-1-4666-0234-2.ch009

gies declined. In order for users to access library resources through mobile devices, the library or database vendor needs to have the technology in place to meet the needs of their users.

In 1981 the first laptop computer, the Osborne, was introduced. It weighed 24 pounds. In the same year, Epson introduced a laptop computer that weighed approximately 4 pounds and had a rechargeable battery (Bellis, 2011). In 1973 Martin Cooper, former general manager of systems at Motorola, made the first cellular phone call (Greene, 2011). As processing chips became smaller and more powerful, handheld devices became readily available. Some of the devices currently available are smartphones, MP3 players, laptop computers, netbook computers, e-book readers such as the Kindle and Nook, and the iPad. Users can take their work with them wherever they go. EBSCO developed a mobile version of their EBSCOhost platform. The mobile platform allows users to search any EBSCO database from a mobile device.

BACKGROUND

Increased use of smartphones will require libraries to design web sites and access to their resources for mobile technology. Designing access for mobile technology will allow libraries to reach users at their point of need. Users will be able to find information about library services and resources without the need of a laptop or desktop computer. Database vendors have developed mobile access to their databases that can be administered by the system librarian. Once the account is created at the library all users, who have access to library resources will be able to use mobile access. Oxford University and Rice University added electronic publication (EPUB) books to iTunes U electronic book collection. The EPUB format allows the books to be read on e-readers and most smartphones. Oxford made Shakespeare's First Folio available and Rice added 18 of their most popular free textbooks. Open U had 100 titles from the Open University web site. One of the biggest changes to mobile technology was the introduction of the iPad (Schaffhauser, 2010).

The iPad with its slim and lightweight design allows users the portability without carrying a laptop. In addition to its lightweight users can purchase or download free a number of applications or apps for their iPad. Sales of tablet devices are expected to increase over the next four years to over 200 million units. Tablet devices, the iPhone and iTouch provide libraries with the opportunity to develop apps for those devices and increasing access to library information and resources. The University of Cambridge in Great Britain is examining the types of library information users' access through their mobile phones.

Kent State University did a similar study and the web sites for the 111 Association of Research Libraries were examined for a mobile web presence. The majority of students using the mobile web to find library information were looking library hours. In the 2010 technology forecast, libraries need to make sure they have a mobile web presence that is easy to access. As early as 2008, the same prediction was made about libraries and the mobile web. In a 2008 report from the Association of Research Libraries noted more people were using their cell phones to search for information and it is important for university libraries to develop ways to meet the needs of users with mobile devices.

MAIN FOCUS OF THE CHAPTER

Mobile technology use is rapidly increasing. From laptops, netbooks, smartphones, iPads and e-book readers people have the ability to obtain remote access library resources. As mobile technology use increases libraries need to design and implement the means for students to use those technologies from remote access to library information. Mobile technologies require libraries to develop applications that will work for the specific devices. Apple has an app development center (http://developer.apple.com/). It provides people with the necessary resources to design and develop applications to work with Apple products. Unfortunately, each type of smartphone has different design specifications so you cannot create a one size fits all mobile web application. Each of the manufacturer's Apple, Blackberry and Android has web sites that provide the specifications for mobile applications (Ragon, 2009).

The University of Virginia Health Sciences Library collaborated with their Library Technology Services and Development, Technology in Education Consulting and Information Services to develop content for mobile computing (Ragon, 2009). Not all information from the library's web site was selected for the mobile web. The developers selected things such as library hours, upcoming classes, study room bookings and chat reference (Ragon, 2009). Some of the other material included was YouTube videos from the University of Virginia's Center for Biomedical Ethics, Humanities, and local resources such as the University of Virginia directory search and information about the Charlottesville area (Ragon, 2009).

Libraries looking to develop content for the mobile web can use the Wireless Universal Resource File (WURFL). This open source is a repository of information about the features and capabilities of many mobile devices. The information is intended to help developers create better applications and services for user. (http://wurfl.sourceforge.net/) If the application or app is not compatible with the mobile device, it will not be purchased or downloaded by users. Designing for the mobile web is important as more people connect via their smartphone, netbook, laptop or iPad.

The iPad is already changing how people connect through mobile devices. It is lighter than a netbook and more versatile than a smartphone or laptop. Some of the features of the latest version of the iPad include front and back cameras, Wi-Fi, 3G, video recording, touch screen, and up to 64GB of storage. Applications can be purchased or in some cases downloaded free. The applications can be used for business, education, social networks, news, entertainment or games. With the success of Apple's iPad, the competition is increasing in the media tablet market. Most computer and smartphone manufacturers are introducing a similar product in the consumer electronics marketplace. Competition is good, driving down the cost of the devices but the manufacturers also need to have the applications available to make consumers want to purchase the device. Many of Apple's applications designed for the iPod Touch will also work on the iPad.

The new entries to the market need to ensure they have the apps in place that users want and need. Smartphones also require applications and depending on the phone, users will have a variety of free apps or apps to purchase. Regardless of whether library users have a smartphone, iPad, netbook or laptop they want the ability to use the device to connect to the information they need when they need it. The expectation is they will always be able to connect and they expect the library to have applications that are compatible with their mobile devices. This includes the library's web site. If the user is unable to connect with their mobile device it becomes a source of frustration in an age where library users expect the library resources will always be available whether it is open. Mobile technology is an enhancement to education because it provides students to access materials anytime or anywhere using different technologies.

Another type of device that grew in popularity but seem to be undergoing changes are e-book readers. The Kindle from Amazon and the Nook from Barnes and Noble are the most widely know but Sony and Kobo offer e-book readers with similar features. The Kindle, Nook, Sony and Kobo e-readers feature Wi-Fi, e-ink screen (designed to replicate the printed page), and newer models have touch screen functionality. The screen sizes range from the 5-inch Sony touch screen reader to the 7-inch Nook color. Amazon announced at the beginning of October 2011, their Kindle Fire a 7-inch color tablet (Falcon, 2011). The iPad offers an app for the Kindle so it can also serve as the e-book reader rather than buying another device. In a recent article in *Computerworld*, it was reported that e-books are outselling print books (Hamblen, 2011). The portability factor is the difference. E-book readers can store approximately 3500 books depending on which model you purchase and are now available in a color version allowing users to read books and magazines in color.

Another advantage to e-readers is the cost of books is lower for the electronic version as opposed to the print version. The books remain in your account until you delete them. If you delete a book by mistake from your e-reader you can download it again from your account. The implications for libraries and the ability for remote access are growing. A few libraries are experimenting with the purchase of Kindle's and lending them to students. Currently not many academic or scholarly works are available for e-book readers but as the use of the devices and the alternative through the iPad it is possible more books that are scholarly will be available for use. Students will then have the ability to download e-books from the library's resources and use it on their e-reader.

The Horizon Report for 2010 and 2011 predicted e-books would continue to gain in popularity and use. As they noted in the report the price is dropping on e-books and they are improving beyond an electronic version of the printed book. Publishers have discovered they can offer enhanced technology with e-books they are not able to offer in the print version (Levine, 2010, 2011). Another option for e-book readers would be the ability to download articles from scholarly journals. Students could access the library's resources download the articles they need and want to their e-reader and use them for their research project. Once the articles are saved the user can access them without having to log into the database or use another device such as a netbook or laptop to access them.

If a web site or software has mobile capabilities students and instructors will be able to access resources through their mobile device. The proliferation of mobile devices is requiring most organizations to develop a web site compatible with mobile technologies. This includes banks, colleges, universities, and public libraries. If the web site or software is not mobile technology compatible it will not display properly on the mobile device and users will not be able to access the resources they need. One thing that must be and probably should be taken into consideration is students can use them to cheat on an exam.

There are numerous possibilities and capabilities available to students and faculty to use their mobile devices for educational purposes. Since most mobile devices have a calendar or scheduling software they can be used by students and faculty to keep track of due dates for assignments, exams or meetings. So how do mobile technologies influence libraries? One way is students will need the ability to access library resources through their mobile device. In order for this to happen libraries will need a web site that is mobile compatible and databases need to allow users to access them from mobile devices.

Database vendors, Gale/Cengage, Elsevier, EBSCO, and ProQuest/Serial Solutions offer applications that allow users to search their databases through their mobile devices. All of the mobile applications from database vendors allow users to do everything from basic searching to e-mailing articles. The library creates a mobile profile through the database administration function. Once the mobile profile is configured users will have the ability to access the databases through their mobile device. This is critical for libraries and their users to have remote access to library resources through their mobile devices. It provides them with access anytime and anywhere without the need for a computer.

Providing remote access to library resources brings them into the 21st century. If libraries are initially reluctant to adopt technology of this nature, they should consider creating focus groups with students and faculty to obtain their input as to why it should or should not be adopted. Meeting user needs is critical for any organization and while the Internet cannot and does not replace the resources and services provided by a library it does provide a place for users to start their research. If users are unable or have a difficult time accessing library resources through their mobile device they will come to rely on the Internet to start and finish their research project. Students know, they can access information on the Internet through their mobile device without entering an ID or password. On the other hand, the library requires them to either come into the library or access the resources through a remote connection. Connecting through a mobile device will require users to be authenticated through a proxy server.

Mobile technology provides library users with ongoing access to educational resources they need. This includes not just library resources but access to course management systems. Mobile technology use for education ties into social networks, blogs, wikis, podcasting, text messaging, video, and photo sharing. Technology enhanced learning will be part of every students life. They will probably use more than one device but will be able to create and connect to a learning environment that is a student centered and participatory. Mobile technology will increase the opportunity for experiential learning. Experiential learning creates knowledge from the experience of the user thus learning takes place both in and outside of the classroom. Wireless or mobile technology provides greater opportunities for this type of learning. Students and faculty are no longer tied to the classroom and they have a greater opportunity to incorporate different pedagogical styles into their instruction (Looi, Seow, Zhang, et al., 2010). Using mobile technology for education provides students and faculty to use information and experiential learning to create new information. They can use images, videos, music and other sources of information and through a mashup develop new information that can be used by others. Mobile technology provides students with the opportunity to be fully engaged in learning. It allows them to use their technology skills and a variety of technology to learn and create new information (Lai, Yang, Chen, Ho, Chan, 2007).

In 2009 the Pew Foundation reported that demand for smartphones had increased 30 percent for the year. The demand is still growing. A follow-up to the original Pew study in 2010 indicated that non-voice use of smartphones was increasing. One example is 38 percent of smartphone users accessed the Internet from their phone versus 25 percent of the people who responded to the survey the previous year. Another example is 23 percent of smartphone users said they accessed a social networking site from their phone. This was just one of seven activities added to the survey in 2010 (Smith, 2010). A smartphone allows users to access the Internet, their e-mail, social networks and make phone calls just to name a few of the many capabilities available to smartphone users.

One word repeated in many articles about the mobile web and technology was ubiquitous. The word was often used in reference to the technology and the proliferation of the devices. In the age of wireless technology, users can connect to the Internet at the nearest coffee shop or bookstore. They can sit in a library, office or their car and receive e-mails or check for information on the Internet. Because of mobile technology, colleges and universities must adapt to meet the needs of their users. Students on campus want the ability to connect to information or the Internet regardless of whether they are at home, in the library or walking across campus. They want apps or applications that will help them get the information they need or be able to connect to the information they need.

An article from EDUCAUSE Quarterly examined how and why people access the mobile web. The article pointed out when access the web through a mobile device it is because they are looking for specific information and want to type as little as possible to get the information they are searching for (Aldrich, 2010). The University of Iowa conducted a survey of their online students to determine what information they accessed from their mobile devices. The top four categories of information accessed were, grades, content, schedule and news (Aldrich, 2010). The University of

Cambridge in the United Kingdom is conducting a similar study to determine the information student's access or would to access through mobile devices. For the students at Cambridge the top four pieces of information they wanted to access were library hours, the catalog, map of the library and contact information (Aldrich, 2010). The two areas that ranked the lowest in the survey were accessing electronic journal articles and databases (Aldrich, 2010).

In a similar study by Kent State University in the United States students' primary reasons for accessing the library using mobile technology was to start their research project (Aldrich, 2010). They wanted to access databases, search for articles and download the citations for later use (Aldrich, 2010). This same article checked the web sites of the 111 members of the Association of Research Libraries and found that only 39 universities or a little over 35 percent of their members had mobile web sites (Aldrich, 2010). Out of the 39 universities, 14 of them had a specific mobile web site for their library (Aldrich, 2010). The top four services found at 25 of the mobile university web sites were an event calendar, directory, and news and campus maps (Aldrich, 2010). Some of top functions accessed on the mobile web site at the Massachusetts Institute of Technology were library hours, directory, catalog and contact us. (Aldrich, 2010). According to this, article students want remote access to library resources through their mobile devices. Allowing students the ability to gain access requires the creation of a web site that is adapted to mobile technologies (Aldrich, 2010). In other words, the college or university will need to create a mobile web site separate from their main web site or the library web site. The other option is to design and develop one web site that is mobile capable. Without a web site that can be accessed by a mobile device, library users will not be able to access library resources requiring them to use remote access from a desktop computer, laptop, or netbook. (Aldrich, 2010).

The proliferation of mobile technologies requires libraries to adapt the new technology to meet the needs of their users. Internally libraries could use the same technology to provide "roving reference" to their users. Using mobile devices librarians could work with users at their point of need for example in residence halls or apartments or student centers or dining halls. Mobile technology provides libraries with the ability to provide text reference services to their users. Any user who has text capabilities on their phone, and most students do, can send a text to the library with their question. Mobile technology moves librarians from the traditional methods of providing service to users, usually from behind a desk or in their office, to one where they can meet the students at their point of need. It also provides users with the ability to gain access to information quickly without having to enter into the library (Sodt & Summey, 2009).

Does the use of mobile technology mean an end to the physical library? No it does not, but it does indicate the use of smartphones and smartphone technology will require libraries to have a web site that is designed specifically for mobile devices it also requires them to provide the technology for users to gain remote access to library resources through their mobile devices. A concern of access to library resources through a mobile device is security. Using a mobile device with a wireless network that might or might not be secure could lead to unauthorized users gaining access to library resources. IT departments and libraries need to address security issues when designing their web site for the mobile web. Currently there are mobile applications, from database vendors, libraries can use in addition to the resources available to help libraries develop mobile applications and web sites.

In the April 2011 College and Research Libraries News section on Internet resources provided a list of resources available for libraries to either adopt or use to develop their own mobile applications. Some of the links provided were Library in Your Pocket: Strategies and Techniques for Developing Successful Mobile Services (Barille, 2011). This site from North Carolina State University Libraries provides information on mobile site development (Barille, 2011). It allows libraries to share their applications and designs that other libraries can then use and adapt to their needs. They also listed a few sites available to mobile learning. Some of the more interesting ones include Dropbox. The site allows users to store synch and share their files online and across computers. The site is compatible with iPhone, iPad, Android and BlackBerry devices (Barile, 2011).

A similar app is Evernote. With Evernote, users can create text, video and audio memos. Users can even include photos with their text. Evernote can be synched with Mac, PC, and the Web. It is compatible with iPhone, iPod touch, and iPad, Android, BlackBerry, Palm and Windows Mobile (Barille, 2011). It is a free application. Meebo had a mobile application that is free and allows users to chat with friends or in the case of libraries; it allows them to monitor their chat service from any location (Barille, 2011). Encyclopedia Britannica has a mobile site, as does WorldCat. For developers there is MobileTuts that provides tutorials on how to create everything from mobile apps to mobile web sites regardless of the platform being used. The World Wide Web Consortium better known as W3C has a web site devoted to mobile web best practices called Mobile Web Best Practices 1.0 Basic Guidelines. It provides specific guidelines needed to develop web based content for mobile devices (Barile, 2011). This list, while not exhaustive, does provide web designers with the resources necessary to create mobile apps and web sites. The information provided would also allow libraries to link some of the applications for learning to their library web site. This would provide students with the ability to obtain information quickly and easily.

The Meebo Mobile app (http://www.meebo.com/meebomobile/) is a great way for libraries to monitor their chat reference service when they are in a meeting or out of the library. This app would provide continuous service to library users. Not all applications are free. Many of the apps or sites previously mentioned are free; some charge anywhere from a few dollars to several hundred dollars per month for their services. Therefore, before selecting an app the library needs to find out if there is a cost associated with the app. The development of mobile apps extends to course management systems.

Blackboard, Moodle, and Sakai offer mobile apps for their course management systems. Blackboard's mobile app allows users to check grades, follow and post to discussion threads, create and upload content from their mobile device. Their mobile application is compatible with every mobile device. Moodle's mobile app works with most mobile devices. According to the Moodle web site users can access the course management system through the web browser on their mobile devices which Moodle does not recommend doing. Alternatively, they can download native apps to access Moodle through the mobile device or the administrator for the system can configure the Moodle site to be accessible through mobile devices with the use of server of server extensions. As with the other mobile apps, the course management system mobile apps provide for learning on the go. Students can use the apps to check for due dates and other course content. Essentially, they can stay connected to the course with their mobile device.

Design is crucial to the mobile web and for users to access the resources at the library. In the Last Byte column that appeared in a 2008 Library Journal Karen Coombs from the University of Houston Libraries discussed the importance having a library's resources ready for the mobile web. At the time of the article, she noted that almost a billion new mobile devices were entering the market every year. In the three years, since the article was written chances are the number has steadily increased. Another dimension of the mobile web she mentioned is for colleges and universities to

Figure 1. Image of iPhone Apps ©Bonnie Brown/ Flickr/CC-BY-2.0

use iTunes U to host audio and video podcasts that students can download to the iPods, iPhones (see also figure 1), or iPads. Mobile technology and designing resources for the mobile web move the library from the building to where users are working. The mobile web and its technologies along with social networks give libraries a presence in locations where users are rather than just the library (Coombs, 2008).

Mobile technologies allow the library to be always open. They expand the presence of the library on campus with the ability to reach beyond the physical building. The previous chapter discussed social networks and social network software. Some of the same technologies can and do fall under mobile technology. Social network sites such as Facebook and Twitter have apps that allow for mobile access. With the ability to design and develop apps and web sites for the mobile web libraries can provide students with the services

they need regardless of whether they are open or closed. As the literature, points out students want the ability to search library resources to develop a list of possible resources to use for their project. Mobile access is just one more option in the arsenal of remote technologies.

Another mobile technology is iTunes U. iTunes U is part of the Apple iTunes store and allows colleges and universities to upload their video or audio podcasts to it. In order to upload podcasts the university first needs to have a podcast server where users can create their podcasts. Once they are created, they will have a link they can use to embed the podcasts into a course management system or a web site. The university also creates an account with iTunes U, which according to the Apple web site is a free service they host. Instructors can upload their podcasts to iTunes U and students can subscribe to the podcasts. Once they subscribe to podcast every time a new podcast is uploaded, the student will receive it. Distance education students in a course taught completely online or students in a face-to-face class by subscribing to the podcast will receive new podcasts added by the instructor. ITunes U is searchable and materials from other colleges and universities can be added to an instructor's course in the course management system because iTunes U does has the option for the instructor to embed the link to the podcast in a course management system.

The podcasts can be embedded into a discussion forum in a course management system. In creating a podcast there are some things faculty need to keep in mind. A student probably is not going to sit through a 45-minute podcast of a lecture. Break the information down into smaller components. It will take less time for the podcast to load and will students will not lose interest and stop watching it because of the length. Another format similar to podcast is screen capture tutorials and narrated PowerPoint presentations. Both should be kept to around two minutes if possible. Once again, anything longer than two minutes will take a long

Figure 2. Cloud computing visual diagram. ©Griner & Butler/Wikimedia Commons/Public Domain

Cloud Computing

Having secure access to all your applications and data from any network device

time to load and students will lose interest in the topic because of the length.

As with any new technology and in this case mobile technology libraries will need to determine what mobile technologies they can and will adopt to meet user needs. In order to determine the technologies they will adopt libraries will need to create focus groups or survey students. The information obtained from student surveys or focus groups should include the type of mobile technology they use and the types of information they would like to obtain through a mobile application from the library. This information will help the library design and develop an app or mobile web site that will meet user needs. As student needs and technology changes, the library will need to redesign their app to meet the requirements. Ragon in his article lists several web sites for mobile developer guides and documentation for the iPhone (http://developer.apple.com/devcenter/ios/index.action), Blackberry (http://docs.blackberry.com/en/developers/?userType=21), Android (http://developer.android.com/guide/index.html), Anyone wishing to develop apps for these devices can use the web sites to find the requirements to develop apps (Ragon, 2009) .

Another aspect of mobile technology and one that should not be overlooked is cloud computing. Cloud computing allows users secure access to a number of applications from any computer or mobile device regardless of their location.

Cloud computing provides the means for hosting computer applications in a distributed network rather than on an individual computer (Tadjer, 2010). An example of this is Google Docs. When a user signs into their Google account, they have access to a number of applications including but not limited to Gmail, Google Docs, iGoogle, and Google Groups. With Google Docs users can create, spreadsheets, presentations, word documents, forms or a drawing. Either users can create new documents within Google Docs or they can upload files from their computer. Within Google Docs, one can organize their documents by creating a collection. Cloud computing refers not only to the software available over the Internet but also the hardware and software used to provide the services to users (figure 2). Once they upload or create a new document they can keep the document private or can share the document with others.

Sharing documents is one of the benefits of cloud computing. It allows for collaboration amongst users whether they are in the same office, classroom or city. In the case of students collaborating on a project, they can provide a link to the document in a message on Facebook or through an e-mail updating others working on the project of any changes they make. The changes are made in real time (Armbrust, Fox, Griffith, et al., 2010). There are security issues associated with cloud computing. The primary security threat is theft of data because a non-locally hosted cloud, such as Google, requires the organization to rely on the host for security. Users of a non-locally hosted cloud need to consider reliability, privacy, anonymity and restrictions to the access and usage of their data (Ovadia, 2010).

Cloud computing can also serve as a backup for documents stored on a computer. Uploading the materials allows the user to access them regardless of their location. They only have to sign into their account to access the materials. If the hard drive dies on a computer, the user can still access the resources they need. The materials can also be accessed through mobile devices, which are another benefit of cloud computing (Armbrust, Fox, Griffith, et al., 2010). Along those same lines as cloud, computing is Zotero (http://www.zotero.org/) a bibliographic management system that is an add-on through Firefox. There is also a standalone version that is in Alpha testing. This software allows users to capture and organize citations to materials for a project. They can share and even publish their list of citations for everyone to see. Once again, for students or anyone working on a project this helps them to share information and allows each of them to contribute and store their data in one location.

In 2008 the Association of Research Libraries (ARL) published a report on mobile technologies and their implication for academic libraries. This short report pointed out several key issues that should be addressed in order to meet the needs of users with mobile devices. As the report, notes it will be important for libraries to determine what users will want to access from their mobile devices and will it be possible to tie library content to online courses that use mobile devices for teaching. As mentioned earlier in the chapter mobile devices provide libraries with the ability to offer reference services through text messaging and this option was also mentioned in the report another service mentioned was providing users with the ability to search the catalog with their mobile device (Lippincott, 2008).

Another aspect of mobile technology is the option for libraries to loan the equipment to users. For example, iPods, video cameras, laptops and e-book readers like the Kindle. The physical space of the library can be configured to incorporate the use of mobile devices by providing areas for students to charge their devices while working on projects and the creation of space for group study that include multimedia production and practice for presentations. Mobile technologies also present the library with the opportunity to provide instruction on using the equipment and accessing materials through mobile devices. The library can take the lead in identifying and targeting

the users who want to access library and campus resources with mobile devices and work with a cross-section of people on campus to develop the necessary infrastructure to meet the needs of those users (Lippincott, 2008).

Every year the New Media Consortium (NMC) publishes their Horizon Report (http://www.nmc.org/horizon) of emerging technologies. This report, first published in 2002, lists up and coming technology trends that will probably be adopted within a period of from one to five years. The report provides information about the technology, its relevance for teaching and learning, links to the technology in practice and a section for further reading. Using the Horizon Report helps colleges and universities and in particular, libraries identify possible technologies they may want to adopt for teaching and learning purposes. Libraries may not adopt some technologies until four or five years in the future. The wait and see approach will provide the institution with the ability to determine how and if they can adopt the technology. It provides institutions with the ability to plan for future needs and demands from their users. Some of the technologies listed in the 2010 report were mobile computing, electronic books (e-books), open content and augmented reality (Levine, 2010).

The 2011 report listed mobile devices, e-books; game based learning, gesture-based computing and learning analytics as some of the technologies looming on the horizon to adopt by education. While most people have strong opinions about e-books, there are advantages to libraries and readers using them. The Horizon Report highlights some of the improvements being made to e-books that make them more robust. One of the improvements noted is developing e-books that are multi-media and interactive. As e-books improve, they will become widely accepted in education providing users with a more robust experience that will enhance their education. Based on the information from the Horizon Report in the next few years students can expect a more technology rich and enhanced learning environment (Levine, 2011).

FUTURE TRENDS

In December of 2010 Campus Technology published a list of five higher education technology trends for 2011. The five technologies were: cloud computing, increased wireless connectivity, increased use of mobile technologies in classrooms, more online education courses and programs, and last but not least a retreat from technology overload (McCrea, 2010). All of the above five items are possible trends for the upcoming year. In particular, cloud, computing will continue to grow. It is an easy way for users to share information for projects regardless of how near or far they are from each other. Distance education or online programs will continue to grow as colleges, universities face a shortage of classroom space the need to offer more courses, and programs will continue to grow to meet the increased enrollment and demand for classes from students (McCrea, 2010).

Mobile devices as the Horizon Report notes will continue to rise in use (Levine, 2011). More users will be accessing information from a mobile device. This is a tremendous opportunity for education to develop the apps and web sites necessary to meet the increased demand. It is also an opportunity for the library to meet with their users to identify the types of resources they would like to access from their mobile device. Libraries will expand their services beyond the four walls of the library allowing them to meet the user's needs where they are working. Media tablets like the iPad will dominate sales in the area of mobile devices and will lead to a decline in the sale of netbooks and laptops. The Horizon Report will continue to be a valuable resource to identify new and emerging technologies that will affect education especially higher education. Libraries will need to work with their users through focus groups and/or surveys to determine what resources they want to

access. They also need the infrastructure in place to develop mobile apps to meet their user needs. Resources available to develop web apps will become more readily available and it is possible there will be a common operating system used by multiple mobile devices making it easier to develop mobile apps (Levine, 2010, 2011).

CONCLUSION

Distance education required libraries to provide remote access to library collections. As a result, students now have access to the resources they need every day, all day throughout the year. Just as distance education played a significant role in access to library resources so are mobile technologies. Mobile technologies consist of smartphones, media tablets, iPods, netbooks, and laptops just to name the primary devices. Before a user can access the library's resources through a mobile device, a couple of things need to take place. The first is the library's web site needs to be mobile ready or they need to provide a link to a mobile library web site. The second is the creation of an app for users to be able to access the library's resources. In order to access the resources the user would need to first download and install the app. Once the app is installed, the user will then be able to access the resources. The library also needs to work with their users through a combination of surveys and focus groups to determine the types of mobile devices they use and the resources they want to access from their mobile devices. Once these areas are addressed, the library can then design the app and web site for users to gain the access they need from their mobile device. Mobile devices have other implications beyond just accessing library resources. They will provide students with a more enhanced and enriched learning environment.

With mobile devices higher education can make better use of podcasts and iTunes U. Students with an iPod will be able to download the podcasts of a lecture or other material they need for their class and listen to it at their convenience. The growth of mobile technology has resulted in the course management systems developers to create mobile versions of their software. Students and faculty can now access course content, grades, and post to discussion forums and even upload materials for the course through their mobile device.

The array of apps available to users of mobile devices makes it possible for them to record a video, edit it and upload to the course management system or to a web site for the course. Mobile devices just like social networks allow students to work collaboratively. Students can access library resources and e-mail links to citations to their fellow students working on the same project. Mobile technology increases real time collaboration. While security can be an issue with users, accessing library resources through mobile device users will need to connect through a proxy server to gain access to the resources they need from the library. Mobile technology provides libraries with the ability to move their services and resources even further beyond the confines of the physical space of the building.

The increased use of mobile technology has opened up new avenues of opportunities for libraries to meet the needs of their users where they work. Just as social networks provide libraries with the ability to meet and work with users in a collaborative environment mobile technologies provide similar opportunities. Most libraries offer reference service in person, e-mail, phone and chat but text messaging is the newest addition to providing reference services. Most students' are comfortable texting. Online reference service systems now include some method of text messaging for users.

The Ask-a-Librarian system in Florida requires users to begin their text message with the text library code. The code is used to route the question to the correct library in the system. A librarian can then answer the question and text the information back to the library user. The physical reference desk is not dead but fewer transactions will take place at the desk as opposed to the use of an online service.

Texting the reference desk allows students to receive the response they need quickly and because the message is limited to a certain number of characters it will be concise and provide only the information they need. (Profit, 2008) Another option is librarians can use a mobile device and provide library services outside of the library. They can meet with students in a classroom, a residence hall or student center. The development of media tablets provides users with lightweight and very portable mobile devices. These devices allow users to create, store and read materials in one device. They can serve as an e-reader by downloading an app. They can be used to record video and then edit and upload the video to a web site or course management system. The sharing of citations from library databases is another possibility with mobile devices. Real time collaboration is another aspect of mobile technology and devices.

Cloud computing is another mobile technology whose use is continuing to grow. Cloud computing allows users to work in real time to make changes to documents such as spreadsheets, forms or presentations. This type of computing can be used to share citations from articles. A bibliography can be created and updated as information is shared. Another advantage of cloud computing is the ability to back-up and access your documents or other materials anytime and from any location. It is not just documents it is also e-mail. The documents created through cloud computing can be shared with a few people or made public and shared with large groups. An example would be the creation of a presentation for a class and the group or instructor posts the link to online course content or sends it in an e-mail to everyone in the class. Cloud computing has no boundaries and whether the user is at home, campus or on vacation they can still access their information (Armbrust, Fox, Griffith, et al., 2010).

With the growth of mobile technologies and devices the shift is away from the print to the electronic and from the physical library to any space outside of the library. Any space physical or virtual becomes a classroom. It provides students and faculty with the ability to engage in experiential learning by using the environment they are working in to create and develop new knowledge. Distance education students are not the only ones using mobile technologies and devices. Students and instructors in classrooms are adopting them. but their proliferation means more teaching and learning can take place outside of the classroom. Libraries will need to rethink how their space will be used and how it incorporates the growing use of mobile devices. A key factor is the infrastructure to meet the needs and demands of users. Wireless networks and bandwidth are two important elements that will be necessary for mobile technology.

Bandwidth in particular is very important because with increased use of mobile devices will come increased streaming of media from movies to music. Mobile technologies will allow libraries to think outside the box and take advantage of mobile technology to meet their user's needs. Many libraries loan laptops to students but as the price of devices like the iPad become lower in cost it is possible they will loan media tablets instead of laptops. E-book readers are items some libraries currently loan to students and as more publications that are scholarly move to e-book platforms that work with e-readers the use of e-book readers will increase in higher education. Database vendors are recognizing the need for mobile access to the information contained in their products. Because of this need, they developed mobile apps that allow users to search their products from a mobile device. Elsevier, Gale/Cengage, ProQuest, and EBSCO offer mobile access to their databases. Once the university installs the application university on their server users with a mobile device can access the database vendor's resources.

In order for libraries to develop apps that meet user needs they need to request student input for the types of apps they want and involve them in the creation of the app. Libraries and higher education institutions tend to rely on committees to develop new ideas and work on projects. The process can be lengthy. Decisions will stretch into months and possibly a year or more. Mobile technology requires the organization to be able to develop the app and make it available in a relatively short period. Committees are not suitable for this type of work. Involving students will shorten the time to complete the project and the app will be designed and developed to meet their needs. Student involvement creates a situation where the library and the student's needs are met. Instead of libraries telling users what they want with mobile technology, it is more important for users to tell the library what they want. In the long term, this creates goodwill between the library and their users. In turn, this could lead to future collaborations. Librarians make every effort to keep abreast of the latest technology but it is not easy to do. Students on the other hand often have the next generation smartphone or MP3 player or the latest media tablet. Observing users and asking question of users will help librarians keep up with new technology. Student centered libraries will lead to better implementation of mobile technology by libraries.

The physical library will always exist but, the space may be reconfigured to meet user needs and new technology as it becomes available. The demand and need for wireless connectivity will continue to increase and libraries will need to ensure they can meet the demand through their wireless network. Another aspect of library design or re-purposing of space will be the need for more outlets for users to charge their devices or places where users can store their devices if they leave their work area. Group study space and multimedia work areas will be necessary. Users will be able to upload content from their mobile devices and edit the material for a class project.

Mobile technology and devices open up new avenues of opportunity for outreach to their users. No longer are librarians tied to the library. Mobile technology provides the means and methods for librarians to work with students in places beyond the classroom and the library. Armed with an iPad or other mobile device the library can go where the users are. They can show someone how to search a database or find a book in the catalog. Likewise, they can do the same with an e-book. Find it in the e-book collection, download it to their device, read it and use it for their research. New opportunities exist for libraries with the proliferation of mobile devices it is their responsibility to incorporate them into their services to meet the needs of their users.

REFERENCES

Aldrich, A. W. (2010). Universities and libraries move to the mobile Web. *EDUCAUSE Quarterly*, *33*(2). Retrieved from http://www.educause.edu/EDUCAUSE+Quarterly/EQVolume332010/EDUCAUSEQuarterlyMagazineVolum/206524

Armbrust, M., Fox, A., Griffith, R., Joseph, A. D., Katz, R., & Knowinski, A. (2010). A view of Cloud Computing. *Communications of the ACM*, *53*(4), 50–58. doi:10.1145/1721654.1721672

Barile, L. (2011, April). Mobile technologies for libraries. *C&RL News, 222-228.*

Bellis, M. (2011). *History of laptop computers.* Retrieved from http://inventors.about.com/library/inventors/bllaptop.htm

Brown, B. (2010). *Most used apps.* Retrieved from http://www.flickr.com/photos/bonnie-brown/4285989531/

Coombs, K. (2008). The mobile iRevolution. *Library Journal*, (Fall): 28.

Falcone, J. P. (2011). Kindle vs. Nook vs. iPad: Which e-book reader should you buy? *CNET.* Retrieved from http://news.cnet.com/8301-17938105-20009738-1/kindle-vs-nook-vs-ipad-which-e-book-reader-should-you-buy/

Greene, B. (2011). *38 years ago he made the first cell phone call.* Retrieved from http://www.cnn.com/2011/OPINION/04/01/greene.first.cellphone.call/index.html

Griner, B. P., & Butler, P. J. (2011). *Cloud Computing visual diagram creative commons public domain.* Retrieved from http://commons.wikimedia.org/wiki/File:Cloudapplications.jpg

Hamblen, M. (2011). Amazon: E-books now outsell print books. Retrieved from http://www.computerworld.com/s/article/9216869/AmazonEbooksnowoutsellprintbooks

Lai, H.-C., Yang, C.-J., Chen, C.-F., Ho, W.-C., & Chan, W.-T. (2007). Affordances of mobile technologies for experiential learning: The interplay of technology and pedagogical practices. *Journal of Computer Assisted Learning*, *23*(4), 326–337. doi:10.1111/j.1365-2729.2007.00237.x

Levine, A. (2010). *2010 horizon report.* Retrieved from http://www.nmc.org/publications/2010-horizon-report

Levine, A. (2011). *2011 horizon report.* Retrieved from http://www.nmc.org/publications/2011-horizon-report

Lippincott, J. K. (2008). Mobile technologies, mobile users: Implications for academic libraries. *ARL*, *261*, 1–4.

Looi, C.-K., Seow, P., Zhang, B. H., So, H.-J., Chen, W., & Wong, L.-H. (2010). Leveraging mobile technology for sustainable seamless learning: A research agenda. *British Journal of Educational Technology*, *41*(2), 154–169. doi:10.1111/j.1467-8535.2008.00912.x

McCrea, B. (2010). *5 higher ed tech trends to watch in 2011.* Retrieved from http://campustechnology.com/articles/2010/12/09/5-higher-ed-tech-trends-to-watch-in-2011.aspx

Ovadia, S. (2010). Navigating the challenges of the Cloud. *Behavioral & Social Sciences Librarian*, *29*(3), 233–236. doi:10.1080/01639269.2010.498764

Profit, S. K. (2008). Text messaging at reference: A preliminary survey. *The Reference Librarian*, *49*(2), 129–134. doi:10.1080/02763870802101328

Ragon, B. (2009). Designing for the mobile Web. *Mobile Computing and the Library*, *6*, 355–361. doi:doi:10.1080/15424060903364875

Schaffhauser, D. (2010). *Oxford, Rice, Open U add to iTunesU electronic book collection.* Retrieved from http://campustechnology.com/articles/2010/11/02/oxford-rice-open-u-add-to-itunes-u-electronic-book-collection.aspx

Smith, A. (2010). *Mobile access 2010.* Pew Internet & American Life Project. Retrieved from http://www.pewinternet.org/Reports/2010/Mobile-Access-2010.aspx

Sodt, J. M., & Summey, P. T. (2009). Beyond the library's walls: Using library 2.0 tools to reach out to all users. *Journal of Library Administration*, *49*(1), 97–109. doi:10.1080/01930820802312854

Tadjer, R. (2010, November 18). What is Cloud Computing? *PC Magazine*. Retrieved from http://www.pcmag.com/article2/0,2817,2372163,00.asp#fbid=v16rIpg9bQ

KEY TERMS AND DEFINITIONS

Apps: Applications created for mobile devices. The apps allow their users to access resources through their mobile devices.

Cloud Computing: A system of computers that hosts applications accessible by anyone. Instead of hosting the applications on a shared network the applications are hosted by a remote vendor. An example are the many applications available from Google that can used or shared by individuals.

E-Book Readers: A portable device that allows readers to download and store e-books. The books can be purchased from an online company or depending on the e-reader they can borrow books from the public library.

Mobile Technology: The array of devices such as, smartphones, iPads or media tablets, iPods, netbooks and laptop computers. Mobile devices have Internet and Wi-Fi capabilities along with cameras to take photos or record videos.

Podcasts: Recorded, audio or video, presentations uploaded to a podcast server. Users can subscribe to the podcasts and store them on a computer or Mp3 player.

Screencasts: Or vidcasts are screen capture videos with audio or captions. Screencasts are used for short instruction videos on library resources.

Chapter 10
Virtual Libraries

ABSTRACT

Virtual libraries are often considered the same as digital collections but in fact, they are different from digital collections given the fact they often contain links to reference sources or subject specific materials including reference books or web sites. Virtual libraries originally intended for distance education students but are available for any researcher or student.

INTRODUCTION

Some people refer to digital collections as virtual libraries but virtual libraries are a collection of materials such as reference books or information that people readily look for when searching the Internet. Virtual libraries are accessible by anyone whether or not they are a student or faculty member at a university or college. Like digital collections, they do not require a password to access the information. It is simply a matter of following the link. One of the shortcomings of virtual libraries is if they are not updated on a regular basis the links to sources might be broken resulting in the dreaded error message page not

DOI: 10.4018/978-1-4666-0234-2.ch010

found. It is important for the owner of the virtual library to maintain the web site and add new material as it becomes available. In addition to updating and maintaining the virtual library, it is equally important to market the site.

BACKGROUND

One of the most widely used and well known virtual libraries is the Internet Public Library. This virtual library was created in 2005. Through the years, the resources were updated and recently the Internet Public Library and the Librarian's Internet Index merged their resources to create IPL2. This virtual library is partnered with the library and information science programs at Drexel, Florida

State, Illinois, Pittsburgh, Rutgers, Syracuse, University of North Carolina, University of Texas at Austin and Washington. Many states offer access to a collection of licensed databases. The New York State Library offers NOVEL (New York Online Virtual Electronic Library) anyone with a valid New York State driver's license can access the resources. Alabama offers a virtual library and Georgia offers GALILEO (Georgia Library Learning Online). The University of Georgia is responsible for the content and maintenance of the Virtual Library of Georgia and the Civil Rights Digital Library.

MAIN FOCUS OF THE CHAPTER

Virtual libraries were created by states to provide their residents with the opportunity to use a collection of electronic resources for research. Researchers through a state supported virtual library will have access to newspapers, magazines and scholarly journals they may not normally have access to without attending college. The difference between a digital library and a virtual library is the content. A digital library usually consists of images, manuscripts, videos, and often materials from special collections or university archives. The University of Georgia has created two very good digital libraries. One is the Digital Library of Georgia. This digital library contains Sanborn Fire Insurance Maps, images from counties in Georgia, slave narratives, Georgia Historic Newspapers and historical broadsides are just a few of the many collections contained within this digital library. The second digital library created by the University of Georgia is the Civil Rights Digital Library. This digital library allows you to search by event by year, places or people. The digital library contains numerous news videos that chronicle the Civil Rights Movement in its early years. Among the events included are the Freedom Rides and the integration of the University of Mississippi. Virtual libraries can contain digital collections but they consist primarily of databases and e-book collections. While most digital collections do not require a password or some type of authentication state supported virtual libraries do have that requirement. In order to access the virtual library you need have a library card for a library in that state, a driver's license or an IP address indicating you are a resident of the state.

Virtual libraries allow you to find materials you would use for research purposes. Most of the virtual libraries contain a selection of databases purchased by the Board of Regents or the state library and are available to all citizens of the state to use for their research purposes. A quick Internet search for state virtual libraries brings up a link for almost every state. While they all have different names, they all provide a collection of databases for use by the public and in particular students in grades K-12. With declining funding for education at the state level virtual libraries, fill the gap for electronic resources for students. All of the virtual libraries allow people to access them remotely. Below are some examples of virtual libraries with information on how to access them.

The Florida Electronic Library:(http://www.flelibrary.org/) contains over 50 resources and library patrons can log into it using the bar code from their library card. The Colorado Virtual Library: (http://coloradovirtuallibrary.org/) provides links for students to free resources in a variety of subjects. The state of Alaska offers SLED (Statewide Library Electronic Doorway)(http://sled.alaska.edu/) that provides access to journals, newspapers, magazines, and selected reference resources. Any citizen of Alaska can call an 800 number to request a password. This virtual library contains electronic resources for students from K-12 and college. The state of Georgia offers GALILEO (GeorgiA LIbrary LEarning Online) (http://www.galileo.usg.edu/welcome/) it is an initiative of the Board of Regents of the University System of Georgia. Remote access to the collection of databases and other resources is determined by IP address. All citizens of Georgia can access the electronic resources once they obtain a password from their local public library. Students at any of the public or private colleges in the state can access the resources using the password supplied by their college. The password is changed four times a year.

The state of New York offers NOVELNY (New York Online Virtual Library)(http://novel-newyork.org/)All New York state residents can access the electronic resources using their public library card, New York state driver's license or the New York state non-driver ID. The resources at the aforementioned virtual libraries can be accessed at the local public library or remotely. Most of the state virtual libraries are supported through funding provided by the state library, department of education or board of regents. The only requirement to access them is be a citizen of the state and have a valid state ID or library card.

Every state offers some form of a virtual library providing the residents of their state with the ability to search databases and similar resources to use for research projects or to find consumer information. This is beneficial to students in grades K-12 who may or may not have access to databases or resources of this nature for school projects. Georgia's virtual library GALILEO divides their resources between grades K-12 and higher education. Students in grades K-12 when they access the GALILEO web site can select the resources for the grade level they need for their project.

State supported virtual libraries provide access to a variety of electronic resources but in addition to state supported libraries there is the Internet Public Library (http://www.ipl.org/) This project is hosted by the *iSchool* at Drexel University, College of Information Science and Technology and the College of Information at Florida State University. The partners who develop and support the project are the information studies programs at Drexel University, the University of Pittsburgh, Rutgers University, University of Illinois, Syracuse University, Florida State University, University of North Carolina, University of Texas-Austin and the University of Washington. The information is organized by subject and within each subject area are sub-categories. From their home page, you can search by subject, newspapers and magazines, special collections created by the Internet Public Library, resources for kids and resources for teens. Users of the site can submit questions to be answered by one of the librarians for the site.

This free virtual library is a collection of free web sites that have been evaluated by librarians and placed into one collection. So rather, than search the Internet on your own users can search the subjects in the Internet Public Library to find the information they need or at least be pointed towards the resources they need. The other nice feature is the fact the site provides virtual reference service. If you cannot find what you need you can ask for help. This holds true for any of the virtual libraries available across the country. In essence, virtual libraries provide not only the resources needed for a research project or find basic information about a subject but they also provide virtual reference service.

Virtual reference services were discussed in a previous chapter; however, they warrant further discussion. Virtual reference services are increasing in scope and use. A physical reference desk is no longer required. Users have the option to call, e-mail, chat or text their reference questions to the librarian. Librarians, on the other hand, no longer have to be confined to a desk to answer questions. Mobile technologies allow librarians to answer user questions any place on campus. Using a media tablet and cell phone librarians can work with users at the places where they normally meet. The reference desk is not truly dead but it is slowly fading away or being repurposed into an information desk or a technology help desk or a combination of the two.

The trend over the past several years in libraries has been the move to an information commons model where there is a combination IT help desk, reference services. The space is designed either for students to work individually or in groups and the librarians can meet one-on-one with the users. There a software packages available that allow the people working at the desk to track the types of questions they receive, the length of time they spent with the user and the question asked and the answer given. In addition to statistical software, the chat reference services provide a transcript of the chat session. The same holds true for text messaging sessions. A transcript of the session is generated at the end of the session.

An issue for libraries is how to integrate virtual reference services into their library. Academic libraries have a reference of information desk that is staffed throughout the day but with virtual reference services, the library has to decide if the person or persons working at the reference desk should provide virtual reference services at the same time. Some libraries do and some create a separate schedule for virtual reference services. Libraries that use QuestionPoint from OCLC are required to have a separate schedule for the service. Their policies stipulate you cannot work at your library's reference desk while answering questions through their chat reference service (OCLC, 2011). In order for libraries to determine their scheduling for virtual reference services they need to keep statistics on the number of questions received and the time of day the majority of the questions are received. A library can compare the statistics from their in-person reference desk and use the comparison to create a staffing model for both services. If more questions are received late in the day through virtual reference then the library will need to have a librarian scheduled for virtual reference during the period. Conversely, if there is fewer in-person reference questions late in the day then the library may schedule the person to answer questions virtually rather than in-person.

Another way to work virtually with users is through social media like Facebook or Twitter. Working with users in social network sites allows librarians to work with users at their point of need. Librarians can provide links to resources by send-

ing the user a message they can also do a quick tutorial video using Jing or Camtasia Studio and send the link to the user. Social network sites are not just for meeting with friends and students often collaborate on projects through social network sites. Tutorials posted to the library's web site provide users with additional training and reference services. Maybe they need to know how to search the catalog or find databases.

Screen capture tutorials or narrated PowerPoint presentations can be created and posted to the library's web site. Users can use them to find the information they need without talking to a librarian. A further extension of the reference desk is an embedded librarian program. This type of program connects a librarian with students in an online class. The librarian can answer student questions about resources through the discussion board and they can provide synchronous or asynchronous instruction to students through the course management system. An embedded librarian program moves the library and its staff beyond the physical space of the library and provides them with a greater ability to reach far larger numbers of students. As the number of online classes continue to grow so will the need to work with students in those classes to meet their needs to access library services and resources from off-campus.

Virtual libraries and virtual library services complement each other in the fact they provide users with remote access to library resources and services. The two go hand in hand. Many academic libraries promote the remote access to collections and at the same time promote their virtual reference services. Embedded librarians, working with teaching faculty they have the opportunity to work in an online class and work with students in the course managements system to provide library help students with library resources of their research projects or class assignments. In other words, they become ebrarians. As libraries compete with other sources of information they can differentiate themselves by offering virtual services and meet students where they work. As more library resources and collections are available electronically librarians need to provide students with services to instruct them on not only on how to find and select the resources they need but also how to search the resources once they identify the type of information they need.

The Rochester Institute of Technology (RIT) libraries are an example of academic libraries whose services to students living off-campus have evolved and grown as technology changed and improved. In the late 1990s, they added a distance-learning librarian and implemented EZproxy to authenticate off-campus users for library resources (Bower & Mee, 2010). By the end of 2010, the library had over 200 electronic database resources and the number of e-books available is over 65,000. The number electronic databases and e-books continue to grow (Bower & Mee, 2010). Because of the growing number of distance education students the libraries at RIT have committed a significant amount of their budget and staffing resources to meet the needs of their distance learners. (Bower & Mee, 2010)

At the time the article was published the 85% of the RIT libraries budget was spent on electronic resources. The libraries provide seamless access to resources for distance education students through their web site, Metalib X-Server (from ExLibris), their course management system, the subject librarian web sites called, "Meet the Librarian," and the use of Skype to communicate with distance education students. They also created a series of instructional tutorials using Adobe Captivate and Camtasia and in 2009, the libraries merged with the RIT Teaching & Learning Services, which allow them to offer more instructional services, and technology improvements to meet the needs of distance education students (Bower & Mee, 2010).

With virtual libraries and library services the access services manager still has responsibilities to ensure library policies and the library and its users comply with copyright laws. Virtual libraries in some ways have increased the responsibilities of the access services manager (Jetton & Bailey,

2010). This person not only oversees circulation and stacks but may also be responsible for e-reserves, interlibrary loan, and copyright or intellectual property rights (Jetton & Bailey, 2010). Because of the responsibilities of the access services manager, they should be included in contract negotiations for electronic resources especially for remote access (Jetton & Bailey, 2010). Since the access services manager will oversee areas responsible for processing copyrighted material they need to ensure the contract provides remote access to library resources and clearly defines who is an authorized user and how the material can be accessed (Jetton & Bailey, 2010).

Virtual libraries have increased the responsibilities of the access services manager because as more materials are available electronically the use of the physical library changes (Jetton & Bailey, 2010). As a result, the access services manager in collaboration with other librarians needs to make sure students can access the materials they need and have the necessary technology to access them through either a laptop or a mobile device. The role of the access services manager will continue to expand as libraries continue to grow their virtual collections and services (Jetton & Bailey, 2010).

The Bucks County Community College (BCCC) in 2007 instituted a student centered information literacy program and developed an embedded ebrarian program. During the spring semester of 2008, the library developed a pilot program to begin integrating the library instruction program into the online courses offered by the college (Hemming & Montet, 2010). The librarian worked with a faculty member who was willing to have the librarian work with his online class (Hemmig & Montet, 2010). This pilot project consisted of having the librarians added as teaching assistants; they created tutorials on how to search databases and monitoring the discussion board to answer student research questions (Hemming & Montet, 2010). By the summer of 2008, the library launched its embedded ebrarian program. During the first year of the program, the library quickly realized there were some challenges and some opportunities associated with this program (Hemming & Montet, 2010). Some of the challenges were the amount of time required to monitor the online class and the need to update the tutorials. Another challenge was faculty members who were uncertain about librarians being in the online class as teaching assistants (Hemmig & Montet, 2010).

One of the best opportunities that arose from this program was the questions posted or e-mailed to the librarians about research and finding the resources they needed. One instructor encouraged the students to contact the librarian for help for another assignment due for the online course (Hemming & Montet, 2010). For the second year of the ebrarian, program the librarians at Bucks County Community College to provide individual research assistance for students (Hemming & Montet, 2010). As part of their change to a more individualized ebrarian program, the library subscribed to LibGuides from Springshare (Hemmig & Montet, 2010). LibGuides is stand-alone software hosted through Springshare that allows libraries to create research guides with information about accessing and using the library's resources. The guides can be embedded into the library's web site or an online class. Because of this change, the librarians at BCCC noted an increase in the use of the LibGuides as opposed to the tutorials they created the previous years (Hemming & Montet, 2010). In a two-year period BCCC was able to develop a student centered information literacy program and expand it into an online embedded ebrarian program that provided individual research help to students in online courses (Hemmig & Montet, 2010).

The librarians at the University of North Texas conducted a survey of the faculty teaching online courses to determine the services and support needed from the libraries to meet the needs of their students. The majority of the faculty surveyed 93 percent, indicated the role of the library was to provide and indicated the library should provide instruction on using electronic resources. Some other issues identified in the survey included 73 percent of the faculty believed students had difficulty finding library resources necessary for their assignments (Thomsett-Scott & May, 2009). This survey helped the University of North Texas libraries identify areas for improvement to meet the needs of both students and faculty in online or distance education courses. It surveyed a number of issues and faculty provided feedback on how the library could improve the marketing of their services to faculty. It also identified opportunities for librarians to embed themselves into an online class through a course page specifically designed to meet students' needs for that course. Another issue raised in the survey was the need for multiple passwords to gain access to library resources through the course management system (Thomsett-Scott & May, 2009). Surveys of this nature help libraries and librarians identify challenges and opportunities to provide virtual services to students and faculty.

The Zell B. Miller Learning Center (MLC) located on the campus of the University of Georgia is another example of a virtual library. The building houses no books or a reference desk but provides a combination of classroom, library and computer facilities (Barratt & White, 2010). Even without books students who use the building have access to group study rooms, practice presentation rooms, a variety of production and media software, and computers including laptops (Barratt & White, 2010). In addition, students can receive research assistance through virtual reference, in-person or instruction sessions (Barratt & White, 2010). The combination of physical space and virtual services for students may become the norm rather than the exception in the near future. While the MLC does not house any books, it still connects students with resources for their research. It redefines library space and the types of services libraries can offer to their users. Facilities of this type while serving multiple purposes provide students with the ability to go from classroom to research without having to leave the building. It is one stop shopping for resources, research and technology (Barratt & White, 2010).

Library collections in academic libraries contain print and electronic or e-books. According to this year's Horizon Report, e-books will grow in use. Currently there are limitations to e-books that make them somewhat unpopular with users. One is the inability to print or download information from the book, which is the result of copyright law. While the prediction is for an increase in use and popularity of e-books, some users may not want an e-book. Some users prefer print and as a result, libraries often purchase the print and electronic version of the book (Levine, 2011).

In February of this year, OverDrive, a distributor of e-books and audio books, released an iPad allowing users to borrow and read e-books and listen to audio books from more than 13,000 libraries around the world (Rapp, 2011). This app will have a significant impact on the e-readers currently available from Amazon, Barnes & Noble and Sony. Amazon's Kindle does not have the capability to download library books while the Nook from Barnes and Noble and the Sony reader provide the option for library lending. With the iPad app from OverDrive, it eliminates the need for a separate e-reader and provides iPad users with the convenience of obtaining e-books from a library. E-books that are part of library collections can be entered into the library's catalog. This allows users to find them during a search and usually the catalog record contains a link to the book. When the user selects the link it will ask them for a user ID and password and once authenticated, they will have access to the book. Including e-books in the library catalog is another remote access technology that allows users access to the resources they need when they are off-campus (Rapp, 2011).

As mentioned in an earlier chapter there are problems with scholarly e-books because they cannot be read from an e-book reader. Often because of the digital rights management technology students can only download and print a limited number of pages from the book. Another problem is books cannot be loaned through interlibrary loan, which becomes a hindrance to patrons at other universities that need the book for research. While e-books have become an integral part of library collections, some improvements to the way the books are accessed, and used need to implemented, before they gain wide acceptance and use by students and faculty. They will grow in popularity but only if changes are made to the digital rights management technology making scholarly e-books more user friendly.

Recent studies of e-book usage and acceptance by college students indicate students prefer a printed book to an e-book. A study by the Head of Electronic Resources at Mount St. Joseph's Alter Library, in the fall of 2004, indicated students liked to use e-books but did not want print books to disappear (Gregory, 2006). Some of the issues students had with e-books were the difficulty in printing, reading from a computer screen, and the unreliability of computers (Gregory, 2008). The Joint Information Systems Committee (JISC), in the United Kingdom, conducted a similar study January 18 and March 1, 2008. They received over 22,000 responses and approximately eight percent of the students indicated it was difficult to read from a computer screen and around six percent preferred a printed book to an e-book. Around one percent of the respondents indicated they had a difficult time printing from e-books. The responses also indicated libraries needed to do more to promote e-books (Jamali, Nicholas & Rowlands, 2009).

Virtual libraries unlike digital libraries or digital collections provide users with access to an array of electronic resources and virtual services. In order for the library to offer virtual services and ensure their virtual resources are fully utilized requires librarians to understand the needs of their users. A few of the examples in this chapter indicate libraries through the use of surveys were able to determine what faculty knew about the resources available for online course and how they utilized the resources they were familiar with for online courses. What do virtual libraries have to do with remote access technologies? In order for users to access the resources available in virtual libraries, they need to be authenticated as authorized users. The examples of the state virtual library resources require the user to enter information to indicate they are a resident of the state where the resources are located. If they are unable to enter the required ID or their IP address cannot be validated they will be unable to access the virtual library for that state.

Virtual library resources provided by a state allow residents of the state to have access to research databases. For students in grades K-12 state resources of this nature provide them with the ability to search electronic resources with scholarly materials instead of using an Internet search engine and using the three or four of the top results for their assignments. Providing students with access to scholarly resources in high school familiarizes them with resources they use in college. They will continue to use an Internet search engine but they will know the library can provide them with scholarly resources beyond their Internet search. Virtual libraries alter the physical space of the library. It provides libraries with the opportunity to reconfigure their physical space to make way for more technology such as, multimedia workspaces where students can create and edit multi-media materials and content for assignments. Create more group study space and include a practice presentation room where students can practice their presentations and possibly record them for their class.

The redesigned space will include more outlets for students to connect their laptops or charge their mobile devices. The 21st century academic library will increasingly be technology driven and oriented. The Miller Learning Center on the campus of the University of Georgia is an example of a newly designed multi-purpose building. It serves as a classroom, technology center and library research facility (Barratt & White, 2010). Students can work in groups, practice presentations, check out a laptop, develop multi-media materials and obtain research help all in one building. While the building does not contain any books students using the MLC can access all of the library's electronic resources and if they are unsure which resources they need to use, they can obtain virtual reference services or in-person reference help. The virtual library resources and services extend the library beyond its physical building. Students can ask for research help whether they are in the library or at home through virtual reference services such as chat, texting or e-mail. They can also access the library's resources on or off-campus (Barratt & White, 2010). Without the development of open URL, EZproxy and VPN library users would not be able to access library resources while off-campus.

The Rochester Institute of Technology provides an excellent example of an academic library that adopted new technology and evolved their library services to meet the needs of students' off-campus in distance education programs. The Wallace center at RIT collaborated with their teaching and learning center in order to offer new services and improved instructional sessions for their students. Most of the colleges and universities mentioned in this chapter focused on virtual collections and services to meet the needs of the distance education students (Bower & Mee, 2010).

The opening chapter of this book indicated distance education was and probably will continue to be the driving force for remote access to library resources and services. Often times virtual services or remote access to library, services are overlooked but they are an integral part of remote access technology. Another aspect of implementing remote access technology understands the resources and services offered by the library that are beneficial to students and faculty in online courses. Working with teaching faculty provides libraries with the opportunity to develop new programs and methods of instruction to meet the needs of distance education students.

The embedded ebrarian program at Bucks County Community College is just one example of such a program. By the second year, the program was growing and improving based on knowledge gained after the first year. Just because materials are available virtually does not mean the access services manager has a declining role in managing library resources on the contrary this individual will have an integral part in managing virtual services. One aspect of virtual services is copyright and access to library resources from off-campus. Because the access services manager will oversee interlibrary loan and e-reserves, they should be included in contract negotiations with database vendors to make sure off-campus users can access the resources and authorized users are clearly defined in the contract. They can also provide input into copyright issues to make sure users have access to the resources they need under the contract and are not denied fair use for materials.

The 2010 and 2011 Horizon Reports indicated that e-books in the next year will increase in use (Levine, 2010, 2011). Some e-book collections have MARC records this record allows the library with the ability to enter the e-book into the catalog. When users search the catalog, they will be able to find the e-books along with print books. Usually a link to the book is included in the catalog record and the user is able to click on the link to the book in the e-book collection. There are still problems with e-books. Many users like to use them to start their research but are frustrated by the fact they cannot download them or print pages because of digital rights management technology. The literature on this topic indicates users are not always willing to sit at a computer to read a book. E-book readers from Sony and Barnes & Noble provide the ability to obtain books through library lending from public libraries. With the creation of the iPad app from OverDrive more users will not be able to download books and audio books from libraries across the world through this app. E-books free up shelf space in the library but users still have not warmed up to the idea of using an e-book. It will be interesting in the course of the next year to determine if the use of e-books will increase or remain the same.

Virtual library services include e-reserves, librarians embedded in online courses, document delivery and reference or research help. These services extend the library beyond their physical location the same as the virtual or electronic collections. Students' off-campus can access the resources they need or seek answers to research questions without coming into the library. Virtual reference services are growing in popularity and use. There are different options available for virtual reference services but the primary forms of service are e-mail, chat and text. Libraries can select from a number of different sources for their chat reference services including Meebo, Libraryh3lp, Ask a librarian and QuestionPoint just to name a few of the choices available. Chat evolved from the late 1990s and early 2000s when libraries were limited to instant messaging (IM) services like AOL.

One of the benefits of chat reference services currently available is the ability to include a chat widget in the library's web site or the subject guides created by the librarians. When a library user opens a subject guide, the library chat widget will appear and if the user has a question, they can chat with the librarian. QuestionPoint is a proprietary chat reference service offered by OCLC. Because this service is part of a nationwide cooperative, subscribers to the service are required to answer questions not only for their institution but also for academic libraries around the country. Once a library subscribes to the service they have to commit to a set number of hours each week for their home institution then an additional set of hours for the cooperative chat reference service.

Another aspect of QuestionPoint is the fact the library may not answer questions while working at the reference desk in their library. The librarians are required to provide service on a schedule separate from their normal reference desk shifts. Instead of one reference desk schedule the library will not have to create two in order to meet the requirements of the service. Separate schedules for chat reference and in person reference are common. Academic libraries depending on their size and staffing will have librarians answer chat reference questions at a separate time from their normally scheduled reference desk hours. A primary reason for this is if the librarian is working with a student in person and a chat reference question is asked the librarian will have the student in front of them wait while they answer the chat reference question. Alternatively, they will have the person in the chat reference queue wait until they finish with the person at the reference.

One study of virtual reference services found that chat reference questions were always answered promptly and users often waited several minutes before someone picked up their question or even acknowledged they had asked a question (Platt & Benson, 2010). One of the pluses to using QuestionPoint is the user of the service receives a survey asking for feedback about the person who answered their question and their overall satisfaction with the service. This type of service is crucial for any type of virtual library service. The library can use the information to provide additional training if necessary in order to improve their level and quality of service to meet the user's needs.

Along those same lines are the marketing of virtual services and collections by the library. Just because the library offers virtual collections or services does not mean faculty and students are aware of them or use them to the extent they could or should be used. A few of the examples in this chapter and previous mentioned surveying faculty regarding their familiarity and use of virtual library services for distance education students. While any students can use these services or faculty it is critical, the faculty who teach distance education courses and the distance education students are aware of how the library can meet their needs. Surveying faculty and/or students is a good place to start. Survey information can help determine what services users are aware of and readily use in their courses.

Conversely, it helps identify the services they are least aware of and underutilized. Libraries have a variety of ways to market their services to students and faculty. One is through the library's web site. Since many library web sites contain a blog, the information can easily found there. Another option is e-mail to faculty members and students. All colleges and universities have a student portal that can be utilized to post announcements or send e-mails to all students. For faculty there is usually a faculty list and anyone subscribed to the list can send an e-mail.

Another option is the use of tent cards in the student dining halls or posters in the residence halls. Libraries can also place the same type of information within the library in student study areas. Marketing is crucial to the success and use of any of the library's services and collections. Working with the teaching faculty as the librarians did in some of the examples used in the chapter is an additional and invaluable way to make a service or resource a success. Word of mouth is one of the best promotions for any service. Collaborating with teaching faculty to design programs and services to meet the needs of distance education ensures the service will meet both their needs.

The embedded ebrarian program developed at Bucks County Community College is a good example of how collaboration can result in better services for students and faculty. Working with faculty in the online courses provided the librarians with a better understanding of what the students needed to complete their assignments and based on their work in the online class the librarians at BCCC were able to make changes to improve the program. The biggest change was the creation of subject guides using LibGuides and offering custom research service to each student based on their needs rather than adopting the one size fits all approach. Some of the topics in this chapter are similar to topics contained in other chapters, however, all the topics are related to one another and each builds on the other.

Virtual libraries are the outcome of remote access technologies. With the development of EZproxy, VPN and OpenURL provided library users with the ability to access the electronic resources of the library from off-campus locations. No longer did users need the librarian's help to obtain materials when they were off-campus. The mediated search was no longer necessary. Articles in journals that are available only in print require the student to contact the access services manager to obtain a copy through document delivery. The document will be copied or scanned and sent to the user through e-mail as an attachment. The development of remote access technologies provides users with access to resources 24 hours a day and every day of the year. Remote access technologies has lead to the creation of a library that is never closed and opened up new opportunities for libraries and librarians to work with students. This is especially true for distance education or online courses.

Librarians can embed themselves into an online course, with the instructor's permission, to provide research help and instruction to students in online classes. The software used for online classes have the capability to link library resources within the course content. This is anything from articles to links to databases or documents on e-reserve. The increase in electronic resources re-purposes the physical space of the library. Instead of endless rows of books, the space can be used for increased group study space or multi-media workstations. While digital collections may be part of virtual libraries, the two have distinct purposes. Digital collections are a resource users can access through a virtual library. A virtual library contains the electronic resources and collections users can access for their research projects or class assignments.

FUTURE TRENDS

Virtual libraries open up a number of future trends for libraries based on the current literature available. States will continue to fund some form a virtual library that is free and open to all residents of that state. With the ongoing economic problems in most states, there may be fewer resources offered to residents but most states will continue to offer some form of a virtual library. This is important for students in grades K-12 to have access to credible and scholarly resources for their class assignments. The education budgets in most states were drastically reduced and do not have the resources to pay for electronic resources on their own. State virtual libraries become a lifeline for K-12 programs and schools. The state virtual libraries do not offer chat reference they do provide links for users to contact them in addition to providing a list of frequently asked questions regarding the resources.

In the future state virtual libraries may want to include chat reference and a series of online tutorials that demonstrate how to search the different resources. Embedded librarian programs or embedded ebrarians as Bucks County Community College called their librarians in online courses will continue to grow. There are some challenges with a program of this nature and the primary one is time. It takes a great amount of time to answer student questions and monitor the discussion board and e-mail for an online class. If the library is using tutorials they will need to be updated on a regular basis as database interfaces change or the library, web site is redesigned or new features are added to the catalog.

Programs of this nature provide increased opportunities for libraries and their users. First, it allows them to work with teaching faculty to help them design assignments and identify the resources the users will need to complete the assignments. Second, it provides students with access to a librarian with class assignments. Students are often reluctant to ask the librarian for help. Third, it provides the library with the opportunity to link their resources and services into the online class. Finally, it provides librarians with the opportunity to provide instruction sessions in the online environment and create course specific subject guides that can be linked into the course content and students can refer back to the information throughout the semester.

E-books will continue to increase in use, but possibly without a significant increase in popularity, providing they become more user friendly. Students using an e-book want the ability to download sections of it and print pages, as they need them. Academic libraries will need to pressure e-book publishers to remove or decrease the digital rights management technology from e-books. In most survey responses about e-books students users stated they did not like reading books on a computer screen and wanted the ability to download them or at least print the pages they need. Virtual reference services will become more widely used than in-person reference services. The physical reference desk will not disappear there will be fewer interactions at the desk between librarians and users who need help.

More campuses will adopt libraries without books, like the Miller Learning Center (MLC) at the University of Georgia. The multi-purpose building will allow students to attend class, work with fellow students and use library resources without leaving the building. Technologies such as the iPad will continue to influence the virtual library. Library users will adopt new technology with the expectation they will be able to use them to gain access to the library resources. They will want the ability to download books, articles and search databases. The expectation is they will have seamless access to library resources on or off campus with any number of different technologies.

CONCLUSION

The Code of Ethics from the American Library Association includes an equal access to information for all users. Virtual libraries provide users with that access. All residents of the state with the proper identification or authentication of their IP address can access the resources. Even if your state does offer access to databases, the option is the Internet Public Library. While it is not the same as searching a database the sources are credible and reliable. Librarians and library students at several major library schools vetted the sites before they were linked to the IPL.

The same holds true for students and faculty at any academic institution. Virtual libraries provide users whether they are on or off campus or taking a class while living half way around the world will have the same access to library resources. In the 21st century the demand for information is increasing along with user expectations, they will be able to access the resources all hours of the day and night anytime of the year. The expectation is the library is never closed. Users also expect they can access the resources from any type of technology be it a laptop, desktop computer or mobile device. No longer is the library confined to its brick and mortar space. The opportunity to work with users outside of the library is ever increasing and as technology improves those types of opportunities will continue to increase.

While an embedded librarian or ebrarian program is time-consuming working with students where they take classes is critical to their success and the library's ability to meet the needs of those students. The technology is already available and being used to create narrated screen capture tutorials and PowerPoint presentations. Librarians also have the technology to provide library instruction synchronously to students in an online class. This type of opportunity will increase and allow libraries to reach more students. The physical space of the library can be re-purposed, as more resources are available electronically. Spaces once taken up by print journals can be converted into group study space or multi-media workstations.

Will virtual libraries mean the end to the physical library. Physical libraries will exist for the time being. Publishers will continue to print books and many of the traditional functions of a library will not disappear anytime in the future. How those functions are performed may change. The biggest change will be in reference services. Libraries who keep statistics of the transactions at their reference desk have been noticing a decline over the past several years. While the reference desk will not disappear completely it, become more of an information desk rather than serving as a primary place for research assistance. Information or learning commons are located in most academic libraries. Because of this transformation, the reference desk has become the place to obtain help with technology or to ask a question about how to find a resource or book. Most academic libraries with an information commons have indicated the types of research questions they receive at the desk are more involved and take longer to answer.

Virtual reference services do not always lend themselves well to complicated reference questions. In some instances, the user should come into the library to receive additional help. However, if this is not possible the librarian will need to get the information to the user. The same technologies used for synchronous instruction in online classes can be used for virtual reference services. Narrated screen captures and be created and the link e-mailed to the student. Technology such as Wimba or Elluminate can be used to provide the user with one-on-one synchronous instruction. There is a variety of methods to make virtual reference services more robust in order to meet the needs of the user. Remote access technologies, mobile technology and virtual libraries transform how and when users access library resources.

The development of remote access technologies combined with the growth in mobile devices and the move from print to electronic resources brought about the virtual libraries we have today.

Virtual libraries will continue to change the way library resources and services are delivered. The role of the access services manager, acquisition librarian and catalogers will not change nor will the role of instruction and reference librarians. Books and other resources will need to be purchased and e-books, if they have a MARC record will need to be added to the catalog so users can find and access them. Articles proclaiming the library is dead or people can find all the information they need on the Internet are not true.

During this most recent economic downturn library usage has increased as people turned to the library to use their computers to look for a job, check out books, music and videos (ALA, 2010). People have come to realize not information on the Internet is readily available or credible. Even students who start their research project or class assignment with an Internet search or an article from Wikipedia eventually turn to the library to find the sources they need to complete the assignment. Virtual services and resources will not turn libraries into buildings without books instead; they extend the library beyond its physical space and turn any space into a classroom. Virtual libraries and services improve equal access to information and sources such as the Internet Public Library allow anyone with access to a computer to find sources of information that are free, reliable and credible. Libraries whether virtual or physical will continue to be a part of our society and promote access to information for all.

REFERENCES

American Library Association. (2010). *Recession drives more Americans to libraries in search of employment resources but funding lags demand.* Retrieved from http://www.ala.org/ala/news-presscenter/news/pressreleases2010/april2010/soalrpio.cfm

Barratt, C. C., & White, E. (2010). Case study for a large research institution library: The University of Georgia's Miller Learning Center. *Journal of Library Administration, 50*(2), 135–144. doi:10.1080/01930820903454977

Bower, S. L., & Mee, S. A. (2010). Virtual delivery of electronic resources and services to off-campus users: A multifaceted approach. *Journal of Library Administration, 50*(5), 468–483. doi:10.1080/01930826.2010.488593

Gregory, C. L. (2010). But I want a real book: An investigation of undergraduates' usage and attitudes toward electronic books. *Reference and User Services Quarterly, 47*(3), 266–273.

Hemmig, W., & Montet, M. (2010). The "just for me" virtual library: Enhancing an embedded ebrarian program. *Journal of Library Administration, 50*(5), 657–669. doi:10.1080/01930826.2010.488943

Jamali, H. R., Nicholas, D., & Rowlands, I. (2009). Scholarly e-books: The views of 16,000 academics: Results from the JISC National E-Book Observatory. *Aslib Proceedings: New Information Perspectives, 61*(1), 33–47. doi:doi:10.1108/00012530910932276

Jetton, L. L., & Bailey, A. S. (2010). The role of the access services manager in the virtual library. *Journal of Access Services, 7*(2), 121–131. doi:10.1080/15367961003617519

Levine, A. (2011). *2011 horizon report*. Retrieved from: http://www.nmc.org/publications/2011-horizon-report

OCLC. (2011). *QuestionPoint*. Retrieved from http://www.oclc.org/questionpoint/about/default.htm

Platt, J., & Benson, P. (2010). Improving the virtual reference experience: How closely do academic libraries adhere to RUSA guidelines? *Journal of Library & Information Services in Distance Learning, 4*(1), 30–42. doi:10.1080/15332901003765811

Rapp, D. (2011, March 15). Infotech: OverDrive unveils iPad app for ebook lending. *Library Journal*, 20.

Thomsett-Scott, B., & May, F. (2009). How may we help you? Online education faculty tell us what they need from libraries and librarians. *Journal of Library Administration, 49*(1), 111–135. doi:10.1080/01930820802312888

KEY TERMS AND DEFINITIONS

E-Books: Electronic versions of printed books. They are protected by digital rights management technology that limits the number of pages that can be downloaded and printed.

OverDrive: A distributor of e-books and audio books that can be downloaded to e-book readers or Mp3 devices.

Virtual Libraries: Collections of electronic resources including e-books, databases, open access materials, and websites. It can also mean a physical building that provides library services but does not contain any books.

Chapter 11
Remote Access
Technology Problems

ABSTRACT

With any remote access technology, problems can and do arise. Some of the common problems with remote access technologies are security, broken links, and privacy. Most remote technology is relatively stable, but unfortunately, problems occur from time to time. It is important that the library has someone monitor the technology to make sure there are no problems. Users become frustrated when trying to access a resource from off-campus only to find they cannot.

INTRODUCTION

Remote access technology for library resources, digital collections or virtual libraries requires a web link, a password or a virtual private network. With any technology problems do occur. EZproxy is one of the most stable software for remote connection to licensed databases but sometimes there are problems with the links to a database or the server goes down preventing the users from accessing the resources they need. The same thing can happen with a link to a virtual library or digital collection. If the server or web site goes down people cannot access the resources. If links are changed and the virtual library is not updated on a regular basis, once again people will not be able to access the resources they need. Another issue that arises at least once a year or more is the database vendor changes the interface, the screen users enter their search criteria, sometimes the change is for the better but sometimes it makes the database more difficult to use.

DOI: 10.4018/978-1-4666-0234-2.ch011

BACKGROUND

One of the biggest debates surrounding remote access is security versus privacy. Librarians support equal access to information and believe everyone should have access to the information they need without restriction. Problems arise when students or other individuals use library computers or other information for inappropriate or abusive behavior. The computer address cannot be authenticated even though an incident is recorded. Even if the computer address is authenticated, librarians and libraries do not share information with third parties. Library records are considered confidential and most libraries destroy or remove information about the books borrowed by a student or faculty member after two weeks. Another issue that arises is the fact students or faculty often needs multiple passwords to access library materials remotely. Unless they are using VPN to connect remotely they will need to access the school's portal using an ID and password then use a separate password to gain access to library materials. Multiple passwords can become a source of frustration for researchers. One other problem related to remote access is if the server for the database vendor goes offline and users get an error message or they are asked for a password or user ID. Another limitation is the number of simultaneous users for an electronic resource. This is driven usually by the cost of the resource.

MAIN FOCUS OF THE CHAPTER

No technology is perfect and we all have experienced at some point a technology or device that suddenly stops working. It could be the result of any one of a number of problems. The network is down and everyone on campus loses their Internet connection or the e-mail server goes down and you are unable to send or receive e-mails. Other times the server from the database publisher may be down or the remote access link does not validate

the user as someone who is authorized to have access to library resources. All of these issues can be frustrating for users and the library because eventually students or faculty will complain about the problems that they have gaining access to library resources when they are off-campus.

While these issues can be minor inconveniences while on campus for an off-campus user they can become a major problem. If the library web site server is down you cannot access the library's web site and as a result will not be able to access the electronic resources you need. You will not be able to access the course management system if their server is down and as a result, you cannot submit your assignment. Technology has become prevalent in our society and as a result, we have come to depend on it and expect it will always work whenever we need it. Each of the technologies discussed in the previous chapters are subject to fail at some point for anyone of a number of reasons. Starting with the first technology distance education this chapter will examine each technology and provide a brief overview of some the technical issues that may cause problems for the end user.

Meeting customer needs is the driving force behind remote access technologies. Users want access to resources without having to come into the library. Understanding how to meet those needs can be determined from surveys and focus groups or a combination of the two. A problem with surveys or focus groups is once the information is received and nothing is done with the information. If library users participate in a survey, their expectation is, they will see changes made or problems corrected. Another problem is not doing a follow-up survey two or three year later to determine if users are still satisfied. Sometimes with implementation of recommended changes, there will still be dissatisfied users.

Another aspect of user surveys is usability studies. If the library changes their web site in the hopes it will be easier for their users to find the resources they need to ask users for feedback regarding the redesigned site. Once again, it is important to use the feedback provided to make further revisions to the site before it is implemented. If a library asks for feedback they must be prepared to hear both good and bad comments, but it is important to use those comments to satisfy the research needs of their users. A drawback to using surveys is the sample size may be too small resulting in a few making changes for the many, which happens in any organization. Usability testing creates an opportunity for more users to participate and provide their feedback on the proposed changes. The examples cited in chapter 2 of the book highlight some of the changes implemented by libraries through different methodologies. Conducting surveys or focus groups is time consuming for the library staff, which is another problem especially when most libraries are, understaffed (Jankowska, Hertel & Young, 2006).

Digital collections created by libraries, archives, museums or colleges and universities provide the opportunity for anyone with an Internet connection to use the online collections. It provides institutions with the ability to display and highlight materials that may otherwise go underutilized. Once an institution begins digitizing materials it will be an ongoing project, time consuming and a significant investment in staffing and monetary resources. Before undertaking projects of this nature, institutions need to secure sources of funding through grants or they may have a difficult time completing their project or projects. The Digital Library of Georgia is an excellent example of an institution that developed partnerships and secured grant funding before undertaking the creation of the digital library. Another problem with digitizing is equipment. The institution must have the equipment and software to scan and edit images or videos. They also need to have trained staff to digitize the materials. Without the financial and personnel resources in place at the start of a digitization project will probably result in the institution taking years to complete their projects if at all. Along with the digitizing of the materials

is the creation of a web site to host the collection and metadata so users can find the materials when searching online (IMLS, 2006).

Digitizing is more than scanning of images it requires an internal infrastructure to complete the project. Once the materials are digitized and the web site created the institution will need to maintain the site and update the site when materials are added or deleted. The collection will only be of use to researchers if it is properly maintained. Site maintenance for a digital collection or a library web site becomes sources of frustration for users because they are unable to find the materials they need. Another aspect of digital collections is copyright and fair use of the materials within the collection. Digital collections need to have clearly defined policies as to how the materials can be used and if the material has, any restrictions or it is considered to be in the public domain (Schlosser, 2006).

Digital collections go beyond images, postcards, scrapbooks, yearbooks and letters. Many colleges and universities transitioned to electronic theses and dissertations. Their digital repositories in addition to digital theses and dissertations include published faculty research or research under consideration for publication. These types of digital repositories also need to have clearly defined polices as to what constitutes fair use of the material. Digital repositories and digital collections do not require users to enter a password or be associated with the campus where the collection is housed.

Copyright law is not a remote access technology; however, it does affect remote access to library resources. When contracts are negotiated for electronic resources the contract needs to define who is authorized to access the materials, how the materials can be accessed on or off campus and what constitutes fair use of the materials. Copyright affects interlibrary loan (ILL) which can be considered another method of remote access to library resources. Database contracts need to include a clause regarding the use of the materials for interlibrary loan (Chou & Zhou, 2005).

Libraries cannot afford to own every journal interlibrary loan is the only method libraries have to meet the research needs of their students and faculty. In order to lend material the library needs to obtain copyright clearance before sending a copy of the article to the borrowing institution. The United States has some of the most complicated copyright laws, which often leave students, faculty and librarians wondering if they have violated copyright law. Copyright law has an impact on e-books because of the digital rights management technology. Digital rights management is intended to protect the intellectual property rights of the author or creator of the copyrighted work.

Digital rights management technology is the biggest impediment for users of e-books or similar electronic resources subscribed to by the library. In the case of e-books, they can only download and print a limited number of pages from the book. DRM technology makes e-books a frustrating source of information for library users. Copyright plays a significant role in how materials can be accessed off campus and who can access them. It also affects materials contained within electronic resources. Copyright law determines how many times an article or articles may be loaned from a journal, how people associated with the university can access materials remotely. The confusing requirements of the law make it difficult to comply with and to explain to students and faculty. What is or is not a violation of copyright law is always subject to interpretation (Eschenfelder, 2008).

Remote access technology to library resources work is relatively stable. However, as with any technology, from time to time problems do occur and sometimes the problems are the result of licensing agreements or the remote access technology infrastructure. One issue is privacy because some systems track user ID. The biggest problem with remote access technology is security. The primary security issue is unauthorized users accessing licensed databases. This can happen by someone gaining access to a database or databases through the proxy server or the verification for authorized users is not updated and someone who is no longer affiliated with the institution is able to gain access to licensed resources.

Firewalls are one way to prevent unauthorized access but they cannot and do not always stop someone from gaining access. For users to gain access to electronic resources at their college or university library requires more than a computer and an Internet connection. In order to gain access they must first be authenticated as an authorized user. This is usually done through their IP address and a password or password and user ID. The authorized users are validated against the list of current students, faculty and staff. This can be a source of problems for the library. If the list is not updated on a timely basis people no longer associated with the university can gain access to their licensed resources. Hacking into systems is another issue (Mitchell & Ennis, 2010).

In 2002 someone gained access to the servers for JSTOR and by the time the unauthorized access was blocked the person had downloaded about 50,000 articles from the database. Database vendors and their customers need to be aware and have mechanisms in place to prevent unauthorized access to their resources. Firewalls are one form of security, but while they can keep unauthorized users out they can also keep authorized users from gaining access. In order for firewall security to be effective when it is implemented the parameters for the security need to be established ensure people who need access are able to gain access to the resources they need. Firewalls combined with a proxy server as one way to ensure only authorized users gain access to licensed library resources.

Virtual private networks (VPN) is another method available to libraries to prevent unauthorized access. However, there is nothing in place to prevent users from sharing their user ID and password with friends or family not associated with the university. The problem with VPN is the flow of information may be slow or the network itself can be offline resulting in users being unable to access the resources they need from off-campus. Another method for users to gain access is through the student portal. Students can log into the student portal and access library resources through this method they will be required to enter another password to gain access to the proxy server (Tyson & Crawford, 2011).

Multiple passwords and/or ID make it frustrating for users when they are trying to gain access to the resources they need. It becomes even more frustrating if the server is offline and they are unable to access the library databases they need. Proxy servers can go offline and so can the server hosting the database. Database publishers sometimes take their databases offline in order to update them or perform maintenance. When they are performing some form of maintenance notification is sent to the library who can post the information to their web site. EZproxy is one of the most reliable products to authorize remote access to users; however, occasionally there are problems with the software.

Another problem that arises is the link to the database changes and it is not changed on EzProxy resulting in users being unable to access to the licensed database. EZproxy is available through OCLC. They provide the support, training and documentation for EZproxy. They also provide the list of links to the licensed products from the database publishers. The information provided tells users how to configure the link to the server so users can gain access. Once the link is configured on the server the systems librarian or acquisitions librarian should test, the link to ensure it is functional and users can access the resource from off-campus. Sometimes the link from the database vendor changes or the configuration becomes corrupted or is entered incorrectly resulting in users being unable to access the resources while off-campus. Once the configuration is corrected, they will regain access to the materials (OCLC, 2011).

Most colleges and universities change their proxy server password at least three or four times a year. Users are notified of the change but if they unaware the password was changed they cannot access the resources they need while off-campus. Sometimes access to information from off-campus locations falls into the category of user error. A user might not know how to access the password for off-campus access, they may have their firewall set at a level that prevents them from gaining off-campus access, and if pop-up windows are blocked, they cannot open a PDF. As with course management systems, users should receive some form of training to know how to access resources from off-campus. Users should receive notification in a timely manner on when the databases will be unavailable.

The other problem that affects remote access is link resolvers. For the most part, they work 99 percent of the time, but the other one percent can be a real headache for remote users. A link resolver provides a remote user with the ability to find an article that is available in a database other than the one they are searching. For example, a student is searching in an EBSCO database but the article they need is a database from ProQuest. There will be a button indicating they need to find where the article is located. By using the link resolver button it should take them to the full-text of the article, they want, unfortunately, this does not always work in the way it was intended to work.

Sometimes you will not get the full-text of the article, or the article will not be in the second database because the subscription to the journal may have ended, and the library does not have access to the backfiles. Anyone who has used a database and selected the link resolver option only to find it did not work properly knows how frustrating it can be. In spite of the occasional problem, link resolvers are one of the best remote access technologies available. Once the user gains access to library resources and begins searching, the link resolver provides them with the ability to find the article, whether it is in the database they are searching, or located in another one. The problems arise when the link resolver indicates the article is available in full text in another database but when they select the link to take them to the article in the other database they receive an error message the article is not found or it is not available in full text in the other resource.

The cause of the problem can be one of many but usually it is caused when publications are listed in the link resolver connection that the library does not subscribe to and therefore do not have full text access to the publication. The solution is to turn off or deselect the publications the library does not subscribe to in full text preventing the user from getting a false positive statement that the articles is available in full text when in fact it is not. Turning off the publications can be time consuming because they have to be turned off at the connection manually. An example would be subscribing only to the backfiles from SAGE and as a result, the link resolver directs users to not the backfiles, but also current issues of the same journals, which the library does not subscribe to, but the journals continue to appear in their search results, which become frustrating for the user. Correctly configuring the link resolver is crucial to remote access to library resources. Yes, they will still be able to access them but they may not get the results they want or need for their assignment.

Distance education at its start used snail mail for students to submit and receive assignments. This is no longer the case as distance education courses use a course management or learning management system. The CMS or LMS can be open source or proprietary software hosted on a server at the college or university where the courses are offered. If the same software is used by the entire university system, it is hosted on servers in one location. An example is the University System of Georgia uses WebCT for all their online courses at all 35 of their campuses. The software is hosted on servers located in Athens, GA. Support during the day for course or software problems are handled locally but 24 hour and weekend support is provided through the help desk in Athens. Every other weekend the University System of Georgia

performs maintenance on WebCT starting at 10pm on Friday and ending on Saturday morning. The problem is not with the maintenance but, with students who do remember, in spite of the reminders from faculty and distance education, and try to submit assignments, take a quiz, or post to the discussion board (University System of Georgia, 2011).

During the maintenance period the site is rendered inoperable and students cannot sign into WebCT. If they are in the middle of submitting an assignment, they are kicked off the system and the assignment does not finish uploading. If they are taking an exam, they become locked out of the exam and need to contact the instructor to reset their attempt. Instructors who teach online are all too familiar with this problem. It happens on more than one occasion with students. This does not happen at every institution with students, but it is a problem with course management systems. Another issue previously stated is course management systems are not always user friendly.

Faculty and students often struggle with the technology and students and faculty when surveyed would like more training in order to navigate the software (ECAR, 2010). Another issue or problem with course management software involves copyrighted materials. In order to link copyright protected materials access needs to be limited to the students enrolled in the class and the material can only be used for the class during that specific semester based on the copyright permission granted to the instructor. At the end of the semester, the material is to be removed from the course management system. The same applies to e-reserves (Copyright Clearance Center, 2011a, 2011b).

The material is to be removed from the e-reserve system at the end of the semester. If the instructor wants to use the same material, again they will have to ask for copyright permission for the new semester. Instructors and libraries encounter problems when they use the same materials semester after semester without renewing the copyright permission another problem is the quantity of material that is sometimes placed on e-reserve. Often it can be whole book chapters, which may or may not border on a violation of copyright law. Copyright law is a problem for faculty and libraries alike. The issue of copyright law was the basis of a lawsuit against Georgia State University.

According to three major university presses the university did not have adequate password protection to their course management and e-reserve system therefore allowing unauthorized users to gain access. The publishers also complained the copyright materials were used repeatedly without obtaining new copyright permission. This is an extreme example of a problem with course management systems and materials under copyright protection. It is a lawsuit being watched carefully by the academic community for the outcome may have a significant impact on academic libraries and their users around the country. It could open the door for additional lawsuits if the publishers win because they would be able to scrutinize the copyright policies of other academic libraries to determine if they are or are not complying with copyright law. Remote access users or distance education students encounter problems when they are unable to access the course management system and the links to articles from the libraries databases. If the instructor has linked e-reserves to the course, management system the student will be unable to access them as well.

There should be an alternative method for students to gain access to the resources and one way is to create a blog or wiki for the class allowing them to gain access to the resources. Another is providing synchronous library instruction to the students in the class so they know how to access resources off-campus when the course management system is down. An embedded librarian program can benefit both students and faculty by instructing them how to use the library's resources but also how to access them from multiple points while off-campus. Meeting students at their point

of need is necessary and with the growth of social networks, libraries need to explore how they can meet their students' needs in those online sites.

Facebook, MySpace, foursquare, and Twitter are just a few of the many social network sites available to users. Originally used by college and high school students the demographic of social network sites is changing to include corporations, and older members of the population. The original intent was for people to meet their friends in an online network to stay connected. In the six years since the creation of Facebook, they have over 500 million users and growing. It is a place where students not only connect with their friends for social events but it is also a place for them to collaborate on projects. This makes it a good environment to provide students with a link to library resources or to connect with one of the librarians.

As with any technology the person who creates the page needs to make sure the page is updated on a regular basis. As the example from the health sciences librarians indicated, many libraries create the page but fail to update the information on a regular basis (Hendrix, et al., 2009). The same survey and a similar one indicated the perceived versus actual use of the site were not as they appeared. The perceived use was much higher than the actual use. Social networking sites are a useful way to update users about changes taking place in the library new resources such as books or databases. They can also be used to post announcements about events taking place at the library but providing access to library resources should be done with limitations. Using a social network site, especially a site like Facebook, to post links to copyright protected materials or other licensed resources has potential problems. A major problem is privacy.

Facebook in particular has not been forthcoming with how they use the information from its members nor how the data is stored and who has access to the information. A link to the library web site is appropriate because from the link provided students could access the libraries databases or other remote services and a link for chat reference. Using Facebook as a course management site would not be appropriate and while there are privacy controls for every Facebook page, there is no guarantee the page cannot or will not be hacked and the information disseminated to others. Linking information from proprietary databases or directly to articles could and probably would be considered a violation of copyright law because the potential is there for unauthorized users to gain access.

Libraries, when it comes to social networks, need to decide the types of information they will place on the social network page and who will maintain the page. Since the page allows you to add a link to a web site, the library can provide the link to their web site and avoid problems with violation of copyright laws. Anyone who uses the link and wants to find articles in a database will have to be authenticated through the proxy server. This protects the library from unauthorized access.

Mobile technologies, like social network sites, have increased in use during the past five years. Mobile technologies are rapidly changing. New technologies include everything from phones to media tablets. When Apple introduced their iPad, it brought a significant shift in mobile technology. Mobile technology created the need for applications or apps for the devices. Each type of device requires different programming in order to work on a particular device or groups of devices. It is not one size fits all design. Mobile devices just like computers use an operating system to function. The application has to be designed and programmed to work on the specific operating system for the device. Creating the application is one part the other part is ensuring the campus IT infrastructure is in place for the app and device to work on campus. Anyone who purchased an iPhone when they first entered the market can probably tell you about the number of problems they encountered because the technology to support the phone or some of its features were not

available where they lived or went to school. Along with the creation of apps for mobile devices, web sites will not display properly on mobile devices (Ragon, 2009).

In a recent article published in the *Chronicle of Higher Education* some colleges and universities are starting to question the need for developing apps for their campuses. The primary reason cited was the cost involved in the development of the app. Instead colleges are focusing their efforts on creating mobile web sites that work on a number of mobile devices. A mobile web site has the ability to reach more people than a single app (Keller, 2011).

In order for users to access library resources a version of the web site that will function on mobile devices needs to be created. Anyone with a mobile device who tries to access a web site that is not designed for mobile devices knows the site will not properly load on their device and if it does load they will not have full functionality of the site. Therefore, it may be impossible for them to access the information they need. Database vendors offer mobile connections to search their databases. While most academic libraries have a mobile version of their web site, some do not and the lack of a mobile version of their web site will make it difficult if not impossible for users to search the library's resources. Another issue with mobile devices is privacy.

Most mobile connections are not considered secure. Yet people will purchase items using their mobile device. This lack of security could result in unauthorized users gaining access to library resources. A mobile device can be thought of as an unsecured wireless network (Friedman & Hoffman, 2008). Anyone driving in their car can gain access to the wireless network and use it. The same thing can happen with a wireless connection on a mobile device. If someone is using the device on a secured network that is entirely different but if the person is using the device walking across campus unless the person logs into the university's network they are using an unsecured connection. Mobile devices are just one aspect of mobile technology.

Cloud computing is another mobile technology that is growing in use. Cloud computing provides many advantages one being the ability to share information or work in real time collaboration for a project. The use of cloud computing to store information allows users to access it from any computer anywhere they are. Most cloud computing applications require a password for users to gain access and access can be limited to certain individuals or groups therefore allowing a more secure sharing of resources. Cloud computing is not problem free. If the servers for the cloud-computing network are down you cannot access your information. Another issue is storage. Where is the information stored and who has access to it? Cloud computing probably provides a more secure environment than a mobile devices but users still should be concerned their documents and accounts are not compromised (Armbrust, Fox, Griffith, et al., 2010).

Last but not least is virtual libraries. Virtual libraries are the collection of electronic resources owned by the library and it includes everything from e-books to databases. Virtual libraries require a password to use the resources. The exception is the Internet Public Library, which is a collection of web sites and other free resources compiled by librarians and library science students at several library science programs. In order to use any of the resources in a virtual library the users must be authenticated that they are affiliated with the university. The same issues that apply to remote access technology apply to virtual libraries. The server could be down for either the database or the proxy server. The user does not have the correct password or their firewall prevents them from gaining access to the library's resources. Security with virtual libraries is a primary concern. Authenticating users through either VPN or a proxy server is required. Another aspect of virtual libraries and electronic collections is the number of simultaneous users allowed to use a database at one time.

Depending on the database and the cost of unlimited versus limited users there may be a limited number of simultaneous users for some databases but not others. When users attempt to use the database they will receive an error message that the maximum number of users has been reached. The user will then have to wait until others exit the database before they can use it. This can be a source of frustration for users but it is an economic reality that academic libraries cannot afford simultaneous users for all of their databases. With virtual libraries, the primary problems for users will be connectivity and a limited number of simultaneous users. Both of these situations can and will be a source of frustration for remote access users. Another aspect of virtual libraries is the services such as, document delivery, interlibrary loan, and reference or research help.

Students no longer have to come into the library to receive these services. Most libraries have an online submission form for document delivery and interlibrary loan. Reference services are available face-to-face. Students can also phone, e-mail, text or chat to receive research help. As with any service involving an Internet connection or the use of a mobile device, the potential exists to lose the connection. A problem with chat, text or e-mail reference service is the fact not every question lends itself well to this type of help. If it as a very involved or complicated question the student should attempt to come to the library to receive the necessary help. Unfortunately, services of this nature are promoted as if they can answer any question in a relatively short period.

If someone is working on a thesis or a senior seminar project the sources of information and the help they may need will take longer and require a lengthy reference interview to determine which resources the student needs. Text messaging for reference limits the librarian and the user to 150 characters. Before the librarian submits their answer to the user, they have to check to make sure their answer falls into the required number of characters before it is sent to the user. Students often grow impatient with the service especially if their question is answered quickly when they first enter the queue. Another problem with virtual reference services is poor communication between the librarian and the user. Sometimes both the librarian terminates the session before the students question is answered and sometimes the student will terminate the session before the librarian can find the resources to help them.

Poor training for library personnel is one cause and students may think they can receive a quick answer before they go to class or they just move onto the next text message without waiting for a response. The service is not perfect and is often used by students seeking information at the last minute for a project that is due in a few days or even a few hours. Training for students on how to use the service would benefit both students and librarians. Since most virtual reference, services were created before the growth in mobile technology it may be time to re-examine the services, especially virtual reference, and make changes that are more user friendly and allow time for longer more involved questions. Virtual reference services will continue to grow in use and it is possible additional formats for service will be added. Regardless of the type of remote access service or technology users, both librarians and students or faculty will encounter a problem at some point.

FUTURE TRENDS

Problems with remote access technology to library resources will not disappear in the future but alternative solutions may be developed to improve connectivity and privacy issues. Internet connections are more stable and reliable than they were in the early years of the Internet. VPN and proxy servers are the primary methods for users to gain access to library resources while off campus. While both types of connections are, relatively stable and

for the most part secure changes to the two types of technology in the future will probably center on making them more secure and improvements in authenticating remote access users. Libraries will continue to use both types of technology as the primary methods for users to gain access to the library's licensed resources when they are on campus.

Social networks while popular with students do provide libraries with the opportunity to connect with students and provide links to their services and web sites. However, because of lack of privacy and the ability for anyone to gain access to information on a person's Facebook page or Twitter account posting links to copyright protected material or using a social network site as a course management system is not a suitable purpose for social network sites. Mobile technology has seen a dramatic increase in use over the last five years. This type of growth will probably continue for many years to come. Because of this growth in mobile technology, academic libraries need to have the apps and mobile web site in place to meet the needs of their users. The biggest problem with mobile technology will be the ability to keep up with the new devices entering the market and identifying the types of apps needed for the devices.

Academic libraries and college IT departments will need someone devoted to mobile technology if they want to meet the remote access needs of their users. Virtual library services will continue to grow both with access to resources and research help. Those types of services need to be re-examined and if necessary redesigned to make them more user friendly and provide better mobile access for users. Link resolvers, whether open source or proprietary, will continue to be used and in all probability will see changes made that will make them more stable and provide for better connections between resources and databases. Problems with remote access technologies whether or not it is a service, a connection or a computer program will never completely go away but with ongoing changes to technology the number of problems and the severity of the problems will decrease. While new problems may appear, they too will be quickly resolved.

CONCLUSION

Problems with remote access technologies will never completely go away. Distance education that once relied on snail mail for students to send and receive their work depended on the mail arriving at the correct address and on time. Chances are it did not always happen. Distance education and online courses are dependent on course management systems both proprietary and open source. Course management systems run on a server hosted either by the college or university or through a system wide IT department. Servers can go offline and neither students nor faculty can access the materials for the class nor can they submit assignments or take an exam. These types of problems will never be eliminated; however, the instructor should have an alternate plan in place when those problems arise. For, example if the student cannot submit the assignment then the alternative is to e-mail the assignment to the instructor.

Another problem that arises with course management systems is the lack of training provided to both instructors and students. Many colleges and universities have some type of faculty development center or instructional design department that works in conjunction with faculty to train them on using the course management system effectively and making it a rich learning environment for the students. Unfortunately, faculty and students are not required to attend training; however, if they do not attend an in-person training center the university can provide online tutorials for their students. Remote connections to library resources include proxy server, virtual private networks (VPN) and link resolvers. These three components provide users with the access to the library's resources off-campus anytime of the day

or night. They intended to allow authorized users access to the library's resources.

Unfortunately, unauthorized users can gain access through a proxy server, as was the case with the theft of thousands of articles from JSTOR. Course management systems, proxy servers, and VPN connections can fail or go offline. This leaves users unable to access the library's resources. The campus IT department should have some form of back up that will allow users to gain access while off-campus. Students become frustrated when the university web site is down and they cannot access the course management system. Their instructor, or distance education department should provide them with an alternate link to the course management system.

Social network sites while widely used by students, and people of all ages for that matter, they do not lend themselves well to providing links to proprietary databases or copyright protected materials. They do lend themselves well to providing students with information about the library or providing them links to the library web site and virtual reference services. Using the links for those specific areas will require students to enter a password to gain access to databases and other licensed electronic resources at the library. Mobile technology will have a significant impact on library services and resources. Libraries in order to meet the needs of their users who want to access their resources with mobile devices will need to have the apps and mobile web sites or other forms of connections available for users to search their resources. Without the resources in place, users will be able to access some but not all of the resources available to them. They might be able to search the catalog but not the databases, which are the resource most students want to access while off-campus.

To meet student needs libraries also need to survey or hold focus groups with their users if they want to stay connected with them. Once the librarians meet with users, it is important for them to use the information to make changes or improvements to existing services or resources. Asking for feedback and doing nothing with the information is just as bad as not asking for user feedback in spite of the complaints from users about services or resources. Problems with technology and remote access technology will never truly disappear and while old problems or issues may be resolved as new technology and devices enter the market new problems will occur. It is important in an environment of ever changing technology, resources and services that libraries stay connected to their users and work with them to meet their ever changing and growing needs. Meeting and solving problems together will help libraries to remain a vital part of their academic community.

REFERENCES

Armbrust, M., Fox, A., Griffith, R., Joseph, A. D., Katz, R., & Knowinski, A. (2010). A view of Cloud Computing. *Communications of the ACM, 53*(4), 50–58. doi:10.1145/1721654.1721672

Chou, M., & Zhou, O. (2005). The impact of licenses on library collections. *Managing Digital Resources in Libraries, 17*(33), 7–23. doi:doi:10.1300/J101v17n3302

Copyright Clearance Center. (2011a). *The TEACH Act.* Retrieved from http://www.copyright.com/content/dam/cc3/marketing/documents/pdfs/CR-Teach-Act.pdf

Copyright Clearance Center. (2011b). *Using course management systems: Guidelines and best practices for copyright compliance.* Retrieved from http://www.copyright.com/content/dam/cc3/marketing/documents/pdfs/Using-Course-Management-Systems.pdf

EDUCAUSE Center for Applied Research. (2010). *ECAR study of undergraduate students and Information Technology 2010.* Retrieved from http://www.educause.edu/Resources/ECARStudyofUndergraduateStuden/217333

Eschenfelder, K. R. (2008). Every library's nightmare? Digital rights management, use restrictions, and licensed scholarly digital resources. *College & Research Libraries, 69*(3), 205–225.

Friedman, J., & Hoffman, D. V. (2008). Protecting data on mobile devices: A taxonomy of security threats to mobile computing and review of applicable defenses. *Information Knowledge Systems Management, 7*(1), 159–180.

Hendrix, D., Chiarella, D., Hasman, L., Murphy, S., & Zafron, M. (2009). Use of Facebook in academic health sciences libraries. *Journal of the Medical Library Association, 97*(1), 44–47. doi:10.3163/1536-5050.97.1.008

Institute of Museum and Library Services. (2006). *Status of technology and digitization in the nation's museums and libraries.* Retrieved from http://www.imls.gov/resources/TechDig05/Technology%2BDigitization.pdf

Jankowska, M. A., Hertel, K., & Young, N. J. (2006). Improving library service quality to graduate students: LibQual+™ survey results in a practical setting. *Portal: Libraries and the Academy, 6*(1), 59–77. doi:10.1353/pla.2006.0005

Keller, J. (2011, 27 June). As mobile devices multiply, some colleges turn away from building campus apps. *The Chronicle of Higher Education.* Retrieved from http://chronicle.com/article/As-Mobile-Devices-Multiply/128060/

Mitchell, N., & Ennis, L. A. (2010). Scaling the (fire) wall. *Journal of Hospital Librarianship, 10*(2), 190–196. doi:10.1080/15323261003681588

OCLC. (2011). *EZproxy.* Retrieved from http://www.oclc.org/ezproxy/support/default.htm

Ragon, B. (2009). Designing for the mobile Web. *Mobile Computing and the Library, 6*, 355–361. doi:doi:10.1080/15424060903364875

Schlosser, M. (2009). Unless otherwise indicated: A survey of copyright statements on digital library collections. *College & Research Libraries, 70*(4), 371–385.

Tyson, J., & Crawford, S. (2011, April 14). How VPNs work. *HowStuffWorks.com.* Retrieved June 7, 2011, from http://www.howstuffworks.com/vpn.htm

University System of Georgia. (2011). *GeorgiaVIEW maintenance schedule--Fall 2011.* Retrieved 24 October, 2011, from http://www.usg.edu/gaview/support/maint-schedule.phtml

Chapter 12
Conclusion

ABSTRACT

Remote access technologies for library collections encompass more than just the technology required to access the resources from an off-campus location. Users no longer have to enter the library to use journals or search the catalog to find books, and remote access technologies have moved the library beyond its physical space to reach a greater numbers of users. Is the library going to cease to exist because of this technology? It is doubtful. The number of electronic resources and collections continues to grow but libraries cannot subscribe to every journal electronically, and not every journal is available electronically. The same holds true for books. E-books can be found in the collections of almost every academic library, yet they are not very popular with students. As more online courses are offered by colleges and universities, remote access to library collections will continue to increase, and libraries will need to make sure their users will be able to access the resources and to offer instruction to students and faculty on how to gain access to the resources from off-campus locations.

BACKGROUND

The catalyst for libraries to offer remote access to library resources was the growth of online courses. Before the advent of the Internet distance, education students could request materials from the library the resources were sent through the mail. Libraries still offer a document delivery service to their online students. Articles are usually sent electronically as an attachment in an e-mail. Books will be sent through the mail. When the books are due, students can renew them online or return them to the library through the mail. The Internet brought changes to the way students access the library's resources on or off-campus. The most significant change came in off-campus access. The growth of electronic resources led to the creation

DOI: 10.4018/978-1-4666-0234-2.ch012

and improvement in access technology for remote access to library collections.

At one-time electronic materials were on CD and the librarian would need to install the material on a computer before it could be used. Digitization led to materials, including images, articles, dissertations and theses being scanned and readily available and accessible to users at an academic library to download, print or save for their assignments. The growth of electronic resources and off-campus access moved the library beyond its physical space and turned any space into a classroom. With the advent and proliferation of mobile devices has brought another change in remote access to library resources. Mobile device users want and expect the same functionality they have on campus when they need off-campus access to library resources. Library users' expectations are they no longer need to come into the library to gain access to library resources. This is partially true because not all materials are available electronically and many students do not like to use e-books because of the limitations imposed by digital rights management technology. Technology and in particular remote access technology brought about significant changes in library collections and services and as technology improves and new technology is developed the future will hold the opportunity for libraries to meet and work with their students beyond the confines of the library, yet at the same time continue to make the library an integral part of the academic community.

MAIN FOCUS OF THE CHAPTER

This book began with a chapter about distance education and its influence on remote access technology. Now and in the near future distance education and online courses will continue to have a significant influence on remote access to library collections. As colleges and universities across the country continue to see increased enrollments while at the same time experience reduction in

funding either through the state, donations or a decline in their endowment they will be unable to fund new construction projects which will result in a reduction in much needed classroom space. To combat the lack of classroom space colleges and universities can offer more online classes. Students will be able to take the classes they need while at the same time the university can provide the required courses to meet the students' needs.

Distance education itself has undergone a transformation from correspondence courses to online instruction through a course management system. As part of the accreditation requirements colleges and universities must provide services, including the library, to distance education services. Distance education students must have access to the same resources available to students' on-campus. Some academic libraries have a librarian who works with distance education services others may have the access services manager oversee the responsibilities of meeting the needs of distance education students. In addition to requirements for accreditation academic libraries should adhere to the guidelines from the American Library Associations' Reference and User Services (RUSA) http://www.ala.org/ala/mgrps/divs/rusa/resources/guidelines/virtual-reference-se.pdf division for implementing and maintaining virtual reference services. The Association of College and Research Libraries (ACRL) http://www.ala.org/ala/mgrps/divs/acrl/standards/guidelinesdistancelearning.cfm has standards for distance education learning services. Using the materials found on the web sites of academic libraries, RUSA, ACRL and in conjunction with the accreditation guidelines from national higher education accrediting agencies, academic libraries can create, develop and maintain the necessary services needed by distance education students. Remote access to library collections is driven primarily by distance and online education but all students need access to library resources when it is closed. Many of the students attending school are working at least one if not two part-time jobs to meet their expenses. Other students are non-traditional and family obligations in addition to the work for school.

Going to the library when it is open is not always possible and assignments are often worked on long after the library has closed. Remote access technology provides all students with the ability to complete their work regardless of whether or not the library is open. Yes, they may have to go to the library to check out a book but for the most part they can search the catalog before going to the library and if necessary they can ask the library to hold the book or use their online library account to place a hold on the book and pick it up when they are on campus. The need for remote access grew throughout the last decade and will continue to grow as a result of increased student need by distance education students and students whose schedules do not meet that of the libraries.

Even with remote access technology to access collections libraries must still work to ensure they are meeting their users' needs. Just because there is a web site with links to resources does not guarantee users can find and access the resources they need. Many libraries have participated in the LibQual® survey administered through the Association of Research Libraries. The purpose of the survey is to provide the library with the level of user satisfaction with library services and resources. Once the library receives the results from their survey the library should do a follow-up survey or create focus groups of students, faculty and staff to obtain additional information about services that need to be improved. Working with users to get a better understanding of what they like and dislike about the library's services is necessary to meet user needs. Even with feedback from users the library will not please everyone. The examples used in chapter two on meeting user needs included several examples of libraries that used their survey results and did additional surveys or follow-up sessions with users to make improvement.

Some of the academic libraries made changes to their web sites that improved the navigation of the web site making it easier for users to find the resources they need. Others used statistics from their database vendors to determine which resources are more widely used than others. Information of this type helps libraries to make better use of their collection development budget. Student and faculty input are important for the library to incorporate into their mission and strategic plan for the library. Providing remote access to library resources is one aspect of meeting user needs, however, if users have a difficult time connecting from off-campus locations then the library is not meeting the distance learning students needs. Part of meeting the user needs is to have the technology including the infrastructure in place to meet off-campus access. Another aspect is having a web site that is easy to navigate allowing users to find the resources quickly without have to click more than two or three times to get to the resource. Part of off-campus resources and access are digital collections.

Digital collections can encompass a variety of resources and materials. They can include everything from postcard collections, old campus yearbooks, photographs, manuscripts or diaries, letters and scrapbooks. Digital collections are often the resources normally found in college archives and special collections. Digitizing the materials makes them available to all users whether or not they are affiliated with the college or university. This type of online collection is often available to anyone with a computer and an Internet connection. No password is required and copyright information is or should be provided to anyone using the collection. Since many college and university special collections and archives do not have the same hours as the library students who are not on campus during the period they are open would need to make an appointment. The digital collections will provide off-campus students with the ability to access resources they might not otherwise be able to use for an assignment.

Digital collections provide the library with the opportunity to highlight resources that might otherwise be overlooked and underutilized. One of the problems with creating digital collections is the cost of digitizing the materials. Projects of this nature require a significant investment in time, money and staffing. A survey from the Institute of Museum and Library Services revealed many libraries; both academic and public had started digitizing their collections but needed additional funding and staffing to digitize more materials. Funding for digital projects focus on preservation of materials that are quickly being eroded by time and in some instances poor quality storage facilities (IMLS, 2006). Digital collections provide users with an opportunity to use primary source materials in their assignments and research. The Digital Library of Georgia and The Civil Rights Digital Library are two very good examples of digital projects developed to preserve photographs and film clips for use by researchers. In order to find the materials the library needs to provide metadata for the items in the collection.

Without metadata a search of the Internet for the collection will yield few if any results. Metadata is the information that describes the items contained within the collection. If the items are in the library online catalog it is this source of information that allows users to find the materials they need. Another type of digital collections is open access journals and articles. The number of open access journals has steadily increased but still have not had a significant impact on the journals available through the major scholarly publishers. Many open access journals require the author to pay a fee to have their article published. The article once it is published can be accessed by anyone without having to subscribe to the journal. An example of this type of scholarly publishing is the Public Library of Science (PLoS) http://www.plos.org/ which publishes seven journals in the sciences. All articles are available in full-text and users can search the publication archives for previous volumes. The creation of open access journals is an attempt to bring down the cost of subscriptions to scholarly publications. Unfortunately, the cost

for subscriptions continues to rise. Open access journals for the most part continue to exist and serve the needs of researchers who are not affiliated with a college or university. The increasing cost of journal subscriptions has an impact on the library's collection development policies.

Collection development policies as with any library policy need revising as the resources available to the library change. Some collection development policies were written before the availability and prevalence of electronic resources. Collection development policies in there simplest form indicate to users the purpose of the collection and what areas the library collects resources. Since libraries do not have an unlimited collection development budget the majority of the funds are used to purchase resources that support faculty and student research and the academic programs of the university. With the proliferation of electronic resources libraries need to work with database publishers to negotiate contracts that clearly specify who can access the electronic resources and how those resources can be accessed both on and off campus. Another aspect of contracts for electronic resources that should be included is how the copyright clause of fair use is interpreted and if the items in the resource can be loaned through interlibrary loan.

The licensing for off-campus use of databases is critical to the library and its users and this part of the contract should state whether the library is or is not responsible for unauthorized access to its proprietary or licensed resources. If the library is responsible they can be sued not only for breach of contract but also for violation of copyright law by allowing users not affiliated with the university to gain access to the resources. Statistics provided by the database publisher can help libraries determine which electronic resources to continue subscribing to and which ones to drop. Another option is to develop consortial agreements with other colleges and universities in the area to reduce the cost of electronic resource. Regardless of how the agreement is negotiated and who is part of the agreement the most important element is the ability of users to access the resources while off-campus. This provision of the contract ensures students will have the ability to use the resource off-campus and also prevents violation of copyright law.

The first copyright law for the United States is part of our Constitution. When the first copyright laws were passed the only media available was print and as other media such as music recordings and movies were created the laws were passed to include protection of those works. The unforeseen aspect of copyright law was the growth of technology and the Internet and with it the ability to download and share files between computers making it easier to pirate movies and music. Copyright law was changed to protect the creators from unlawful copying of materials electronically and with the new changes to the law digital rights management technology came into existence. The technology is intended to protect the intellectual property rights of the creator and to prevent unlawful reproduction of the material. Unfortunately, it limits the amount of material users can download and print from e-books they need for educational purposes. The technology impedes fair use of the resources for research and as a result makes e-books one of the least favorite sources of material for research. Copyright law impacts interlibrary loan, e-reserves and embedding copyright protected materials in course management systems.

Contracts for electronic resources grant libraries the right to loan articles from databases to other libraries, however, in order to do that they must first obtain copyright clearance. If the library has loaned an article from a journal more than a certain number of times then they may not loan additional articles from the journal for the remainder of the year. E-reserves are articles or book chapters scanned into a reserve system that students can access from the library web site for a specific course. Students are required to enter a password created and provided to them by the professor. At the end of the semester the instructor is to remove all items from the e-reserve system. If they want to use the same materials for the next semester they need to request another copyright permission or clearance. Permission is to be obtained before the start of each semester and the library is to include the copyright clearance with the e-reserve request. The same holds true for copyright protected materials in course reserve systems.

Instructors need to obtain copyright clearance before posting the material in the course management system. At the end of the semester it needs to be removed and a new permission obtained for the next semester. Copyright only allows the material to be used for a specific number of students who are authorized to access the material for a set period of time. Using the material repeatedly violates copyright law because once the course has ended and to prevent students from the previous semester from gaining access to the material or sharing it with friends before the material is removed from the course management system. United States copyright law is complicated and confusing to librarians, instructors and students. Most libraries have at least one person who is responsible for overseeing copyright law compliance and in most instances it is the person who oversees interlibrary loan or access services. Training for librarians, students and faculty is important in order to make sure everyone understands the basics of complying with copyright law. Complying with copyright law is part of accessing library resources through remote access technology.

Remote access technology comes in a variety of formats. Users can access library resources through proxy servers, virtual private networks, course management systems and link resolvers. Proxy servers allow a user to access their library's resources remotely by authenticating them as an authorized user and with the entry of the password the user can then search the library's databases. EZproxy has made it easier for libraries to link their electronic resources to the proxy servers.

With this technology the library is given the configuration for the database and when a user accesses the resource remotely it redirects them to the database once they enter the password. There can be problems with proxy servers for example the server can be down or the database vendor's server may be offline preventing the user from gaining access to the resource. Another problem is the database vendor creates a new interface and also their configuration to link to the server. Users can enter an error when they attempt to access the database. For the most part EZproxy is relatively stable and used by most libraries for remote access by their users.

Another option for remote access is virtual private networks or VPN. This type of connection is more secure and allows the user to access the resources they need as if they were on campus. Information travels between the user's computer and the network and is encrypted in the process to prevent unauthorized access to the network. Using a VPN allows the user access with a single sign-on. Some colleges and universities allow students to single sign-on access through their course management systems. Once the user is authenticated through the course management system they will not need an additional password to use the library's resources. Link resolvers allow users to find resources in other databases without having to leave the database they are using for their search. They prevent users from having to sign in multiple times or search multiple databases. Libraries that have connected their resources to Google Scholar through their link resolver provide users with the ability to access the articles through Google Scholar through the proxy server. A link appears next to the article with a "Find it @" by selecting the link the user will be taken to the proxy server sign on and gain access to the article.

Google Scholar is another remote access technology or resource for library users. When searching Google if the user selects scholar from the list of options they will be taken to the scholarly articles available on their topic. They also have the option to set their preferences for their university library and when they search off-campus through Google Scholar the links to articles will be show if they are available at their university library. Selecting the link will connect via the proxy server to the database and if the article is not available it will provide them with the option to obtain it through interlibrary loan. Google Scholar provides users with another remote access technology to connect with library resources. Course management systems are another method for remote access to library collections.

Colleges and universities have a choice between open source and proprietary course management systems. Course management systems (CMS) provide instructors with a platform to upload and link materials for their online classes. The use of a course management system is not limited to online classes because instructors in both face-to-face and hybrid classes can and often do use the CMS for their classes to post lecture notes and supplemental material for the class. The types of materials can range from Word documents, PowerPoint slides, links to web sites, videos, podcasts and links to e-reserves or articles. Online courses and course management systems provide the library with the opportunity to develop an embedded librarian program.

Chapter 7 provides examples from two similar embedded librarian programs and how they were developed and expanded based on the experiences of the librarians involved in the programs. Even though such a program can be time consuming for the librarians involved it allows the library to connect with students in their online classes. In the online environment librarians can answer student's questions about library resources for their projects and provide synchronous instruction. This moves library services beyond the physical space of the library. Since the course management system can be accessed from any computer librarians can be at work, home or a conference and when answering student questions.

The ECAR report about undergraduate use of technology in 2010 indicated the majority of students used a course management system but many responded they found them difficult to use and thought instructors had problems using the technology. The types of responses seem to indicate training on how to use course management systems is needed for both students and faculty. Users of open source course management systems such as Sakai and Moodle indicate they are more users friendly and easier to navigate then some of the proprietary systems. Regardless of the course management system used by the university it can and often does provide users with the ability to gain remote access to library resources. Links to the catalog and databases can be included in the course homepage.

Depending on how the proxy server is configured once a user signs into the CMS they will be authenticated as an authorized user and can search the databases without having to enter another password. This type of access provides students with seamless access to library resources off-campus. Students can work on an assignment in the CMS and search the library's resources at the same time. This is the goal and objective of remote access technology to provide users with seamless access to resources. Users should not be frustrated by multiple identification requirement or passwords. With a single sign on they should be able to gain access to the resources they need for their assignments. Course management systems include the ability to link library resources to course homepage without violating the database agreement or copyright law because the material is password protected. Social network sites on the other hand do not afford the same type of password protection.

Facebook was started in a dormitory room at Harvard University in 2005 and has grown to over 500 million users in a six year period. It dominates the social network sites and students check the site repeatedly throughout the day and night. It is site where students can meet up with friends and make plans for the day, night or weekend. It is also the site where students can collaborate with each other on an assignment. The question is does a Facebook page created by an academic library create new opportunities for the library?

In May 2011 a discussion took place on the information literacy instruction list (ili-l) about using Facebook as surrogate course management system. Most responses to the discussion indicated they had concerns about using Facebook for an online course citing privacy as the major concern and in particular posting links to copyright protected materials to the site. Since the privacy controls are minimal and students can freely share materials it would not be in the best interest of the library or the instructor to attempt to use the site for an online course. The Academic Newswire from Library Journal dated 2 June 2011, contained a column from Steven Bell, Associate University Librarian at Temple University, titled "What are we doing with social media?" The focus was library's need to create a social media plan if they want to develop a community of users who will follow the library on Facebook. The occasional post or Tweet will not create a robust and engaged group of users who will follow the library in the social network community. Libraries embraced social network sites and social network media as a way to meet students where they work but as two examples used in the chapter on this topic point out the pages are created then infrequently updated and seldom used by students.

Mississippi State University Libraries used Facebook as a method to communicate with their student workers and for the student workers to share information with each other including swapping shifts when necessary. Library's can use the space to provide announcements about events or the availability of new resources and links to the library's web site and virtual services. This type of information should be prominently displayed on the Facebook page. Conceivably users could be in Facebook and use the library's page to connect to resources or to contact the virtual reference service.

With Facebook or any social media or network libraries need to examine how it fits in with their mission and strategic plan. Incorporating a social media plan within the library's strategic plan will help the library identify their expectations for using social networks or media to reach their users. Social media and social networks do have a place in libraries and can provide limited remote access to library services and resources but libraries to make the most effective use of this type of site need to define their expectations before trying to adopt it to their purposes.

A number of mobile devices is available for use and some can be used for and with a variety of media. The proliferation of smart phones, media tablets, MP3 players, laptops and netbooks allow their users to connect to the Internet anytime and anywhere. Walk across a college campus and you will see students using one or more of the devices. As with social network sites libraries need to identify the types of mobile technologies being used by their students and the types of library information the users would like to find with their mobile devices. Two different studies explored the use of mobile devices to gain access to library resources and the libraries then developed a mobile accessible web site for users to easily obtain the information they needed.

A problem for libraries and IT departments will be keeping up with the ever changing type of devices available and the applications users will want or need to gain access to the resources they need and want. IT departments in conjunction with systems librarians will need to base their designs on current operating systems available for mobile devices and create apps that will work on different platforms to meet user needs. Incorporating information technology resources into campus and library strategic plans will help both departments with the ability to leverage their resources to design and implement mobile services for users. The database vendors EBSCO and ProQuest both offer the technology for users to search their resources from their mobile devices

and others are beginning to add mobile apps to their list of resources.

A study by Pew Research Foundation indicates the use of mobile devices will continue to grow in use and the need for remote access to library resources will more than likely continue in its growth (Smith, 2010). In addition to designing and implementing apps for mobile devices colleges and universities will need to have the security in place to prevent unauthorized users from gaining access to resources through the use of mobile devices. Since connections to resources require a password to gain access it needs to be a secure connection to prevent unauthorized users from obtaining the password. Mobile devices are just one aspect of mobile technology the other is cloud computing, the ability to share documents and other resources through a common application.

Google Docs is just one example of cloud computing. Collaboration can take place in real time and users can share materials by providing a link to the documents for the assignment or project. The links can be posted to a web site or copied and pasted into an e-mail. With Google the users can create a group and share information through the group without the need for e-mails. Cloud computing makes it easy to store information and use it for a presentation. It serves as back-up for a presentation stored on a thumb drive. Mobile technology will make it easier for students to access and share resources in the virtual world.

The proliferation of electronic resources, course management systems and mobile technology has turned the library into a virtual as well as a physical space. Users are no longer required to walk into a library to obtain access to its resources. Yes, they will still need to enter the library to check out books but the library's catalog can be searched from off-campus. The end of the card catalog was the beginning of the move toward electronic resources and remote access. Gone are the days when the librarian needed to load the information onto a computer for the user. The library has moved beyond it physical location and any space can now become a classroom. Electronic resources provide libraries with the opportunity to work with students in online classes or across campus. Instruction no longer has to take place in a classroom it can take place online. Interlibrary loan makes it possible for users to obtain materials from libraries from across the country. The Miller Learning Center is an example of a building that combines library services and resources plus classroom space and group study areas without a physical library collection. Publishers will not cease publishing books; especially in the humanities and the arts. An increase in electronic collections means libraries can weed their collections of bound periodicals and the newfound space can be repurposed for student study space and multimedia design and work areas for students. Electronic resources and new technology have brought about significant changes in library services and collections.

Reference service once restricted to a librarian sitting at a desk has also moved from the desk to the virtual world. Virtual reference services include, e-mail, chat, and text. Some services such as QuestionPoint are available 24 hours a day with an exception during the holidays in December. Virtual reference may not lend itself well to every question but it allows users with the ability to seek the help they need for their assignment whether they are on or off campus. Some colleges and universities are experimenting with loaning e-readers to students loaded with books or course reserves. This is an experiment that is worth observing to see the long-term success of the project. Virtual services and resources will allow libraries to meet students where they work whether it is at home or off-campus. Remote access to library resources provides users with seamless access the materials they need whether the library is opened or closed. With more students working part-time jobs or in the case of non-traditional students they can access the library's resources while juggling family, work and school obligations. In the year 2011 it appears remote access

and virtual library resources will not disappear in the future.

Each of the different types of technology can encounter a problem at some point. In the case of digital collections if the site is not maintained on a regular basis broken links will result in users being unable to access all the materials contained in the collection. Users may not be able to connect through the proxy server or the virtual private network if the server is down. In the case of the virtual private network if the authentication comes from the e-mail server and it is down then users will be unable to connect through VPN. If the materials are linked incorrectly through the link resolvers then they will find the wrong article at the end of their link resolver connection. Course management systems can be down for maintenance or links within the CMS will not work when users try the link.

If the student is using a wireless connection they may be unable to connect because there are not enough ports or the wireless network develops connectivity issues and they cannot sign into the network. Any technology can fail for any reason at any given time. Mobile technology and devices can also encounter problems and the major one is being unable to connect to network or being unable to find a strong enough signal to connect the device to the network. While technology has improved our access to library resources when it does not work the way in which it was intended to work it becomes a source of frustration for users.

When technology fails within the library users may not be able to search the catalog or the databases. There were many times while sitting at the reference desk I had to inform users we lost our Internet connection and as a result they would be unable to use any of the libraries electronic resources until the connection was restored. When a user is off-campus and working an assignment and they lose their connection it becomes even more frustrating especially if the assignment is due the next day. While technology works most of the time but it is the times when it fails that become the source of frustration for library users and librarians. It is necessary to always have options or a work-around for the moments when the technology is not working.

FUTURE TRENDS

Remote access technology will continue to improve and users will probably be able to access more collections over the next several years. The Horizon Report for 2011 identified several technology trends that may impact libraries, their users and services in the years to come. Technology will continue to influence how libraries meet the needs of their users. Will the physical library completely disappear? Probably not and the same can be said for printed books and journals. The number printed may decrease but they will still be available. If improvements are made to e-books allowing users to download and print the pages they need for research. E-book use and popularity among library users will increase in the years to come. Should libraries adopt every new technology or social media that comes along?

Before adopting new technology libraries need to determine how it will benefit their users. The technology to access library resources off-campus will improve providing more secure connections for library users. Regardless of the type of connection or the technology used to access library resources from off-campus users will encounter a problem at some point. It can be a bad link from the database to the proxy server or a server that is offline or a course management system that is down for maintenance or the university or library web site server is down making it impossible to access library resources. At some point technology will fail or at the very least disappoint the user. Remote access technologies have created a new avenue for libraries to connect with users beyond their physical space. The virtual world makes it easier to meet students where they meet, study and work. It is important for libraries to continue to

explore, adopt and implement those technologies that will increase their ability to meet or exceed their users' expectations for the services and resources they can provide whether they are on or off-campus.

The next several years will see a growth in services offered to distance education students. New technology will improve the quality of services to provide seamless access to library resources. Libraries will develop assessment plans for their distance library services. The assessment plans will lead to improved services to students both on and off-campus. Faculty and students in off-campus locations or satellite campuses should have the same level of service as students and faculty at the main campus. Libraries will need to survey students and faculty at satellite campuses to determine their level of satisfaction with distance education library services (Ismail, 2010). Surveying distance education students is critical to understanding and meeting their needs. A survey will provide the opportunity to develop and implement new services or improve existing services to distance learning services. Library instruction or information literacy instruction for distance education students is one service libraries need to offer to distance education students. Libraries should promote library services and resources to distance education students through a section on their web site. Making distance education students aware of library services will increase their use and connect them to the resources they need for their courses (Hensley & Miller, 2010).

FINAL THOUGHTS

Remote access for libraries will present new opportunities for libraries to meet their users at their point of need. Technology, especially mobile technology, will be a key factor in the types of services libraries offer to their users. Libraries will not go out of existence but they will offer more services to their remote users because of improvements in technology. Social media will increasingly be incorporated into the services offered by libraries. The library of 21st Century will be a place where users can find the resources they need without having to set foot into the building.

REFERENCES

Hensley, M. K., & Miller, R. (2010). Listening from a distance: A survey of University of Illinois distance learners and its implications for meaningful instruction. *Journal of Library Administration, 50*(5-6), 670-683. DOI: 10.1080.01930826.2010.488946

Institute of Museum and Library Services. (2006). *Status of technology and digitization in the nation's museums and libraries.* Retrieved from http://www.imls.gov/resources/TechDig05/ Technology%2BDigitization.pdf

Ismail, L. (2010). Revelations of an off-campus user group: Library use and needs of faculty and students at a satellite graduate social work program. *Journal of Library Administration, 50*(5-6), 712-736. DOI: 10.1080/01930826.2010.488957

Smith, A. (2010). *Mobile access 2010.* Pew Internet & American Life Project. Retrieved from http://www.pewinternet.org/Reports/2010/ Mobile-Access-2010.aspx

Appendix

Technology Information

Apple--Makers of the iPad and iPod plus numerous apps: http://www.apple.com/

Archivists Toolkit: Open source archival data management system: http://www.archiviststoolkit.org/

Blackboard--Proprietary course management systems. Their products include, Blackboard, WebCT, Elluminate and Wimba. http://www.blackboard.com/

Creative Commons--provides licensing agreements allowing people to share their knowledge and creativity: http://creativecommons.org/

DSpace--Open Source software developed by MIT and Hewlett Packard to build open digital repositories http://www.dspace.org/#

Kindle--E-reader from Amazon: https://kindle.amazon.com/

Kobo: E-book reader: http://www.kobo.com/

Moodle--Open source course management system: http://moodle.org/

Nook: E-reader from Barnes & Noble: http://www.barnesandnoble.com/nook/index.asp

Open DLib--Open source software to create digital libraries: http://opendlib.iei.pi.cnr.it/home.html

Sakai--Open source course management system: http://sakaiproject.org/

Skype--VoIP phone calls and video calls http://www.skype.com/intl/en-us/home

Sony: E-book reader: http://store.sony.com/webapp/wcs/stores/servlet/CategoryDisplay?catalogId=10551&storeId=10151&langId=-1&identifier=SPortableReader

Compilation of References

(2003). *In Webster's New World Computer Dictionary* (10th ed.). Proxy Server.

Aldrich, A. W. (2010). Universities and libraries move to the mobile Web. *EDUCAUSE Quarterly, 33*(2). Retrieved from http://www.educause.edu/EDUCAUSE+Quarterly/EQVolume332010/EDUCAUSEQuarterlyMagazineVolum/206524

American Library Association Public Libraries Interest Group. (2011). *Distance education and the TEACH Act.* Retrieved from http://www.ala.org/Template.cfm?Section=DistanceEducationandtheTEACHAct&Template=/ContentManagement/ContentDisplay.cfm&ContentID=25939

American Library Association. (2005). *Intellectual freedom issues.* Retrieved from http://www.ala.org/template.cfm?section=ifissues&template=/contentmanagement/contentdisplay.cfm&contentid=21654

American Library Association. (2006). Digital Rights Management. Retrieved from http://www.ala.org/ala/issuesadvocacy/copyright/digitalrights/index.cfm

American Library Association. (2008). Guidelines for distance learning services. Retrieved from http://www.ala.org/ala/mgrps/divs/acrl/standards/guidelinesdistancelearning.cfm

American Library Association. (2010). *Recession drives more Americans to libraries in search of employment resources but funding lags demand.* Retrieved from http://www.ala.org/ala/newspresscenter/news/pressreleases2010/april2010/soalrpio.cfm

Armbrust, M., Fox, A., Griffith, R., Joseph, A. D., Katz, R., & Knowinski, A. (2010). A view of Cloud Computing. *Communications of the ACM, 53*(4), 50–58. doi:10.1145/1721654.1721672

Barile, L. (2011, April). Mobile technologies for libraries. *C&RL News,* 222-228.

Barratt, C. C., & White, E. (2010). Case study for a large research institution library: The University of Georgia's Miller Learning Center. *Journal of Library Administration, 50*(2), 135–144. doi:10.1080/01930820903454977

Beall, J. (2010). How Google uses metadata to improve search results. *The Serials Librarian, 59*(1), 40–53. doi:10.1080/03615260903524222

Beckman, M. (2010, September). SSL VPN 101. *Windows IT Pro,* 71-74.

Bellis, M. (2011). *History of laptop computers.* Retrieved from http://inventors.about.com/library/inventors/bllaptop.htm

Belliston, J. C., Howland, J. L., & Roberts, B. C. (2007). Undergraduate use of federated searching: A survey of preferences and perceptions of value-added functionality. *College & Research Libraries, 68*(6), 472–486.

Black, E. L., & Blankenship, B. (2010). Linking students to library resources through the learning management system. *Journal of Library Administration, 50*(4).

Blecic, D. D., Fiscella, J. B., & Wiberly, S. E. Jr. (2007). Measurement of use of electronic resources: Advances in use statistics and innovations in resource functionality. *College & Research Libraries, 68*(1), 26–44.

Bosch, S., Henderson, K., & Klusendorf, H. (2011, April 14). Periodicals price survey 2011: Under pressure, times are changing. *Library Journal*. Retrieved from http://www.libraryjournal.com/lj/home/890009264/periodicalsprice-survey2011under.html.csp

Bower, S. L., & Mee, S. A. (2010). Virtual delivery of electronic resources and services to off-campus users: A multifaceted approach. *Journal of Library Administration*, *50*(5), 468–483. doi:10.1080/01930826.2010.488593

Boyd-Barnes, M. K., & Rosenthal, M. (2005). Remote access revisited: Disintermediation and its discontents. *Journal of Academic Librarianship*, *31*(3), 216–224. doi:10.1016/j.acalib.2005.03.002

Boyd, D. M., & Ellison, N. B. (2007). Social network sites: Definition, history, and scholarship. *Journal of Computer-Mediated Communication*, *13*(1). doi:10.1111/j.1083-6101.2007.00393.x

Breeding, M. (2001). Offering remote access to restricted resources. *Information Today*, *18*(5), 52–53.

Brown, B. (2010). *Most used apps*. Retrieved from http://www.flickr.com/photos/bonnie-brown/4285989531/

Cahoy, E. S., & Moyo, L. M. (2005). Faculty perspective on e-learner research needs. *Journal of Library & Information Services in Distance Learning*, *2*(4). doi:doi:10.1300/J192v02n0401

Carter, H. V. (2008). Why the Technology, Education, and Copyright Harmonization Act matters to librarians. *Journal of Interlibrary Loan. Document Delivery & Electronic Reserves*, *18*(1), 49–56. doi:10.1300/J474v18n01_06

Charnigo, L., & Barnett-Ellis, P. (2007). Checking out Facebook.com: The impact of a digital trend on academic libraries. *Information Technology and Libraries*, *26*(1), 23–34.

Chisman, J., Matthews, G., & Brady, C. (2007). Electronic resource management. *The Serials Librarian*, *52*(3), 297–303. doi:10.1300/J123v52n03_08

Chou, M., & Zhou, O. (2005). The impact of licenses on library collections. *Managing Digital Resources in Libraries*, *17*(33), 7–23. doi:doi:10.1300/J101v17n3302

Chrzastowski, T. E., Norman, M., & Miller, S. E. (2009). SFX statistical reports: A primer for collection assessment librarians. *Collection Management*, *34*(4), 286–303. doi:10.1080/01462670903177912

Cohen, L. (2004). Issues in URL management for digital collections. *Information Technology and Libraries*, *23*(2), 42–49.

Connell, R. S. (2009). Academic libraries, Facebook and MySpace, and student outreach: A survey of student opinion. *Portal: Libraries and the Academy*, *9*(1), 25–36. doi:10.1353/pla.0.0036

Coombs, K. (2008). The mobile iRevolution. *Library Journal*, (Fall): 28.

Copyright Clearance Center. (2011a). *The TEACH Act*. Retrieved from http://www.copyright.com/content/dam/cc3/marketing/documents/pdfs/CR-Teach-Act.pdf

Copyright Clearance Center. (2011a). *The TEACH Act*. Retrieved from http://www.copyright.com/content/dam/cc3/marketing/documents/pdfs/CR-Teach-Act.pdf

Copyright Clearance Center. (2011b). *Using course management systems: Guidelines and best practices for copyright compliance*. Retrieved from http://www.copyright.com/content/dam/cc3/marketing/documents/pdfs/Using-Course- Management-Systems.pdf

Copyright Clearance Center. (2011b). *Using course management systems: Guidelines and best practices for copyright compliance*. Retrieved from http://www.copyright.com/content/dam/cc3/marketing/documents/pdfs/Using-Course-Management-Systems.pdf

Copyright Clearance Center. (2011c). *Interlibrary loan: Copyright guidelines and best practices*. Retrieved from http://www.copyright.com/content/dam/cc3/marketing/documents/pdfs/ILL-Brochure.pdf

Copyright Clearance Center. (2011d). *Using electronic reserves: Guidelines and best practices for copyright compliance*. Retrieved from http://www.copyright.com/content/dam/cc3/marketing/documents/pdfs/Using-Electronic-Reserves.pdf

Copyright Clearance Center. (2011e). *Get it now*. Retrieved from http://www.copyright.com/content/cc3/en/toolbar/productsAndSolutions/getitnow.html

Cotter, G., Carroll, B., Hodge, G., & Japzon, A. (2005). Electronic collection management and electronic information services. *Information Services & Use, 25*, 23–34.

Covey, D. T. (2003). The need to improve remote access to online library resources: Filling the gap between commercial vendor and academic user practice. *Portal: Libraries and the Academy, 3*(4), 577–599. doi:10.1353/pla.2003.0082

Crawford, A. R. (2008). Licensing and negotiations for electronic content. *Resource Sharing & Information Networks, 19*, 15–38. doi:10.1080/07377790802498523

Creaser, C. (2006). User surveys in academic libraries. *New Review of Academic Librarianship, 12*(1), 1–15. doi:10.1080/13614530600913419

Creative Commons. (2011). *Frequently asked questions*. Retrieved from http://wiki.creativecommons.org/FAQ

Croft, J. B. (2005). Interlibrary loan and licensing: Tools for proactive contract management. *Licensing in Libraries: Practical and Ethical Aspects, 42*(3), 41–53. doi:doi:10.1300/J111v42n0303

DaCosta, J. W., & Jones, B. (2007). Developing students' information and research skills via blackboard. Communications in Information Literacy, 1(1).

Daly, E. (2010). Embedding library resources into learning management systems: A way to reach Duke undergrads at their points of need. C&RL News, April.

Dixon, L., Duncan, C., Fagan, J. C., Mandernach, M., & Warlick, S. E. (2010). Finding articles and journals via Google Scholar, journal portals, and link resolvers: Usability study results. *Reference and User Services Quarterly, 50*(2), 170–181.

Edgar, W. B. (2006). Questioning Liquid+™ expanding its assessment of academic library effectiveness. *Portal: Libraries and the Academy, 6*(4), 445–465. doi:10.1353/pla.2006.0050

EDUCAUSE Center for Applied Research. (2010). *ECAR study of undergraduate students and Information Technology 2010*. Retrieved from http://www.educause.edu/Resources/ECARStudyofUndergraduateStuden/217333

EDUCAUSE. (2008). E-books in higher education: Nearing the end of the era of hype? *EDUCAUSE Center for Applied Research Bulletin, 1*, 2-13. Retrieved from http://www.educause.edu/ECAR/EBooksinHigherEducation-Nearing/162438

Emery, J. (2007). Ghosts in the machine. *The Serials Librarian, 51*(3), 201–208. doi:10.1300/J123v51n03_14

Encyclopædia Britannica. (2011). Distance learning. Retrieved from http://www.britannica.com.ezproxy.lib.usf.edu/EBchecked/topic/1482174/distance-learning

Eschenfelder, K. R. (2008). Every library's nightmare? Digital rights management, use restrictions, and licensed scholarly digital resources. *College & Research Libraries, 69*(3), 205–225.

Escobar, H. Jr. (2010). Reserves through Sakai: University of Dayton's primary tool for electronic reserves. Journal of Interlibrary Loan. *Document Delivery & Electronic Reserve, 20*(4). doi:doi:10.1080/1072303X.2010.507457

Eyambi, L., & Suleman, H. (2004). A digital library component assembly environment. *Proceedings of the SAICSIT, 2004*, 15–22.

Fagan, J. C. (2009). Marketing the virtual library. *Computers in Libraries, 29*(7), 25–30.

Falcone, J. P. (2011). Kindle vs. Nook vs. iPad: Which e-book reader should you buy? *CNET*. Retrieved from http://news.cnet.com/8301-17938105-20009738-1/kindle-vs-nook-vs-ipad-which-e-book-reader-should-you-buy/

Fletcher, D. (2010). Facebook: Friends without borders. *Time, 175*(21), 32–38.

Foster, N. F., & Gibbons, S. (Eds.). (2007). *Studying students: The undergraduate research project at the University of Rochester*. Chicago, IL: Association of College and Research Libraries.

Fox, R., & Stuart, C. (2009). Creating learning spaces through collaboration: How one library refined its approach. *EDUCAUSE Quarterly, 32*(1). Retrieved from http://www.educause.edu/EDUCAUSE+Quarterly/EDUCAUSEQuarterlyMagazineVolum/CreatingLearningSpacesThroughC/163850

Friedman, J., & Hoffman, D. V. (2008). Protecting data on mobile devices: A taxonomy of security threats to mobile computing and review of applicable defenses. *Information Knowledge Systems Management, 7*(1), 159–180.

Garibay, C. G., & Figueroa, A. (2010). Evaluation of a digital library by means of quality function deployment (QFD) and the Kano model. *Journal of Academic Librarianship, 36*(2), 125–132. doi:10.1016/j.acalib.2010.01.002

Gerke, J., & Maness, J. M. (2010). The physical and the virtual: The relationship between the library as place and electronic collections. *College & Research Libraries, 71*(1), 20–31.

Gerlich, B. K., & Beard, L. G. (2010). Testing the validity of the READ scale (Reference Effort Assessment Data) ©: Qualitative statistics for academic reference services. *College & Research Libraries, 71*(2), 116–137.

Ge, X. (2010). Information -seeking behavior in the digital age: A multidisciplinary study of academic researchers. *College & Research Libraries, 71*(5), 435–455.

Gibbons, S. (2005). Course management systems. *Library Technology Reports, 41*(3), 12–20.

Gibbons, S. (2005). Integration of libraries and course-management systems. *Library Technology Reports, 41*(3).

Gorley, D. (2001). *An architecture for the evolving digital library*. Conference Paper, EDUCAUSE Annual Conference 2001. Retrieved from http://net.educause.edu/ir/library/html/edu0122/edu0122.html

Greene, B. (2011). *38 years ago he made the first cell phone call*. Retrieved from http://www.cnn.com/2011/OPINION/04/01/greene.first.cellphone.call/index.html

Gregory, C. L. (2010). But I want a real book: An investigation of undergraduates' usage and attitudes toward electronic books. *Reference and User Services Quarterly, 47*(3), 266–273.

Griner, B. P., & Butler, P. J. (2011). *Cloud Computing visual diagram creative commons public domain*. Retrieved from http://commons.wikimedia.org/wiki/File:Cloudapplications.jpg

Grogg, J. (2006). Linking without a stand-alone link resolver. *Library Technology Reports, 42*(1), 31–34.

Grossman, L. (2011). 2010 person of the year Mark Zuckerberg. *Time, 176*(26), 46–75.

Hamblen, M. (2011). Amazon: E-books now outsell print books. Retrieved from http://www.computerworld.com/s/article/9216869/AmazonEbooksnowoutsellprintbooks

Hansen, B. (2001, December 7). Distance learning. CQ Researcher, 11, 993-1016. Retrieved from http://library.cqpress.com/cqresearcher/

Head, A. J., & Eisenberg, M. B. (2010). *Lessons learned: How college students seek information in the digital age*. Retrieved from http://projectinfolit.org/pdfs/PILFall-2009finalvYR1122009v2.pdf

Hemmig, W., & Montet, M. (2010). The "just for me" virtual library: Enhancing an embedded ebrarian program. *Journal of Library Administration, 50*(5), 657–669. doi:10.1080/01930826.2010.488943

Hendrix, D., Chiarella, D., Hasman, L., Murphy, S., & Zafron, M. (2009). Use of Facebook in academic health sciences libraries. *Journal of the Medical Library Association, 97*(1), 44–47. doi:10.3163/1536-5050.97.1.008

Hensley, M. K., & Miller, R. (2010). Listening from a distance: A survey of University of Illinois distance learners and its implications for meaningful instruction. *Journal of Library Administration, 50*(5-6), 670-683. DOI: 10.1080.01930826.2010.488946

Hightower, B., Rawl, C., & Schutt, M. (2007). Collaborations for delivering the library to students through WebCT. *RSR. Reference Services Review, 35*(4).

Hillyer, N., & Parker, L. (2007). Video reference--It's not your typical virtual reference. Internet Reference Services Quarterly, 11(4), 41-54. DOI: 10-1300/J136v11n0403

Hobbs, R. (2010). *Copyright clarity: How fair use supports digital learning*. Thousand Oaks, CA: Corwin.

Horva, T. (2010). Challenges and possibilities for collection management in a digital age. *Library Resources & Technical Services, 54*(3), 142–152.

HujiStat. (2007). *Schematic representation of a proxy server, CC-by-SA-3.0 & GFDL*. Retrieved from http://commons.wikimedia.org/wiki/File:SchematicProxyServer.png

Hunter, K. (2005). Access management. *Journal of Library Administration, 42*(2), 57–70. doi:10.1300/J111v42n02_05

Institute of Museum and Library Services. (2006). *Status of technology and digitization in the nation's museums and libraries.* Retrieved from http://www.imls.gov/resources/TechDig05/Technology%2BDigitization.pdf

Ismail, L. (2010). Revelations of an off-campus user group: Library use and needs of faculty and students at a satellite graduate social work program. *Journal of Library Administration, 50*(5- 6), 712-736. DOI: 10.1080/01930826.2010.488957

Jamali, H. R., Nicholas, D., & Rowlands, I. (2009). Scholarly e-books: The views of 16,000 academics: Results from the JISC National E-Book Observatory. *Aslib Proceedings: New Information Perspectives, 61*(1), 33–47. doi:doi:10.1108/00012530910932276

Jankowska, M. A., Hertel, K., & Young, N. J. (2006). Improving library service quality to graduate students: LibQual+™ survey results in a practical setting. *Portal: Libraries and the Academy, 6*(1), 59–77. doi:10.1353/pla.2006.0005

Jayaraman, S., & Harker, K. (2009). Evaluating the quality of a link resolver. *Journal of Electronic Resources in Medical Libraries, 6*(2), 152–162. doi:10.1080/15424060902932250

Jetton, L. L., & Bailey, A. S. (2010). The role of the access services manager in the virtual library. *Journal of Access Services, 7*(2), 121–131. doi:10.1080/15367961003617519

Jones, S., & Kayonga, J. (2008). Identifying student and faculty needs through LibQual+™: An analysis of qualitative survey comments. *College & Research Libraries, 69*(6), 493–509.

JSTOR. (2002). Open proxy servers: Gateways to unauthorized use of licensed resources. *JSTOR News, 6(3),* 1-2. Retrieved from http://news.jstor.org/newsPDFs/dec2002.pdf

Keller, J. (2011, 27 June). As mobile devices multiply, some colleges turn away from building campus apps. *The Chronicle of Higher Education.* Retrieved from http://chronicle.com/article/As-Mobile-Devices-Multiply/128060/

Kneivel, J. E., Wicht, H., & Connaway, L. S. (2006). Use of circulation statistics and interlibrary loan data in collection management. *College & Research Libraries, 67*(1), 35–49.

Korah, A., & Cassidy, D. E. (2010). Students and federated searching. *Reference and User Services Quarterly, 49*(4), 325–332.

Koutsomitropoulos, D., Alexopoulos, A. D., Solomou, G. D., & Papatheodorou, T. S. (2010). The use of metadata for educational resources in digital repositories: Practices and perspectives. *D-Lib Magazine, 16*(1/2). Retrieved from http://www.dlib.org/dlib/january10/kout/01kout.htmldoi:10.1045/january2010-koutsomitropoulos

Kranch, D. A. (2008). Who owns online course intellectual property? *The Quarterly Review of Distance Education, 9*(4), 349–356.

Krishnamurthy, M. (2007). Open access, open source and digital libraries: A current trend in university libraries around the world. *Program: Electronic Library and Information Systems, 42*(1). doi:doi:10.1108/00330330810851582

Lai, H.-C., Yang, C.-J., Chen, C.-F., Ho, W.-C., & Chan, W.-T. (2007). Affordances of mobile technologies for experiential learning: The interplay of technology and pedagogical practices. *Journal of Computer Assisted Learning, 23*(4), 326–337. doi:10.1111/j.1365-2729.2007.00237.x

Lawrence, P. (2009, January). Access, when and where they want it. *Information Today,* 40-43.

Lei, S. A., & Gupta, R. K. (2010). College distance education courses: Evaluating benefits and costs from institutional, faculty and students' perspectives. *Education, 130*(4).

Lenhart, A., Purcell, K., Smith, A., & Zickuhr, K. (2010). *Social media & mobile Internet use among teens and young adults.* Pew Internet, Pew Internet & American Life Project. Retrieved from http://www.pewinternet.org/Reports/2010/Social-Media-and-Young-Adults.aspx

Levine, A. (2011). *2011 horizon report.* Retrieved from: http://www.nmc.org/publications/2011-horizon-report

Library of Congress. (2010). *Twitter donates entire tweet archive to Library of Congress.* Retrieved from http://www.loc.gov/today/pr/2010/10-081.html

Lipinski, T. A. (2006). *The complete copyright liability handbook for librarians and educators.* New York, NY: Neal-Schuman.

Lippincott, J. K. (2008). Mobile technologies, mobile users: Implications for academic libraries. *ARL, 261,* 1–4.

Looi, C.-K., Seow, P., Zhang, B. H., So, H.-J., Chen, W., & Wong, L.-H. (2010). Leveraging mobile technology for sustainable seamless learning: A research agenda. *British Journal of Educational Technology, 41*(2), 154–169. doi:10.1111/j.1467-8535.2008.00912.x

Lynch, C. (2005). Where do we go from here? *D-Lib Magazine, 11*(7/8). Retrieved from http://www.dlib.org/dlib/july05/lynch/07lynch.html

Markgraf, J. S., & Erffmeyer, R. C. (2002). Providing library service to off-campus business students: Access, resources and instruction. Library Services for Business Students in Distance Education: Issues and Trends, 7(2/3).

Matthew, V., & Schroeder, A. (2006). The embedded librarian program: Faculty and librarians partner to embed personalized library assistance into online courses. *EDUCAUSE Quarterly, 4.*

McCrea, B. (2010). *5 higher ed tech trends to watch in 2011.* Retrieved from http://campustechnology.com/articles/2010/12/09/5-higher-ed-tech-trends-to-watch-in-2011.aspx

McDonald, R. H., & Thomas, C. (2006). Disconnects between library culture and millennial generation values. *EDUCAUSE Quarterly, 29*(4), 4–6.

McLean, E., & Dew, S. H. (2006). Providing library instruction to distance learning students in the 21st century. *Journal of Library Administration, 45*(3-4), 315–337. doi:10.1300/J111v45n03_01

Mikesell, B. L. (2004). Anything, anytime, anywhere: Proxy servers, Shibboleth, and the dream of the digital library. *The Eleventh Off-Campus Library Services Conference Proceedings, 41*(1). DOI: 10.1300/J111v41n0122

Mitchell, N., & Ennis, L. A. (2010). Scaling the (fire) wall. *Journal of Hospital Librarianship, 10*(2), 190–196. doi:10.1080/15323261003681588

Munson, D. M. (2006). Link resolvers: An overview for reference librarians. *Internet Reference Services Quarterly, 11*(1), 17–27. doi:10.1300/J136v11n01_02

National Center for Education Statistics. (2011). Fast facts: How many postsecondary institutions offer distance learning programs? Retrieved from http://nces.ed.gov/fastfacts/display.asp?id=80

OCLC. (2011). *EZproxy.* Retrieved from http://www.oclc.org/ezproxy/support/default.htm

OCLC. (2011). *QuestionPoint.* Retrieved from http://www.oclc.org/questionpoint/about/default.htm

Open, U. R. L. (2011). *Website.* Retrieved from http://www.exlibrisgroup.com/category/sfxopenurl

OpenVPN. (2011) *OpenVPN.* Retrieved from http://openvpn.net/

Ovadia, S. (2010). Navigating the challenges of the Cloud. *Behavioral & Social Sciences Librarian, 29*(3), 233–236. doi:10.1080/01639269.2010.498764

Pfleeger, C. O. (2008). *Computer security in Access-Science.* McGraw-Hill.

Platt, J., & Benson, P. (2010). Improving the virtual reference experience: How closely do academic libraries adhere to RUSA guidelines? *Journal of Library & Information Services in Distance Learning, 4*(1), 30–42. doi:10.1080/15332901003765811

Powers, A. C., Schmidt, J., & Hill, C. (2008). Why can't we be friends? The MSU libraries find friends on Facebook. *Mississippi Libraries, 72*(1), 3–5.

Profit, S. K. (2008). Text messaging at reference: A preliminary survey. *The Reference Librarian, 49*(2), 129–134. doi:10.1080/02763870802101328

Puckett, J. (2010). Digital rights management as information access barrier. *Progressive Librarian, 34/35,* 11–24.

Ragon, B. (2009). Designing for the mobile Web. *Mobile Computing and the Library, 6,* 355–361. doi:doi:10.1080/15424060903364875

Rainie, L., Purcell, K., & Smith, A. (2011). *The social side of the Internet.* Pew Internet, Pew Internet & American Life Project. Retrieved from http://www.pewinternet.org/Reports/2011/The-Social-Side-of-the-Internet.aspx

Raphael, J. R. (2010). Myspace's Facebook 'mashup'--Why bother? *PC World.* Retrieved from http://www.pcworld.com/article/211127/myspacesfacebookmashupwhybother.html

Rapp, D. (2011, March 15). Infotech: OverDrive unveils iPad app for ebook lending. *Library Journal, 20.*

Ribaric, T. J. (2009, January). How well do you proxy? *Computers in Libraries,* •••, 19–21.

Ross, L., & Sennyey, P. (2008). The library is dead, long live the library! The practice of academic librarianship and the digital revolution. *Journal of Academic Librarianship, 34*(2), 145–152. doi:10.1016/j.acalib.2007.12.006

Rudestam, K. E., & Schoenholtz-Read, J. (2010). *Handbook of online learning.* Thousand Oaks, CA: SAGE Publications.

Saunders, E. S. (2008). Meeting academic needs for information: A customer service approach. *Portal: Libraries and the Academy, 8*(4), 357-371. DOI: 10.1353/pla.0.0020

Schaffhauser, D. (2010). *Oxford, Rice, Open U add to iTunes U electronic book collection.* Retrieved from http://campustechnology.com/articles/2010/11/02/oxford-rice-open-u-add-to-itunes-u-electronic-book-collection.aspx

Schlosser, M. (2009). Unless otherwise indicated: A survey of copyright statements on digital library collections. *College & Research Libraries, 70*(4), 371–385.

Shank, J. D., & Dewald, N. H. (2003). Establishing our presence in courseware: Adding library services to the virtual classroom. Information Technology and Libraries, 22(1).

Sharifabadi, S. R. (2006). How digital libraries can support e-learning. *The Electronic Library, 24*(3), 389–401. doi:10.1108/02640470610671231

Sheeya, N. K. (2010). Undergraduate students' perceptions of digital library: A case study. *The International Information & Library Review, 42,* 149–153. doi:10.1016/j.iilr.2010.07.003

Shibboleth. (2011). *Website.* Retrieved from http://shibboleth.internet2.edu/

Sloan Consortium. (2010a). Learning on demand: Online education in the United States, 2009. Retrieved from http://sloanconsortium.org/publications/survey/learningondemandsr2010

Sloan Consortium. (2010b). Class differences: Online education in the United States, 2010. Retrieved from http://sloanconsortium.org/publications/survey/classdifferences

Smith, A. (2010). *Mobile access 2010.* Pew Internet & American Life Project. Retrieved from http://www.pewinternet.org/Reports/2010/Mobile-Access-2010.aspx

Smith, K. L. (2010). Copyright renewal for libraries: Seven steps toward a user-friendly law. *Portal: Libraries and the Academy, 10*(1), 5–27. doi:10.1353/pla.0.0089

Sodt, J. M., & Summey, P. T. (2009). Beyond the library's walls: Using library 2.0 tools to reach out to all users. *Journal of Library Administration, 49*(1), 97–109. doi:10.1080/01930820802312854

Starr, J. (2010). California digital library in Twitter-land. *Computers in Libraries, 30*(7), 23–27.

Sutton, L., Bazirijian, R., & Zerwas, S. (2009). Library perceptions: A study of two universities. *College & Research Libraries, 70*(5), 474–494.

Tadjer, R. (2010, November 18). What is Cloud Computing? *PC Magazine.* Retrieved from http://www.pcmag.com/article2/0,2817,2372163,00.asp#fbid=v16rlpg9bQ

Thomsett-Scott, B., & May, F. (2009). How may we help you? Online education faculty tell us what they need from libraries and librarians. *Journal of Library Administration, 49*(1), 111–135. doi:10.1080/01930820802312888

Thong, J. Y. L., Hong, W., & Tam, K. Y. (2004). What leads to user acceptance of digital libraries? *Communications of the ACM, 47*(11), 79–83. doi:10.1145/1029496.1029498

Tibbo, H. R. (2002). *Primarily history: Historians and the search for primary source materials.* Joint Conference on Digital Libraries. New York, NY: ACM

Tyson, J., & Crawford, S. (2011, April 14). How VPNs work. *HowStuffWorks.com.* Retrieved June 7, 2011, from http://www.howstuffworks.com/vpn.htm

United States Copyright Office. (2009). *Fair use.* Retrieved from http://www.copyright.gov/fls/fl102.html

United States Copyright Office. (2011a). *Copyright basics.* Retrieved from http://www.copyright.gov/circs/circ1.pdf

United States Copyright Office. (2011b). *Duration of copyright.* Retrieved from http://www.copyright.gov/circs/circ15a.pdf

United States Department of Education. (2008). Distance education at degree-granting postsecondary institutions: 2006-07. Washington, DC: National Center for Education Statistics. Retrieved from http://nces.ed.gov/pubs2009/2009044.pdf

University of South Florida. (2011). *Screen capture of NetID single sign-on.*

University System of Georgia. (2011). *GeorgiaVIEW maintenance schedule--Fall 2011.* Retrieved 24 October, 2011, from http://www.usg.edu/gaview/support/maint-schedule.phtml

Wakimoto, J. C., Walker, D. S., & Dabbour, K. S. (2006). The myths and realities of SFX in academic libraries. *Journal of Academic Librarianship, 32*(2), 127–136. doi:10.1016/j.acalib.2005.12.008

Waller, A., & Bird, G. (2006). We own it. *The Serials Librarian, 50*(1), 179–196. doi:10.1300/J123v50n01_17

Webster, P. (2002). Remote patron validation: Posting a proxy server at the digital doorway. *Computers in Libraries, 22*(8), 18–23.

Wikipedia. (2011). *Digital rights management.* Retrieved June 8, 2011, from http://en.wikipedia.org/w/index.php?title=Digitalrightsmanagement&oldid=432654426

Xu, C., Ouyang, F., & Chu, H. (2009). The academic library meets Web 2.0: Applications and implications. *Journal of Academic Librarianship, 35*(4), 324–331. doi:10.1016/j.acalib.2009.04.003

Yang, Z. Y. (2005). Distance education librarians in the US: ARL libraries and library services provided to their distance users. *Journal of Academic Librarianship, 31*(2).

Young, J. (2008). Blackboard customers consider alternatives. *The Chronicle of Higher Education, 55*(3).

Young-Wiles, S., Landesman, B., & Terrill, L. J. (2007). E-resources=e-opportunity. *The Serials Librarian, 52*(3), 253–258. doi:doi:10.1300/J123v52n0301

Related References

To continue our tradition of advancing information science and technology research, we have compiled a list of recommended IGI Global readings. These references will provide additional information and guidance to further enrich your knowledge and assist you with your own research and future publications.

REFERENCES

Abbas, J. (2010). Social software use in public libraries. In Dumova, T., & Fiordo, R. (Eds.), *Handbook of research on social interaction technologies and collaboration software: Concepts and trends* (pp. 451–461).

Abbasi, M., & Stergioulas, L. K. (2011). Hybrid wireless networks for e-learning and digital literacy: Testing and evaluation. *International Journal of Digital Literacy and Digital Competence, 2*(2), 40–52. doi:10.4018/jdldc.2011040104

Abresch, J. (2008). Geographic Information Systems research and data centers. In Tomei, L. A. (Ed.), *Online and distance learning: Concepts, methodologies, tools, and applications* (pp. 1714–1723). doi:10.4018/978-1-59140-106-3.ch004

Abresch, J., Hanson, A., Heron, S., & Reehling, P. J. (2008). Integrating geographic Information Systems into library services: A guide for academic libraries (pp. 1-318). doi:10.4018/978-1-59904-726-3

Abresch, J., Hanson, A., & Rheeling, P. J. (2008). Geographic information and library education. In Abresch, J., Hanson, A., Heron, S., & Reehling, P. J. (Eds.), *Integrating Geographic Information Systems into library services: A guide for academic libraries* (pp. 239–266). doi:10.4018/978-1-59904-726-3.ch009

Abresch, J., Reehling, P. J., & Hanson, A. (2008). Spatial databases and data infrastructure. In Abresch, J., Hanson, A., Heron, S., & Reehling, P. J. (Eds.), *Integrating Geographic Information Systems into library services: A guide for academic libraries* (pp. 53–81). doi:10.4018/978-1-59904-726-3.ch003

Achugbue, E. I., & Anie, S. O. (2011). Attitudes of librarians in selected Nigerian universities towards digital libraries in e-learning. *International Journal of Digital Library Systems, 2*(1), 52–57. doi:10.4018/jdls.2011010103

Adamich, T. (2011). The new age "information dowser" and mobile learning opportunities: The use of library classification and subject headings in K-20 education – Today and tomorrow. In Kitchenham, A. (Ed.), *Models for interdisciplinary mobile learning: Delivering information to students* (pp. 265–284). doi:10.4018/978-1-60960-511-7.ch015

Adedibu, L. O., Akinboro, E. O., & Abdussalam, T. A. (2012). Cataloguing and classification of library resources in the 21st century. In Tella, A., & Issa, A. (Eds.), *Library and information science in developing countries: Contemporary issues* (pp. 313–326). doi:10.4018/978-1-61350-335-5.ch023

Adogbeji, O. B., & Adomi, E. E. (2008). Computer networking of cybercafés in Delta State, Nigeria. In Putnik, G. D., & Cruz-Cunha, M. M. (Eds.), *Encyclopedia of networked and virtual organizations* (pp. 305–310). doi:10.4018/978-1-59904-885-7.ch040

Afifi, M. (2008). Process mapping for electronic resources: A Lesson from business models. In Yu, H., & Breivold, S. (Eds.), *Electronic resource management in libraries: Research and practice* (pp. 90–104). doi:10.4018/978-1-59904-891-8.ch006

Ahmad, F., Sumner, T., & Devaul, H. (2009). New roles of digital libraries. In Theng, Y., Foo, S., Goh, D., & Na, J. (Eds.), *Handbook of research on digital libraries: Design, development, and impact* (pp. 520–532). doi:10.4018/978-1-59904-879-6.ch054

Akporhonor, B. A. (2010). Library photocopy policies. In Adomi, E. (Ed.), *Handbook of research on information communication technology policy: Trends, issues and advancements* (pp. 520–526). doi:10.4018/978-1-61520-847-0.ch031

Al-Suqri, M. N., & Fatuyi, E. O. (2009). Digital library service system; digital library system; document model; grid computing; grid infrastructure; institutional repository; service oriented architecture. In Theng, Y., Foo, S., Goh, D., & Na, J. (Eds.), *Handbook of research on digital libraries: Design, development, and impact* (pp. 8–15). doi:10.4018/978-1-59904-879-6.ch002

Alonge, A. J. (2012). Social media in library and information centres. In Tella, A., & Issa, A. (Eds.), *Library and information science in developing countries: Contemporary issues* (pp. 293–302). doi:10.4018/978-1-61350-335-5.ch021

Alpert, S. R. (2009). User-centered evaluation of personalized Web sites: What's unique? In Ang, C., & Zaphiris, P. (Eds.), *Human computer interaction: Concepts, methodologies, tools, and applications* (pp. 177–191).

Ameen, K., & Rafiq, M. (2009). Development of digital libraries in Pakistan. In Theng, Y., Foo, S., Goh, D., & Na, J. (Eds.), *Handbook of research on digital libraries: Design, development, and impact* (pp. 482–491). doi:10.4018/978-1-59904-879-6.ch050

Anaraki, L. N., & Heidari, A. (2010). Bridging the digital divide: A review of critical factors in developing countries. In Ashraf, T., Sharma, J., & Gulati, P. A. (Eds.), *Developing sustainable digital libraries: Socio-technical perspectives* (pp. 286–310). doi:10.4018/978-1-61520-767-1.ch016

Andriole, S. J., & Monsanto, C. (2008). Herding 3,000 cats: Enabling continuous real estate transaction processing. In Nemati, H. (Ed.), *Information security and ethics: Concepts, methodologies, tools, and applications* (pp. 1603–1610).

Ansari, M. A. (2012). Modernization of a traditional library. In Tella, A., & Issa, A. (Eds.), *Library and information science in developing countries: Contemporary issues* (pp. 32–44).

Arora, J. (2010). Digitisation: Methods, tools and technology. In Ashraf, T., Sharma, J., & Gulati, P. A. (Eds.), *Developing sustainable digital libraries: Socio-technical perspectives* (pp. 40–63). doi:10.4018/978-1-61520-767-1.ch003

Ashraf, D., & Gulati, M. A. (2010). Digital libraries: a sustainable approach. In Ashraf, T., Sharma, J., & Gulati, P. A. (Eds.), *Developing sustainable digital libraries: Socio-technical perspectives* (pp. 1–18). doi:10.4018/978-1-61520-767-1.ch001

Ashraf, T., Sharma, J., & Gulati, P. A. (2010*). Developing sustainable digital libraries: Socio-technical perspectives* (pp. 1-378). doi:10.4018/978-1-61520-767-1

Baim, S. A. (2006). Distance learning applications using virtual communities. In Dasgupta, S. (Ed.), *Encyclopedia of virtual communities and technologies* (pp. 140–144). doi:10.4018/978-1-59140-563-4.ch027

Baker, A. B., Gil-Garcia, J. R., Canestraro, D., Costello, J., & Werthmuller, D. (2008). Public sector participation in open communities. In Garson, G. D., & Khosrow-Pour, M. (Eds.), *Handbook of research on public Information Technology* (pp. 41–49). doi:10.4018/978-1-59904-857-4.ch005

Barker, S. (2008). Business graduates as end-user developers: Understanding information literacy skills required. In Clarke, S. (Ed.), *End-user computing: Concepts, methodologies, tools, and applications* (pp. 1–1). doi:10.4018/978-1-59904-945-8.ch029

Barnaghi, P. M., Wang, W., & Kurian, J. C. (2009). Semantic association analysis in ontology-based information retrieval. In Theng, Y., Foo, S., Goh, D., & Na, J. (Eds.), *Handbook of research on digital libraries: Design, development, and impact* (pp. 131–141). doi:10.4018/978-1-59904-879-6.ch013

Bartolacci, M., & Powell, S. R. (2012). *Research, practice, and educational advancements in telecommunications and networking* (pp. 1–506). doi:10.4018/978-1-46660-050-8

Bartsch, R. A. (2008). Misuse of online databases for literature searches. In Kidd, T. T., & Song, H. (Eds.), *Handbook of research on instructional systems and technology* (pp. 373–380). doi:10.4018/978-1-59904-865-9.ch027

Beale, R. (2009). Socially-aware design: The 'slanty' approach. *International Journal of Sociotechnology and Knowledge Development, 1*(2), 1–7. doi:10.4018/jskd.2009040101

Béjar, R., Nogueras-Iso, J., Latre, M. Á., Muro-Medrano, P. R., & Zarazaga-Soria, F. J. (2009). Digital libraries as a foundation of spatial data infrastructures. In Theng, Y., Foo, S., Goh, D., & Na, J. (Eds.), *Handbook of research on digital libraries: Design, development, and impact* (pp. 382–389). doi:10.4018/978-1-59904-879-6.ch039

Bermón-Angarita, L., Amescua-Seco, A., Sánchez-Segura, M. I., & García-Guzmán, J. (2009). Software process asset libraries using knowledge repositories. In Theng, Y., Foo, S., Goh, D., & Na, J. (Eds.), *Handbook of research on digital libraries: Design, development, and impact* (pp. 465–475). doi:10.4018/978-1-59904-879-6.ch048

Bhatt, M. I. (2010). Harnessing technology for providing knowledge for development: New role for libraries. In Ashraf, T., Sharma, J., & Gulati, P. A. (Eds.), *Developing sustainable digital libraries: Socio-technical perspectives* (pp. 252–264). doi:10.4018/978-1-61520-767-1.ch014

Bodomo, A. B. (2010). Digital literacy: Reading in the age of ICT. In Bodomo, A. B. (Ed.), *Computer-mediated communication for linguistics and literacy: Technology and natural language education* (pp. 17–35).

Boston, G., & Gedeon, R. J. (2009). Beyond OpenURL: Technologies for linking library resources. In Erickson, J. (Ed.), *Database technologies: Concepts, methodologies, tools, and applications* (pp. 1405–1419). doi:10.4018/978-1-60566-058-5.ch084

Bothmann, R. L., & Holmberg, M. (2008). Strategic planning for electronic resource management. In Yu, H., & Breivold, S. (Eds.), *Electronic resource management in libraries: Research and practice* (pp. 16–28). doi:10.4018/978-1-59904-891-8.ch002

Buchanan, E. (2009). Library services for distance education students in higher education. In Rogers, P. L., Berg, G. A., Boettcher, J. V., Howard, C., Justice, L., & Schenk, K. D. (Eds.), *Encyclopedia of distance learning* (2nd ed., pp. 1380–1383). doi:10.4018/978-1-60566-198-8.ch197

Burke, M. (2009). E-libraries and distance learning. In Khosrow-Pour, M. (Ed.), *Encyclopedia of Information Science and technology* (2nd ed., pp. 1349–1353).

Burke, M., Levin, B. L., & Hanson, A. (2008). Online academic libraries and distance learning. In Tomei, L. A. (Ed.), *Online and distance learning: Concepts, methodologies, tools, and applications* (pp. 3449–3464).

Butterworth, R. (2008). A case study of use-centered descriptions: Archival descriptions of what can be done with a collection. In Goh, D., & Foo, S. (Eds.), *Social information retrieval systems: Emerging technologies and applications for searching the Web effectively* (pp. 67–86).

Camarihna-Matos, L. M., & Afsarmanesh, H. (2008). Concept of collaboration. In Putnik, G. D., & Cruz-Cunha, M. M. (Eds.), *Encyclopedia of networked and virtual organizations* (pp. 311–315). doi:10.4018/978-1-59904-885-7.ch041

Candela, L., Castelli, D., & Pagano, P. (2009). OpenDLib: A digital library service system. In Theng, Y., Foo, S., Goh, D., & Na, J. (Eds.), *Handbook of research on digital libraries: Design, development, and impact* (pp. 1–7). doi:10.4018/978-1-59904-879-6.ch001

Candela, L., Castelli, D., & Pagano, P. (2011). History, evolution, and impact of digital libraries. In Iglezakis, I., Synodinou, T., & Kapidakis, S. (Eds.), *E-publishing and digital libraries: Legal and organizational issues* (pp. 1–30). doi:10.4018/978-1-60960-031-0.ch001

Carroll, J. M. (2009). Introducing digital case library. In Pagani, M. (Ed.), *Encyclopedia of multimedia technology and networking* (2nd ed., pp. 782–788).

Cartelli, A. (2008). ICT, CoLs, CoPs, and virtual communities. In Van Slyke, C. (Ed.), *Information communication technologies: Concepts, methodologies, tools, and applications* (pp. 2350–2356). doi:10.4018/978-1-59904-949-6.ch171

Cartelli, A. (2012). *Current trends and future practices for digital literacy and competence* (pp. 1–421).

Cartelli, A., Daltri, A., Errani, P., Palma, M., & Zanfini, P. (2009). The open catalogue of manuscripts in the Malatestiana library. In Cartelli, A., & Palma, M. (Eds.), *Encyclopedia of information communication technology* (pp. 656-661). doi:10.4018/978-1-59904-845-1.ch086

Casbas, O. C., Nogueras-Iso, J., & Zarazaga-Soria, F. J. (2009). DL and GIS: Path to a new collaboration paradigm. In Theng, Y., Foo, S., Goh, D., & Na, J. (Eds.), *Handbook of research on digital libraries: Design, development, and impact* (pp. 390–399). doi:10.4018/978-1-59904-879-6.ch040

Cater-Steel, A. (2010). IT services departments struggle to adopt a service-oriented philosophy. In St.Amant, K. (Ed.), *IT outsourcing: Concepts, methodologies, tools, and applications* (pp. 1447–1455). doi:10.4018/jisss.2009040105

Cater-Steel, A., & Toleman, M. (2009). Education for IT service management standards. In Kelley, G. (Ed.), *Selected readings on Information Technology Management: Contemporary issues* (pp. 293–306).

Chailla, A. M., Dulle, F. W., & Malekani, A. W. (2009). Digitization initiatives and knowledge management: Institutionalization of e-governance in teaching, learning and research in East African universities. In Rahman, H. (Ed.), *Social and political implications of data mining: Knowledge management in e-government* (pp. 288–301). doi:10.4018/978-1-60566-230-5.ch017

Chakraborty, A. K. (2010). Web 2.0 and social Web approaches to digital libraries. In Ashraf, T., Sharma, J., & Gulati, P. A. (Eds.), *Developing sustainable digital libraries: Socio-technical perspectives* (pp. 108-132). doi:10.4018/978-1-61520-767-1.ch006Chandrasekaran, M., & Upadhyaya, S. (2009). A multistage framework to defend against phishing attacks. In Gupta, M., & Sharman, R. (Eds.), *Handbook of research on social and organizational liabilities in information security* (pp. 175-192). doi:10.4018/978-1-60566-132-2.ch011

Chavez, T. (2008). Staffing the transition to the virtual academic library: Competencies, characteristics, and change. In Tomei, L. A. (Ed.), *Online and distance learning: Concepts, methodologies, tools, and applications* (pp. 3416–3432).

Chen, E. (2012). Web 2.0 social networking technologies and strategies for knowledge management. In Boughzala, I., & Dudezert, A. (Eds.), *Knowledge management 2.0: Organizational models and enterprise strategies* (pp. 84–102).

Chew-Hung, C., & Hedberg, J. G. (2009). The Future of learning with digital libraries. In Theng, Y., Foo, S., Goh, D., & Na, J. (Eds.), *Handbook of research on digital libraries: Design, development, and impact* (pp. 543–551). doi:10.4018/978-1-59904-879-6.ch056

Chías, P., Abad, T., & Rivera, E. (2010). The project of the ancient Spanish cartography e-library: Main targets and legal challenges. In Portela, I. M., & Cruz-Cunha, M. M. (Eds.), *Information communication technology law, protection and access rights: Global approaches and issues* (pp. 384–396). doi:10.4018/978-1-61520-975-0.ch023

Choudhary, P. K. (2010). Tools and techniques for digital conversion. In Ashraf, T., Sharma, J., & Gulati, P. A. (Eds.), *Developing sustainable digital libraries: Socio-technical perspectives* (pp. 64–89). doi:10.4018/978-1-61520-767-1.ch004

Christenson, H., & Willhite, S. (2008). Working with database and e-journal vendors to ensure quality for end users. In Yu, H., & Breivold, S. (Eds.), *Electronic resource management in libraries: Research and practice* (pp. 194–212). doi:10.4018/978-1-59904-891-8.ch011

Chudamani, K. S., & Nagarathna, H. C. (2009). Metadata interoperability. In Theng, Y., Foo, S., Goh, D., & Na, J. (Eds.), *Handbook of research on digital libraries: Design, development, and impact* (pp. 122–130). doi:10.4018/978-1-59904-879-6.ch012

Ciaramitaro, B. L. (2012). *Mobile technology consumption: Opportunities and challenges* (pp. 1-256). doi:10.4018/978-1-61350-150-4

Clough, P., & Eleta, I. (2010). Investigating language skills and field of knowledge on multilingual information access in digital libraries. *International Journal of Digital Library Systems, 1*(1), 89–103. doi:10.4018/jdls.2010102705

Crummett, C., & Perrault, A. (2008). The use of CMC technologies in academic libraries. In Kelsey, S., & St.Amant, K. (Eds.), *Handbook of research on computer mediated communication* (pp. 705–719). doi:10.4018/978-1-59904-863-5.ch050

Cusack, B. (2009). Managing IT security relationships within enterprise control frameworks. In Cater-Steel, A. (Ed.), *Information Technology governance and service management: Frameworks and adaptations* (pp. 191–201). doi:10.4018/978-1-60566-008-0.ch010

Daniel, B. K. (2009). User-centered design principles for online learning communities: A sociotechnical approach for the design of a distributed community of practice. In Ang, C., & Zaphiris, P. (Eds.), *Human computer interaction: Concepts, methodologies, tools, and applications* (pp. 979–991).

Daniel Licthnow, S. L., & Tiago Primo, T. B. (2009). Mining chat discussions. In Wang, J. (Ed.), *Encyclopedia of data warehousing and mining* (2nd ed., pp. 1243–1247).

Darby, S., Priest, S. J., Fill, K., & Leung, S. (2009). Using digital libraries to support undergraduate learning in geomorphology. In Rees, P., MacKay, L., Martin, D., & Durham, H. (Eds.), *E-learning for geographers: Online materials, resources, and repositories* (pp. 76-99). doi:10.4018/978-1-59904-980-9.ch005

Das, A. K., Sen, B. K., & Dutta, C. (2010). Collaborative digital library development in India: A network analysis. In Ashraf, T., Sharma, J., & Gulati, P. A. (Eds.), *Developing sustainable digital libraries: Socio-technical perspectives* (pp. 206–222). doi:10.4018/978-1-61520-767-1.ch011

De Smedt, A. (2008). Ubiquitous communication via residential gateways. In Dwivedi, Y. K., Papazafeiropoulou, A., & Choudrie, J. (Eds.), *Handbook of research on global diffusion of broadband data transmission* (pp. 655–669). doi:10.4018/978-1-59904-851-2.ch041

de Souza Baptista, C., & Schiel, U. (2009). Towards multimedia digital libraries. In Theng, Y., Foo, S., Goh, D., & Na, J. (Eds.), *Handbook of research on digital libraries: Design, development, and impact* (pp. 361–370). doi:10.4018/978-1-59904-879-6.ch037

De Troyer, O. (2009). Audience-drive design approach for Web systems. In Khosrow-Pour, M. (Ed.), *Encyclopedia of Information Science and Technology* (2nd ed., pp. 274–278).

188

Deb, S. (2008). Multimedia systems and content-based retrieval. In Syed, M. R. (Ed.), *Multimedia technologies: Concepts, methodologies, tools, and applications* (pp. 268–278). doi:10.4018/978-1-59904-953-3.ch022

Deng, H. (2009). An empirical analysis of the utilization of university digital library resources. In Theng, Y., Foo, S., Goh, D., & Na, J. (Eds.), *Handbook of research on digital libraries: Design, development, and impact* (pp. 344–351). doi:10.4018/978-1-59904-879-6.ch035

Draghici, A., Matta, N., Molcho, G., & Draghici, G. (2008). Networks of excellence as virtual communities. In Putnik, G. D., & Cruz-Cunha, M. M. (Eds.), *Encyclopedia of networked and virtual organizations* (pp. 1022–1030). doi:10.4018/978-1-59904-885-7.ch134

Dunn, H. S. (2010). Information literacy and the digital divide: Challenging e-exclusion in the global South. In Ferro, E., Dwivedi, Y. K., Gil-Garcia, J., & Williams, M. D. (Eds.), *Handbook of research on overcoming digital divides: Constructing an equitable and competitive information society* (pp. 326–344).

Dybdahl Sorby, I., Melby, L., Dahl, Y., & Seland, G. (2010). The MOBEL Project: Experiences from applying user-centered methods for designing mobile ICT for hospitals. In Khoumbati, K., Dwivedi, Y. K., Srivastava, A., & Lal, B. (Eds.), *Handbook of research on advances in health informatics and electronic healthcare applications: Global adoption and impact of information communication technologies* (pp. 52–73).

Echeverri, M., & Abels, E. G. (2008). Opportunities and obstacles to narrow the digital divide: Sharing scientific knowledge on the Internet. In Bolisani, E. (Ed.), *Building the knowledge society on the Internet: Sharing and exchanging knowledge in networked environments* (pp. 146–171). doi:10.4018/978-1-59904-816-1.ch008

Eckert, K., Meusel, R., & Stuckenschmidt, H. (2011). User-centered maintenance of concept hierarchies. In Wong, W., Liu, W., & Bennamoun, M. (Eds.), *Ontology learning and knowledge discovery using the Web: Challenges and recent advances* (pp. 105-128). doi:10.4018/978-1-60960-625-1.ch006

Ellis, K. (2012). *Partnerships and collaborations in public library communities: Resources and solutions* (pp. 1-489). doi:10.4018/978-1-61350-387-4

Engel, D., & Robbins, S. (2008). Evolving roles for electronic resources librarians. In Yu, H., & Breivold, S. (Eds.), *Electronic resource management in libraries: Research and practice* (pp. 105–120). doi:10.4018/978-1-59904-891-8.ch007

Eom, S. (2009). *Author co-citation analysis: Quantitative methods for mapping the intellectual structure of an academic discipline* (pp. 1-368). doi:10.4018/978-1-59904-738-6

Espinoza Matheus, N., & Pérez Reyes, M. (2009). A literacy integral definition. In Khosrow-Pour, M. (Ed.), *Encyclopedia of Information Science and technology* (2nd ed., pp. 2445–2449).

Everhart, D., & Shelton, K. (2010). From information literacy to scholarly identity: Effective Pedagogical strategies for social bookmarking. In Yang, H. H., & Yuen, S. C. (Eds.), *Collective intelligence and e-learning 2.0: Implications of Web-based communities and networking* (pp. 167-184). doi:10.4018/978-1-60566-729-4.ch010

Fabbro, E. (2009). Information literacy. In Rogers, P. L., Berg, G. A., Boettcher, J. V., Howard, C., Justice, L., & Schenk, K. D. (Eds.), *Encyclopedia of distance learning* (2nd ed., pp. 1178–1182). doi:10.4018/978-1-60566-198-8.ch168

Fahmi, I. (2005). Development of Indonesia's national digital library network. In Theng, Y., & Foo, S. (Eds.), *Design and usability of digital libraries: Case studies in the Asia Pacific* (pp. 38–54). doi:10.4018/978-1-59140-441-5.ch003

Fan, L., & Li, B. (2009). A user-driven ontology guided image retrieval model. *International Journal of Cognitive Informatics and Natural Intelligence, 3*(3), 61–72. doi:10.4018/jcini.2009070106

Fang Fang, C. (2009). Adaptation of cognitive walkthrough in response to the mobile challenge. In Cartelli, A., & Palma, M. (Eds.), *Encyclopedia of information communication technology* (pp. 10-13). doi:10.4018/978-1-59904-845-1.ch002

Fantin, M. (2010). Perspectives on media literacy, digital literacy and information literacy. *International Journal of Digital Literacy and Digital Competence, 1*(4), 10–15. doi:10.4018/jdldc.2010100102

Fantin, M., & Girardello, G. (2010). Digital literacy and cultural mediations to the digital divide. In Pullen, D. L., & Cole, D. R. (Eds.), *Multiliteracies and technology enhanced education: Social practice and the global classroom* (pp. 231–253). doi:10.4018/978-1-59904-798-0.ch018

Farmer, L. (2008). Affective collaborative instruction with librarians. In Kelsey, S., & St.Amant, K. (Eds.), *Handbook of research on computer mediated communication* (pp. 15–24). doi:10.4018/978-1-59904-863-5.ch002

Farmer, L. (2009). Using real case studies to teach ethics collaboratively to library media teachers. In Demiray, U., & Sharma, R. (Eds.), *Ethical practices and implications in distance learning* (pp. 268–283). doi:10.4018/978-1-59904-867-3.ch016

Farmer, L. S. (2011). Technology-enhanced information literacy in adult education. In Wang, V. (Ed.), *Encyclopedia of information communication technologies and adult education integration* (pp. 184–203).

Ferri, F., & Paolozzi, S. (2009). Analyzing multimodal interaction. In Grifoni, P. (Ed.), *Multimodal human computer interaction and pervasive services* (pp. 19–33). doi:10.4018/978-1-60566-386-9.ch002

Fill, K., & Mackay, L. (2009). Evaluating the geography e-learning materials and activities: Student and staff perspectives. In Rees, P., MacKay, L., Martin, D., & Durham, H. (Eds.), *E-learning for geographers: Online materials, resources, and repositories* (pp. 222-235). doi:10.4018/978-1-59904-980-9.ch013

Fons, T. (2008). The future of electronic resource management systems: Inside and out. In Yu, H., & Breivold, S. (Eds.), *Electronic resource management in libraries: Research and practice* (pp. 363–373). doi:10.4018/978-1-59904-891-8.ch020

Foo, S., Theng, Y., Goh, D. H., & Na, J. (2009). From digital archives to virtual exhibitions. In Theng, Y., Foo, S., Goh, D., & Na, J. (Eds.), *Handbook of research on digital libraries: Design, development, and impact* (pp. 88–100). doi:10.4018/978-1-59904-879-6.ch009

Ford, N. (2008). Library and Information Science. In Ford, N. (Ed.), *Web-based learning through educational informatics: Information Science meets educational computing* (pp. 110–144). doi:10.4018/978-1-59904-741-6.ch004

Fox, E. A., Suleman, H., Gaur, R. C., & Madalli, D. P. (2005). Design architecture: An introduction and overview. In Theng, Y., & Foo, S. (Eds.), *Design and usability of digital libraries: Case studies in the Asia Pacific* (pp. 22–37).

Galvez, C. (2009). Standardization of terms applying finite-state transducers (FST). In Theng, Y., Foo, S., Goh, D., & Na, J. (Eds.), *Handbook of research on digital libraries: Design, development, and impact* (pp. 102–112). doi:10.4018/978-1-59904-879-6.ch010

Ganguly, S., & Pandey, S. (2010). Managing change in reference and information services in digital environment. In Ashraf, T., Sharma, J., & Gulati, P. A. (Eds.), *Developing sustainable digital libraries: Socio-technical perspectives* (pp. 160–183). doi:10.4018/978-1-61520-767-1.ch009

Garfinkel, S. L. (2011). Providing cryptographic security and evidentiary chain-of-custody with the advanced forensic format, library, and tools. In Li, C., & Ho, A. T. (Eds.), *New technologies for digital crime and forensics: Devices, applications, and software* (pp. 1–28). doi:10.4018/978-1-60960-515-5.ch001

Garland, V. E. (2009). Wireless technologies and multimedia literacies. In Tan Wee Hin, L., & Subramaniam, R. (Eds.), *Handbook of research on new media literacy at the K-12 level: Issues and challenges* (pp. 471–479). doi:10.4018/978-1-60566-120-9.ch030

Garrido Picazo, P., Tramullas Saz, J., & Coll Villalta, M. (2009). Digital libraries beyond cultural heritage information. In Theng, Y., Foo, S., Goh, D., & Na, J. (Eds.), *Handbook of research on digital libraries: Design, development, and impact* (pp. 400–411). doi:10.4018/978-1-59904-879-6.ch041

Garten, E. D. (2005). The birth of virtual libraries. In Howard, C., Boettcher, J. V., Justice, L., Schenk, K. D., Rogers, P. L., & Berg, G. A. (Eds.), *Encyclopedia of distance learning* (pp. 166–171). doi:10.4018/978-1-59140-555-9.ch023

Garten, E. D., & Meyer, D. K. (2009). Expanding desktop libraries. In Rogers, P. L., Berg, G. A., Boettcher, J. V., Howard, C., Justice, L., & Schenk, K. D. (Eds.), *Encyclopedia of distance learning* (2nd ed., pp. 995–1002). doi:10.4018/978-1-60566-198-8.ch140

Gaur, R. C. (2010). Facilitating access to Indian cultural heritage: Copyright, permission rights and ownership issues vis-à-vis IGNCA collections. In Ashraf, T., Sharma, J., & Gulati, P. A. (Eds.), *Developing sustainable digital libraries: Socio-technical perspectives* (pp. 235–251). doi:10.4018/978-1-61520-767-1.ch013

Geerts, D. (2009). Sociability heuristics for evaluating social interactive television systems. In Cesar, P., Geerts, D., & Chorianopoulos, K. (Eds.), *Social interactive television: Immersive shared experiences and perspectives* (pp. 78–98). doi:10.4018/978-1-60566-656-3.ch006

Geiger, C. (2011). Copyright and digital libraries: Securing access to information in the digital age. In Iglezakis, I., Synodinou, T., & Kapidakis, S. (Eds.), *E-publishing and digital libraries: Legal and organizational issues* (pp. 257–272).

Gena, C., & Ardissono, L. (2009). A user-centered approach to the retrieval of information in an adaptive Web site. In Szewczak, E. J. (Ed.), *Selected readings on the human side of Information Technology* (pp. 125–140). doi:10.4018/9781878289919.ch051

Gergory, V. L. (2008). The changing library education curriculum. In Tomei, L. A. (Ed.), *Online and distance learning: Concepts, methodologies, tools, and applications* (pp. 3484–3489).

Giaretta, D. (2010). Digital preservation challenges, infrastructures and evaluations. In Ashraf, T., Sharma, J., & Gulati, P. A. (Eds.), *Developing sustainable digital libraries: Socio-technical perspectives* (pp. 145–159). doi:10.4018/978-1-61520-767-1.ch008

Gibson, S. E. (2010). Developing digital literacy skills with WebQuests and Web inquiry projects. In Tatnall, A. (Ed.), *Web technologies: Concepts, methodologies, tools, and applications (4 volume)* (pp. 1554–1569). doi:10.4018/978-1-60566-120-9.ch026

Goh, D. H. (2009). Learning geography with the g-portal digital library. In Rees, P., MacKay, L., Martin, D., & Durham, H. (Eds.), *E-learning for geographers: Online materials, resources, and repositories* (pp. 260-269). doi:10.4018/978-1-59904-980-9.ch016

Goh, D. H., Razikin, K., Chua, A. Y., Lee, C. S., & Foo, S. (2009). On the effectiveness of social tagging for resource discovery. In Theng, Y., Foo, S., Goh, D., & Na, J. (Eds.), *Handbook of research on digital libraries: Design, development, and impact* (pp. 251–260). doi:10.4018/978-1-59904-879-6.ch025

Golian-Lui, L. M., & Westenkirchner, S. (2011). Library issues in adult online education. In Wang, V. (Ed.), *Encyclopedia of information communication technologies and adult education integration* (pp. 485–505).

Górski, M., & Marcinek, M. (2010). Application of selected software tools for data collection and analysis in library management and their effectiveness assessment: Results of the research conducted at Polish academic libraries. *International Journal of Decision Support System Technology, 2*(2), 24–35. doi:10.4018/jdsst.2010040103

Govindarajulu, C., & Arinze, B. (2010). End user types: An instrument to classify users based on the user cube. In Clarke, S. (Ed.), *Computational advancements in end-user technologies: Emerging models and frameworks* (pp. 142–158).

Gregory, V. L. (2009). Education for library and information science professionals. In Khosrow-Pour, M. (Ed.), *Encyclopedia of Information Science and Technology* (2nd ed., pp. 1251–1254). doi:10.4018/978-1-60566-026-4.ch198

Guan, S., & Zhang, X. (2008). Networked Memex based on personal digital library. In Putnik, G. D., & Cruz-Cunha, M. M. (Eds.), *Encyclopedia of networked and virtual organizations* (pp. 1044–1051). doi:10.4018/978-1-59904-885-7.ch136

Gulliksen, J., Cajander, Å., Sandblad, B., Eriksson, E., & Kavathatzopoulos, I. (2009). User-centred systems design as organizational change: A longitudinal action research project to improve usability and the computerized work environment in a public authority. *International Journal of Technology and Human Interaction, 5*(3), 13–53. doi:10.4018/jthi.2009070102

Gunjal, B., Gaitanou, P., & Yasin, S. (2012). Social networks and knowledge management: An explorative study in library systems. In Boughzala, I., & Dudezert, A. (Eds.), *Knowledge management 2.0: Organizational models and enterprise strategies* (pp. 64–83).

Gunn, M., & Kraemer, E. W. (2012). The agile teaching library: Models for integrating information literacy in online learning experiences. In Kelsey, S., & St. Amant, K. (Eds.), *Computer-mediated communication: Issues and approaches in education* (pp. 191–206).

Habib, S. J. (2009). Empirical prediction of computer-network evolution. In Bose, I. (Ed.), *Breakthrough perspectives in network and data communications security, design and applications* (pp. 14–27).

Hagenhoff, S., Ortelbach, B., & Seidenfaden, L. (2009). A classification scheme for innovative types in scholarly communication. In Theng, Y., Foo, S., Goh, D., & Na, J. (Eds.), *Handbook of research on digital libraries: Design, development, and impact* (pp. 216–226). doi:10.4018/978-1-59904-879-6.ch021

Hanewald, R., & Ng, W. (2011). The digital revolution in education: Digital citizenship and multi-literacy of mobile technology. In Ng, W. (Ed.), *Mobile technologies and handheld devices for ubiquitous learning: Research and pedagogy* (pp. 1-14). doi:10.4018/978-1-61692-849-0.ch001

Harboe, G., Huang, E., Massey, N., Metcalf, C., Novak, A., Romano, G., & Tullio, J. (2010). Getting to know social television: One team's discoveries from library to living room. In Symonds, J. (Ed.), *Ubiquitous and pervasive computing: Concepts, methodologies, tools, and applications* (pp. 678–706).

Hatzimihail, N. (2011). Copyright infringement of digital libraries and private international law: Jurisdiction issues. In Iglezakis, I., Synodinou, T., & Kapidakis, S. (Eds.), *E-publishing and digital libraries: Legal and organizational issues* (pp. 447–460).

Hawthorne, D. (2008). History of electronic resources. In Yu, H., & Breivold, S. (Eds.), *Electronic resource management in libraries: Research and practice* (pp. 1–15). doi:10.4018/978-1-59904-891-8.ch001

Heilesen, S. (2009). The case of Roskilde University e-services. In Scupola, A. (Ed.), *Cases on managing e-services* (pp. 189–203).

Hogarth, M., & Bloom, V. (2008). Panorama of electronic resource management systems. In Yu, H., & Breivold, S. (Eds.), *Electronic resource management in libraries: Research and practice* (pp. 322–349). doi:10.4018/978-1-59904-891-8.ch018

Hopkinson, A. (2012). Establishing the digital library: Don't ignore the library standards and don't forget the training needed. In Tella, A., & Issa, A. (Eds.), *Library and information science in developing countries: Contemporary issues* (pp. 195–204).

Iden, J. (2009). Implementing IT service management: Lessons learned from a university IT department. In Cater-Steel, A. (Ed.), *Information Technology governance and service management: Frameworks and adaptations* (pp. 333–349).

Iglezakis, I. (2011). Personal data protection in digital libraries. In Iglezakis, I., Synodinou, T., & Kapidakis, S. (Eds.), *E-publishing and digital libraries: Legal and organizational issues* (pp. 413–429).

Iglezakis, I., Synodinou, T., & Kapidakis, S. (2011). *E-publishing and digital libraries: Legal and organizational issues* (pp. 1-552). doi:10.4018/978-1-60960-031-0

Ihlström Eriksson, C., & Svensson, J. (2009). A user centered innovation approach identifying key user values for the e-newspaper. *International Journal of E-Services and Mobile Applications, 1*(3), 38–78. doi:10.4018/jesma.2009070103

Iivari, N., & Molin-Juustila, T. (2009). Listening to the voices of the users in product based software development. *International Journal of Technology and Human Interaction, 5*(3), 54–77. doi:10.4018/jthi.2009070103

Ing Tiong, C., Cater-Steel, A., & Tan, W. (2009). Measuring return on investment from implementing ITIL: A review of the literature. In Cater-Steel, A. (Ed.), *Information Technology governance and service management: Frameworks and adaptations* (pp. 408–422).

Inoue, Y. (2009). Adult education and adult learning processes with ICT. In Cartelli, A., & Palma, M. (Eds.), *Encyclopedia of information communication technology* (pp. 14-20). doi:10.4018/978-1-59904-845-1.ch003

Inoue, Y. (2009). Electronic government and integrated library systems. In Khosrow-Pour, M. (Ed.), *Encyclopedia of Information Science and Technology* (2nd ed., pp. 1229–1334).

Issa, A. O. (2012). An assessment of the perception of library school students towards librarianship at the University of Ilorin: A pilot study. In Tella, A., & Issa, A. (Eds.), *Library and Information Science in developing countries: Contemporary issues* (pp. 148–168).

Jaeger, P. T., & Bertot, J. C. (2010). Designing, implementing, and evaluating user-centered and citizen-centered e-government. In Reddick, C. (Ed.), *Citizens and e-government: Evaluating policy and management* (pp. 1–19). doi:10.4018/978-1-61520-931-6.ch001

Jefsioutine, M. (2009). Design methods for experience design. In Ang, C., & Zaphiris, P. (Eds.), *Human computer interaction: Concepts, methodologies, tools, and applications* (pp. 432–447).

Jeng, J. (2009). Usability evaluation of digital library. In Theng, Y., Foo, S., Goh, D., & Na, J. (Eds.), *Handbook of research on digital libraries: Design, development, and impact* (pp. 278–286). doi:10.4018/978-1-59904-879-6.ch028

Jesness, R. (2009). High school online learning. In Rogers, P. L., Berg, G. A., Boettcher, J. V., Howard, C., Justice, L., & Schenk, K. D. (Eds.), *Encyclopedia of distance learning* (2nd ed., pp. 1072–1078). doi:10.4018/978-1-60566-198-8.ch152

Jewels, T., & Albon, R. (2011). Reconciling culture and digital literacy in the United Arab Emirates. *International Journal of Digital Literacy and Digital Competence, 2*(2), 27–39. doi:10.4018/jdldc.2011040103

Jindal, S. C. (2010). Digital libraries and scholarly communication: A perspective. In Ashraf, T., Sharma, J., & Gulati, P. A. (Eds.), *Developing sustainable digital libraries: Socio-technical perspectives* (pp. 19–39). doi:10.4018/978-1-61520-767-1.ch002

Johnson, M. R. (2008). Investigating and encouraging student nurses' ICT engagement. In Kidd, T. T., & Chen, I. (Eds.), *Social Information Technology: Connecting society and cultural issues* (pp. 313–335). doi:10.4018/978-1-59904-774-4.ch020

Joshipura, S. (2008). Selecting, acquiring, and renewing electronic resources. In Yu, H., & Breivold, S. (Eds.), *Electronic resource management in libraries: Research and practice* (pp. 48–70). doi:10.4018/978-1-59904-891-8.ch004

Juan, M. C., Furió, D., Alem, L., Ashworth, P., & Giménez, M. (2011). An augmented reality library for mobile phones and its application for recycling. In Chao, L. (Ed.), *Open source mobile learning: Mobile Linux applications* (pp. 124–139). doi:10.4018/978-1-60960-613-8.ch009

Kallinikou, D., Papadopoulos, M., Kaponi, A., & Strakantouna, V. (2011). Intellectual property issues for digital libraries at the intersection of law, technology, and the public interest. In Iglezakis, I., Synodinou, T., & Kapidakis, S. (Eds.), *E-publishing and digital libraries: Legal and organizational issues* (pp. 294–341). doi:10.4018/978-1-60960-031-0.ch015

Kamthan, P. (2009). A pattern-oriented methodology for engineering high-quality e-commerce applications. *Journal of Electronic Commerce in Organizations*, 7(2), 1–21. doi:10.4018/jeco.2009040101

Kan, M. (2005). Using multi-document summarization to facilitate semi-structured literature retrieval: A case study in consumer healthcare. In Theng, Y., & Foo, S. (Eds.), *Design and usability of digital libraries: Case studies in the Asia Pacific* (pp. 111–128).

Kani-Zabihi, E., Ghinea, G., & Chen, S. Y. (2010). Experiences with developing a user-centered digital library. *International Journal of Digital Library Systems*, 1(1), 1–23. doi:10.4018/jdls.2010102701

Kanyengo, C. W. (2012). Fostering and developing leadership amongst library staff at the University of Zambia library. In Tella, A., & Issa, A. (Eds.), *Library and Information Science in developing countries: Contemporary issues* (pp. 1–10). doi:10.4018/978-1-61350-335-5.ch001

Kapellakou, G., Markellou, M., & Vagena, E. (2011). Open content in libraries: Contractual issues. In Iglezakis, I., Synodinou, T., & Kapidakis, S. (Eds.), *E-publishing and digital libraries: Legal and organizational issues* (pp. 342–361).

Kapidakis, S. (2011). Emerging challenges of the digital information. In Iglezakis, I., Synodinou, T., & Kapidakis, S. (Eds.), *E-publishing and digital libraries: Legal and organizational issues* (pp. 141–156).

Kennedy, D. M. (2008). Digital literacy research. In Tomei, L. A. (Ed.), *Encyclopedia of Information Technology curriculum integration* (pp. 228–234). doi:10.4018/978-1-59904-881-9.ch037

Kettunen, J. (2009). The strategic plan of digital libraries. In Theng, Y., Foo, S., Goh, D., & Na, J. (Eds.), *Handbook of research on digital libraries: Design, development, and impact* (pp. 457–464). doi:10.4018/978-1-59904-879-6.ch047

Kheng Grace, S. W. (2009). Digital libraries overview and globalization. In Theng, Y., Foo, S., Goh, D., & Na, J. (Eds.), *Handbook of research on digital libraries: Design, development, and impact* (pp. 562–573). doi:10.4018/978-1-59904-879-6.ch058

Kichuk, D. (2008). Using consistent naming conventions for library electronic resources. In Yu, H., & Breivold, S. (Eds.), *Electronic resource management in libraries: Research and practice* (pp. 275–293). doi:10.4018/978-1-59904-891-8.ch015

Kidd, T. T., & Keengwe, J. (2010). Information literacy in the digital age: Implications for adult learning. In Kidd, T. T., & Keengwe, J. (Eds.), *Adult learning in the digital age: Perspectives on online technologies and outcomes* (pp. 126–133).

Kim, W., & Hansen, J. H. (2009). Speechfind: Advances in rich content based spoken document retrieval. In Theng, Y., Foo, S., Goh, D., & Na, J. (Eds.), *Handbook of research on digital libraries: Design, development, and impact* (pp. 173–187). doi:10.4018/978-1-59904-879-6.ch017

Kimani, S., Panizzi, E., Catarci, T., & Antona, M. (2009). Digital library requirements: A questionnaire-based study. In Theng, Y., Foo, S., Goh, D., & Na, J. (Eds.), *Handbook of research on digital libraries: Design, development, and impact* (pp. 287–297). doi:10.4018/978-1-59904-879-6.ch029

Kismihók, G., & Vas, R. (2011). Empirical research on learners' thoughts about the impact of mobile technology on learning. *International Journal of Mobile and Blended Learning, 3*(1), 73–88. doi:10.4018/jmbl.2011010105

Ko, C. C., Chen, B. M., & Cheng, C. D. (2009). Web-based remote experimentation. In Rogers, P. L., Berg, G. A., Boettcher, J. V., Howard, C., Justice, L., & Schenk, K. D. (Eds.), *Encyclopedia of distance learning* (2nd ed., pp. 2306–2318). doi:10.4018/978-1-60566-198-8.ch341

Koppel, T. (2008). In the eye of the storm: ERM systems are guiding libraries' future. In Yu, H., & Breivold, S. (Eds.), *Electronic resource management in libraries: Research and practice* (pp. 374–382). doi:10.4018/978-1-59904-891-8.ch021

Koppel, T. (2008). Standards, the structural underpinnings of electronic resource management systems. In Yu, H., & Breivold, S. (Eds.), *Electronic resource management in libraries: Research and practice* (pp. 295–305). doi:10.4018/978-1-59904-891-8.ch016

Korres, S., & Kokotsaki, E. (2011). Preservation of cultural and scientific heritage by means of digital libraries. In Iglezakis, I., Synodinou, T., & Kapidakis, S. (Eds.), *E-publishing and digital libraries: Legal and organizational issues* (pp. 462–481). doi:10.4018/978-1-60960-031-0.ch022

Kovacevic, A., & Devedzic, V. (2009). Duplicate journal title detection in references. In Theng, Y., Foo, S., Goh, D., & Na, J. (Eds.), *Handbook of research on digital libraries: Design, development, and impact* (pp. 235–242). doi:10.4018/978-1-59904-879-6.ch023

Kowalczyk, S. (2008). Digital preservation by design. In Raisinghani, M. S. (Ed.), *Handbook of research on global Information Technology management in the digital economy* (pp. 406–431). doi:10.4018/978-1-59904-875-8.ch019

Kromwijk, K., Balkesen, Ç., Boder, G., Dindar, N., Keusch, F., Sengül, A., & Tatbul, N. (2010). Connecting the real world with the virtual world: The SmartRFLib RFID-supported library system on Second Life. In Murugesan, S. (Ed.), *Handbook of research on Web 2.0, 3.0, and X.0: Technologies, business, and social applications* (pp. 720–732).

Kumar, B. (2010). Digital library and repositories: An Indian initiative. In Ashraf, T., Sharma, J., & Gulati, P. A. (Eds.), *Developing sustainable digital libraries: Socio-technical perspectives* (pp. 184–205). doi:10.4018/978-1-61520-767-1.ch010

196

Kumar, B. (2010). Digital library and repositories: An Indian initiative. In Ashraf, T., Sharma, J., & Gulati, P. A. (Eds.), *Developing sustainable digital libraries: Socio-technical perspectives* (pp. 184–205). doi:10.4018/978-1-61520-767-1.ch010

Kyprouli, N. (2011). Newspapers and digital libraries. In Iglezakis, I., Synodinou, T., & Kapidakis, S. (Eds.), *E-publishing and digital libraries: Legal and organizational issues* (pp. 363–381).

Lai, M., Fu, X., Zhang, L., & Wang, L. (2009). Information resources development in China. In Khosrow-Pour, M. (Ed.), *Encyclopedia of Information Science and Technology* (2nd ed., pp. 1973–1978).

Lammintakanen, J. (2008). Curriculum development in Web-based education. In Tomei, L. A. (Ed.), *Online and distance learning: Concepts, methodologies, tools, and applications* (pp. 1219–1251).

Landoni, M. (2011). E-books in digital libraries. In Iglezakis, I., Synodinou, T., & Kapidakis, S. (Eds.), *E-publishing and digital libraries: Legal and organizational issues* (pp. 131–140).

Lappas, G. (2009). Machine learning and Web mining: Methods and applications in societal benefit areas. In Rahman, H. (Ed.), *Data mining applications for empowering knowledge societies* (pp. 76–95).

Lasnik, V. E. (2009). Developing prescriptive taxonomies for distance learning instructional design. In Rogers, P. L., Berg, G. A., Boettcher, J. V., Howard, C., Justice, L., & Schenk, K. D. (Eds.), *Encyclopedia of distance learning* (2nd ed., pp. 616–630). doi:10.4018/978-1-60566-198-8.ch088

Lastrucci, E., Infante, D., & Pascale, A. (2009). Evaluating usability to improve efficiency in e-learning programs. In Cartelli, A., & Palma, M. (Eds.), *Encyclopedia of information communication technology* (pp. 315-320). doi:10.4018/978-1-59904-845-1.ch042

Lavariega, J. C., Gomez, L. G., Sordia-Salinas, M., & Garza-Salazar, D. A. (2009). Personal digital libraries. In Theng, Y., Foo, S., Goh, D., & Na, J. (Eds.), *Handbook of research on digital libraries: Design, development, and impact* (pp. 41–50). doi:10.4018/978-1-59904-879-6.ch005

Law, W. K. (2006). Public sector data management in a developing economy. In Khosrow-Pour, M. (Ed.), *Cases on database technologies and applications* (pp. 125–134). doi:10.4018/978-1-59904-399-9.ch007

Lee, C. (2009). Client computer system and remote access. In Chao, L. (Ed.), *Utilizing open source tools for online teaching and learning: Applying Linux technologies* (pp. 251–278). doi:10.4018/978-1-60566-376-0.ch009

Lee, L. L. (2009). ITIL and value networks. In Lock Lee, L. (Ed.), *IT governance in a networked world: Multi-sourcing strategies and social capital for corporate computing* (pp. 210–237). doi:10.4018/978-1-60566-084-4.ch009

Letic-Gavrilovic, A. (2009). Digital library for dental biomaterials. In Daskalaki, A. (Ed.), *Dental computing and applications: Advanced techniques for clinical dentistry* (pp. 232–272). doi:10.4018/978-1-60566-292-3.ch015

Li, Y. (2011). A survey of digital forensic techniques for digital libraries. *International Journal of Digital Library Systems*, 2(3), 49–66. doi:10.4018/jdls.2011070106

Li, Y. (2011). Decomposed PRNU library for forensics on photos. *International Journal of Digital Library Systems*, 2(1), 38–51. doi:10.4018/jdls.2011010102

Li, Y., & Wei, C. (2011). Digital image authentication: A review. *International Journal of Digital Library Systems, 2*(2), 55–78. doi:10.4018/jdls.2011040104

Lightsom, F. L., & Allwardt, A. O. (2009). USGS digital libraries for coastal and marine science. In Theng, Y., Foo, S., Goh, D., & Na, J. (Eds.), *Handbook of research on digital libraries: Design, development, and impact* (pp. 421–430). doi:10.4018/978-1-59904-879-6.ch043

Lim, E., & Hwang, S. (2005). Implementation of next generation digital libraries. In Theng, Y., & Foo, S. (Eds.), *Design and usability of digital libraries: Case studies in the Asia Pacific* (pp. 97–110).

Loucky, J. P. (2008). Improving online readability and information literacy. In Hansson, T. (Ed.), *Handbook of research on digital information technologies: Innovations, methods, and ethical issues* (pp. 284–305). doi:10.4018/978-1-59904-970-0.ch019

Lourdi, I., & Nikolaidou, M. (2009). Guidelines for developing digital cultural collections. In Theng, Y., Foo, S., Goh, D., & Na, J. (Eds.), *Handbook of research on digital libraries: Design, development, and impact* (pp. 198–205). doi:10.4018/978-1-59904-879-6.ch019

Lucas-Schloetter, A. (2011). Digital libraries and copyright issues: Digitization of contents and the economic rights of the authors. In Iglezakis, I., Synodinou, T., & Kapidakis, S. (Eds.), *E-publishing and digital libraries: Legal and organizational issues* (pp. 159–179).

Luong, M., Nguyen, T. D., & Kan, M. (2010). Logical structure recovery in scholarly articles with rich document features. *International Journal of Digital Library Systems, 1*(4), 1–23. doi:10.4018/jdls.2010100101

Ma, Y., Clegg, W., & O'Brien, A. (2009). A review of progress in digital library education. In Theng, Y., Foo, S., Goh, D., & Na, J. (Eds.), *Handbook of research on digital libraries: Design, development, and impact* (pp. 533–542). doi:10.4018/978-1-59904-879-6.ch055

Mackert, M., Whitten, P., & Krol, E. (2009). Planning successful telemedicine and e-health systems. In Dwivedi, A. N. (Ed.), *Handbook of research on Information Technology management and clinical data administration in healthcare* (pp. 433–446). doi:10.4018/978-1-60566-356-2.ch027

Madden, A. D., Baptista Nunes, J. M., McPherson, M., Ford, N. J., Miller, D., & Rico, M. (2005). A new generation gap? Some thoughts on the consequences of early ICT first contact. *International Journal of Information and Communication Technology Education, 1*(2), 19–32. doi:10.4018/jicte.2005040102

Magara, E. (2012). The future of readership development: How ICTs have influenced user habits and library acquisitions. In Tella, A., & Issa, A. (Eds.), *Library and Information Science in developing countries: Contemporary issues* (pp. 125–140).

Mairn, C. (2012). Acquiring, promoting, and using mobile-optimized library resources and services. In Polanka, S. (Ed.), *E-reference context and discoverability in libraries: Issues and concepts* (pp. 178–198). doi:10.4018/978-1-61350-308-9.ch016

Mandl, T. (2009). User-adapted information services. In Theng, Y., Foo, S., Goh, D., & Na, J. (Eds.), *Handbook of research on digital libraries: Design, development, and impact* (pp. 336–343). doi:10.4018/978-1-59904-879-6.ch034

Markgren, S., Eastman, C., & Bloom, L. M. (2010). Librarian as collaborator: Bringing e-learning 2.0 into the classroom by way of the library. In Yang, H. H., & Yuen, S. C. (Eds.), *Handbook of research on practices and outcomes in e-learning: Issues and trends* (pp. 260-277). doi:10.4018/978-1-60566-788-1.ch016

Markless, S., & Streatfield, D. (2010). Reconceptualising information literacy for the Web 2.0 environment? In Tatnall, A. (Ed.), *Web technologies: Concepts, methodologies, tools, and applications* (pp. 2115–2133). doi:10.4018/978-1-60566-208-4.ch022

Martin, H., & Hesseldenz, P. (2012). Library resources and services in 21st century online education. In Kelsey, S., & St. Amant, K. (Eds.), *Computer-mediated communication: Issues and approaches in education* (pp. 33–49).

Martínez-González, M. M. (2009). Document versioning and XML in digital libraries. In Ferraggine, V. E., Doorn, J. H., & Rivero, L. C. (Eds.), *Handbook of research on innovations in database technologies and applications: Current and future trends* (pp. 137–144). doi:10.4018/978-1-60566-242-8.ch016

Masterson-Smith, J. (2008). Electronic reading programs. In Tomei, L. A. (Ed.), *Online and distance learning: Concepts, methodologies, tools, and applications* (pp. 1655–1660).

Matzen, N. J., Ochoa, L., & Purpur, G. (2011). At the intersection of learning: The role of the academic library in 3D environments. In Cheney, A., & Sanders, R. L. (Eds.), *Teaching and learning in 3D immersive worlds: Pedagogical models and constructivist approaches* (pp. 99–111). doi:10.4018/978-1-60960-517-9.ch006

Mauro, A. (2009). Patient-centered e-health design. In Wilson, E. (Ed.), *Patient-centered e-health* (pp. 10–25).

McCarthy, C. (2006). Promoting the culture and development of regional communities with digital libraries. In Marshall, S., Taylor, W., & Yu, X. (Eds.), *Encyclopedia of developing regional communities with information and communication technology* (pp. 593-597). doi:10.4018/978-1-59140-575-7.ch105

McCarthy, C. (2007). Portal features of major digital libraries. In Tatnall, A. (Ed.), *Encyclopedia of portal technologies and applications* (pp. 724–736). doi:10.4018/978-1-59140-989-2.ch120

McCarthy, C. (2009). Digital library structure and software. In Tiako, P. (Ed.), *Software applications: Concepts, methodologies, tools, and applications* (pp. 1742–1749). doi:10.4018/978-1-60566-060-8.ch102

McLachlan, R., & Sullivan, K. (2012). E-reference in public libraries: Phoenix public library case study, our website is your 24/7 reference librarian. In Polanka, S. (Ed.), *E-reference context and discoverability in libraries: Issues and concepts* (pp. 220–229).

McNaught, C. (2008). Information literacy in the 21st century. In Tomei, L. A. (Ed.), *Encyclopedia of Information Technology curriculum integration* (pp. 406–412). doi:10.4018/978-1-59904-881-9.ch067

Meletiou, A. (2010). The evaluation of library services methods: Cost per use and users' satisfaction. *International Journal of Decision Support System Technology, 2*(2), 10–23. doi:10.4018/jdsst.2010040102

Menzin, M. (2008). Resources on Web-centric computing. In Brandon, D. M. (Ed.), *Software engineering for modern Web applications: Methodologies and technologies* (pp. 292–353). doi:10.4018/978-1-59904-492-7.ch016

Merchant, G. (2009). Learning for the future: Emerging technologies and social participation. In Tan Wee Hin, L., & Subramaniam, R. (Eds.), *Handbook of research on new media literacy at the K-12 level: Issues and challenges* (pp. 1–13). doi:10.4018/978-1-60566-120-9.ch001

Mills, S. C. (2006). Information problem-solving using the Internet. In Tan Wee Hin, L., & Subramaniam, R. (Eds.), *Handbook of research on literacy in technology at the K-12 level* (pp. 357–371). doi:10.4018/978-1-59140-494-1.ch020

Mirijamdotter, A., & Somerville, M. M. (2009). Collaborative design: An SSM-enabled organizational learning approach. *International Journal of Information Technologies and Systems Approach, 2*(1), 48–69. doi:10.4018/jitsa.2009010104

Mittal, A., Pagalthivarthi, K. V., & Altman, E. (2007). Integrating multimedia cues in e-learning documents for enhanced learning. In Khan, B. H. (Ed.), *Flexible learning in an information society* (pp. 164–177). doi:10.4018/978-1-59904-325-8.ch016

Mohamedally, D., Zaphiris, P., & Petrie, H. (2009). User-centered mobile computing. In Taniar, D. (Ed.), *Mobile computing: Concepts, methodologies, tools, and applications* (pp. 2019–2026).

Mutula, S. M. (2010). Capacity building in SMEs. In Mutula, S. M. (Ed.), *Digital economies: SMEs and e-readiness* (pp. 248–264).

Mutula, S. M. (2010). Conclusion and the way forward. In Mutula, S. M. (Ed.), *Digital economies: SMEs and e-readiness* (pp. 322–330).

Mutula, S. M. (2010). Local content and SMEs. In Mutula, S. M. (Ed.), *Digital economies: SMEs and e-readiness* (pp. 176–190).

Mutula, S. M. (2012). Demystifying digital scholarship. In Tella, A., & Issa, A. (Eds.), *Library and information science in developing countries: Contemporary issues* (pp. 170–194).

Na, J., Thet, T. T., Goh, D. H., Theng, Y., & Foo, S. (2009). Word segmentation in Indo-China languages for digital libraries. In Theng, Y., Foo, S., Goh, D., & Na, J. (Eds.), *Handbook of research on digital libraries: Design, development, and impact* (pp. 243–250). doi:10.4018/978-1-59904-879-6.ch024

Nesset, V. (2009). Elementary school students, information retrieval, and the Web. In Pagani, M. (Ed.), *Encyclopedia of multimedia technology and networking* (2nd ed., pp. 469–476). doi:10.4018/978-1-60566-014-1.ch063

Neumayer, R., & Rauber, A. (2009). Map-based user interfaces for music information retrieval. In Theng, Y., Foo, S., Goh, D., & Na, J. (Eds.), *Handbook of research on digital libraries: Design, development, and impact* (pp. 321–329). doi:10.4018/978-1-59904-879-6.ch032

Ng, W. (2010). Empowering students to be scientifically literate through digital literacy. In Rodrigues, S. (Ed.), *Multiple literacy and science education: ICTs in formal and informal learning environments* (pp. 11–31). doi:10.4018/978-1-61520-690-2.ch002

Nichols, D. M., Bainbridge, D., Marsden, G., Patel, D., Cunningham, S. J., Thompson, J., & Boddie, S. J. (2005). Evolving tool support for digital librarians. In Theng, Y., & Foo, S. (Eds.), *Design and usability of digital libraries: Case studies in the Asia Pacific* (pp. 171–190).

Nicholson, S. (2009). Bibliomining for library decision-making. In Wang, J. (Ed.), *Encyclopedia of data warehousing and mining* (2nd ed., pp. 153–159).

Nicholson, S., & Stanton, J. (2008). Gaining strategic advantage through bibliomining: Data mining for management decisions in corporate, special, digital and, traditional libraries. In Wang, J. (Ed.), *Data warehousing and mining: Concepts, methodologies, tools, and applications* (pp. 2673–2687). doi:10.4018/978-1-59904-951-9.ch165

O'Connell, T. A., & Murphy, E. D. (2009). The usability engineering behind user-centered processes for website development lifecycles. In Ang, C., & Zaphiris, P. (Eds.), *Human computer interaction: Concepts, methodologies, tools, and applications* (pp. 192–211).

O'Connell, T. A., & Murphy, E. D. (2009). Usability engineering of user-centered websites. In Khosrow-Pour, M. (Ed.), *Encyclopedia of Information Science and Technology* (2nd ed., pp. 3890–3896).

Ofua, O. J., & Emiri, O. T. (2011). Perceptions and attitude of students in relation to vandalism in university libraries in South-South zone of Nigeria. *International Journal of Digital Library Systems, 2*(3), 23–28. doi:10.4018/jdls.2011070103

Ofua, O. J., & Emiri, O. T. (2011). Role of public libraries in bridging the digital divide. *International Journal of Digital Library Systems, 2*(3), 14–22. doi:10.4018/jdls.2011070102

Ogbomo, M. O. (2012). The significance of marketing in library and Information Science. In Tella, A., & Issa, A. (Eds.), *Library and Information Science in developing countries: Contemporary issues* (pp. 70–81). doi:10.4018/978-1-61350-335-5.ch006

Ogola, S. A., & Otike, J. (2012). Strategies for marketing an academic library in an African setting. In Tella, A., & Issa, A. (Eds.), *Library and information science in developing countries: Contemporary issues* (pp. 61–69). doi:10.4018/978-1-61350-335-5.ch005

Oguz, F. (2009). Adoption of Web services in digital libraries: An exploratory study. In Khan, K. M. (Ed.), *Managing Web service quality: Measuring outcomes and effectiveness* (pp. 307–320).

Oliver, E. I. (2009). The evolution of online composition pedagogy. In Rogers, P. L., Berg, G. A., Boettcher, J. V., Howard, C., Justice, L., & Schenk, K. D. (Eds.), *Encyclopedia of distance learning* (2nd ed., pp. 981–986). doi:10.4018/978-1-60566-198-8.ch138

Onohwakpor, J. E., & Adogbeji, B. O. (2010). The implications of Alireza Noruzi's laws of the Web for library Web-based services. In Adomi, E. (Ed.), *Handbook of research on information communication technology policy: Trends, issues and advancements* (pp. 724–733). doi:10.4018/978-1-61520-847-0.ch046

Oreku, G. S., & Li, J. (2011). End user authentication (EUA) model and password for security. In Clarke, S., & Dwivedi, A. (Eds.), *Organizational and end-user interactions: New explorations* (pp. 149–164). doi:10.4018/978-1-60960-577-3.ch007

Osman, T., Thakker, D., & Schaefer, G. (2009). Semantic annotation and retrieval of images in digital libraries. In Theng, Y., Foo, S., Goh, D., & Na, J. (Eds.), *Handbook of research on digital libraries: Design, development, and impact* (pp. 261–268). doi:10.4018/978-1-59904-879-6.ch026

Osondu, M. C., & Solomon-Uwakwe, B. (2010). Positioning library and information services for user satisfaction through ICT policy formulation in Nigeria. In Adomi, E. (Ed.), *Handbook of research on information communication technology policy: Trends, issues and advancements* (pp. 581–589). doi:10.4018/978-1-61520-847-0.ch036

Ou, S., Khoo, C. S., & Goh, D. H. (2009). Automatic text summarization in digital libraries. In Theng, Y., Foo, S., Goh, D., & Na, J. (Eds.), *Handbook of research on digital libraries: Design, development, and impact* (pp. 159–172). doi:10.4018/978-1-59904-879-6.ch016

Paberza, K. (2010). Towards an assessment of public library value: Statistics on the policy makers' agenda. *International Journal of Decision Support System Technology, 2*(2), 42–51. doi:10.4018/jdsst.2010040105

Paganelis, G. I. (2010). Recruitment experiences in area studies library organizations: The case of ACRL's Western European studies section (WESS). In Pankl, E., Theiss-White, D., & Bushing, M. C. (Eds.), *Recruitment, development, and retention of information professionals: Trends in human resources and knowledge management* (pp. 112–138). doi:10.4018/978-1-61520-601-8.ch006

Paiano, R., Guido, A. L., & Pandurino, A. (2009). A case study for external users. In Paiano, R., Guido, A., & Pandurino, A. (Eds.), *Designing complex Web Information Systems: Integrating evolutionary process engineering* (pp. 179–194). doi:10.4018/978-1-60566-300-5.ch007

Paiano, R., Guido, A. L., & Pandurino, A. (2009). Code generators. In Paiano, R., Guido, A., & Pandurino, A. (Eds.), *Designing complex Web Information Systems: Integrating evolutionary process engineering* (pp. 287–310). doi:10.4018/978-1-60566-300-5.ch013

Pallotta, V., Bruegger, P., & Hirsbrunner, B. (2009). Kinetic user interfaces: Physical embodied interaction with mobile ubiquitous computing systems. In Szewczak, E. J. (Ed.), *Selected readings on the human side of Information Technology* (pp. 154–175).

Pan, J., Yang, H., & Faloutsos, C. (2007). Cross-modal correlation mining using graph algorithms. In Zhu, X., & Davidson, I. (Eds.), *Knowledge discovery and data mining: Challenges and realities* (pp. 49–73). doi:10.4018/978-1-59904-252-7.ch004

Pang, N. (2009). Digital libraries as centres of knowledge: Historical perspectives from European ancient libraries. In Theng, Y., Foo, S., Goh, D., & Na, J. (Eds.), *Handbook of research on digital libraries: Design, development, and impact* (pp. 506–513). doi:10.4018/978-1-59904-879-6.ch052

Pankl, E., & Ryan, J. (2008). Information commons and Web 2.0 technologies: Creating rhetorical situations and enacting Habermasian ideals in the academic library. In Kelsey, S., & St. Amant, K. (Eds.), *Handbook of research on computer mediated communication* (pp. 845–854). doi:10.4018/978-1-59904-863-5.ch060

Paolozzi, S., Ferri, F., & Grifoni, P. (2009). Improving multimedia digital libraries usability applying NLP sentence similarity to multimodal sentences. In Theng, Y., Foo, S., Goh, D., & Na, J. (Eds.), *Handbook of research on digital libraries: Design, development, and impact* (pp. 227–234). doi:10.4018/978-1-59904-879-6.ch022

Papadopoulou, A. (2011). The digitization of contents in digital libraries: Moral right and limits. In Iglezakis, I., Synodinou, T., & Kapidakis, S. (Eds.), *E-publishing and digital libraries: Legal and organizational issues* (pp. 180–197).

Papadopoulou, M. (2011). The issue of 'orphan' works in digital libraries. In Iglezakis, I., Synodinou, T., & Kapidakis, S. (Eds.), *E-publishing and digital libraries: Legal and organizational issues* (pp. 198–231). doi:10.4018/978-1-60960-031-0.ch011

Paul, S. (2010). Digital divide and economic wealth: Evidence from Asia-Pacific countries. In Ashraf, T., Sharma, J., & Gulati, P. A. (Eds.), *Developing sustainable digital libraries: Socio-technical perspectives* (pp. 311–320). doi:10.4018/978-1-61520-767-1.ch017

Perry, J. C., Andureu, J., Cavallaro, F. I., Veneman, J., Carmien, S., & Keller, T. (2011). Effective game use in neurorehabilitation: User-centered perspectives. In Felicia, P. (Ed.), *Handbook of research on improving learning and motivation through educational games: Multidisciplinary approaches* (pp. 683–725). doi:10.4018/978-1-60960-495-0.ch032

Pimienta, D. (2009). Digital divide, social divide, paradigmatic divide. *International Journal of Information Communication Technologies and Human Development, 1*(1), 33–48. doi:10.4018/jicthd.2009010103

Pitariu, H. D., Andrei, D. M., & Guran, A. M. (2010). Social research methods used in moving the traditional usability approach towards a user-centered design approach. In Spiliotopoulos, T., Papadopoulou, P., Martakos, D., & Kouroupetroglou, G. (Eds.), *Integrating usability engineering for designing the Web experience: Methodologies and principles* (pp. 225–242). doi:10.4018/978-1-60566-896-3.ch012

Poda, I., & Brescia, W. F. (2008). Improving electronic information literacy in West African higher education. In Tomei, L. A. (Ed.), *Online and distance learning: Concepts, methodologies, tools, and applications* (pp. 2121–2129). doi:10.4018/978-1-59140-575-7.ch074

Poe, J., Bevis, M., Graham, J., Latham, B., & Stevens, K. W. (2008). Sharing the albatross of e-resources management workflow. In Yu, H., & Breivold, S. (Eds.), *Electronic resource management in libraries: Research and practice* (pp. 71–89). doi:10.4018/978-1-59904-891-8.ch005

Polanka, S. (2012). *E-reference context and discoverability in libraries: Issues and concepts* (pp. 1-294). doi:10.4018/978-1-61350-308-9

Prakash, K. (2011). Library support to distance learners: Case of a university's distance library services in India. In Huffman, S., Albritton, S., Wilmes, B., & Rickman, W. (Eds.), *Cases on building quality distance delivery programs: Strategies and experiences* (pp. 122-134). doi:10.4018/978-1-60960-111-9.ch009

Prakash, K., Pannone, J. A., & Swarup, K. S. (2010). Building digital libraries: Role of social (open source) software. In Ashraf, T., Sharma, J., & Gulati, P. A. (Eds.), *Developing sustainable digital libraries: Socio-technical perspectives* (pp. 90–107). doi:10.4018/978-1-61520-767-1.ch005

Purvis, M., Ebadi, T., & Savarimuthu, B. T. (2009). An agent-based library management system using RFID technology. In Symonds, J., Ayoade, J., & Parry, D. (Eds.), *Auto-identification and ubiquitous computing applications* (pp. 195–204). doi:10.4018/978-1-60566-298-5.ch012

Pyrounakis, G., & Nikolaidou, M. (2009). Comparing open source digital library software. In Theng, Y., Foo, S., Goh, D., & Na, J. (Eds.), *Handbook of research on digital libraries: Design, development, and impact* (pp. 51–60). doi:10.4018/978-1-59904-879-6.ch006

Raisinghani, M. S., & Hohertz, C. (2009). Integrating library services into the Web-based learning curriculum. In Rogers, P. L., Berg, G. A., Boettcher, J. V., Howard, C., Justice, L., & Schenk, K. D. (Eds.), *Encyclopedia of distance learning* (2nd ed., pp. 1222–1227). doi:10.4018/978-1-60566-198-8.ch176

Ramos, M. (2008). Sharing digital knowledge with end-users: Case study of the international rise research institute library and documentation service in the Philippines. In Clarke, S. (Ed.), *End-user computing: Concepts, methodologies, tools, and applications* (pp. 1–1). doi:10.4018/978-1-59904-945-8.ch032

Ramos, M. M., Alvaré, L. M., Ferreyra, C., & Shelton, P. (2009). The CGIAR virtual library bridging the gap between agricultural research and worldwide users. In Theng, Y., Foo, S., Goh, D., & Na, J. (Eds.), *Handbook of research on digital libraries: Design, development, and impact* (pp. 308–320). doi:10.4018/978-1-59904-879-6.ch031

Ratzek, W. (2009). The European approach towards digital library education: Dead end or recipe for success? In Theng, Y., Foo, S., Goh, D., & Na, J. (Eds.), *Handbook of research on digital libraries: Design, development, and impact* (pp. 514–519). doi:10.4018/978-1-59904-879-6.ch053

Rennard, J. (2006). Producing and sharing free advanced scientific and technological knowledge using the Internet. In Marshall, S., Taylor, W., & Yu, X. (Eds.), *Encyclopedia of developing regional communities with information and communication technology* (pp. 587-592). doi:10.4018/978-1-59140-575-7.ch104

Rennard, J. (2008). Open access to scholarly publications and public policies. In Garson, G. D., & Khosrow-Pour, M. (Eds.), *Handbook of research on public Information Technology* (pp. 284–293). doi:10.4018/978-1-59904-857-4.ch027

Ribble, M. (2009). Becoming a digital citizen in a technological world. In *Handbook of research on technoethics* (pp. 250–262). Hershey, PA: IGI Global. doi:10.4018/978-1-60566-022-6.ch017

Rix, R. W. (2012). Changes in customer behavior: A case study in reference service at the Santa Monica public library. In Polanka, S. (Ed.), *E-reference context and discoverability in libraries: Issues and concepts* (pp. 230–236).

Rodriguez, J. C., & Zhang, B. (2008). Authentication and access management of electronic resources. In Yu, H., & Breivold, S. (Eds.), *Electronic resource management in libraries: Research and practice* (pp. 250–274). doi:10.4018/978-1-59904-891-8.ch014

Romero, N. L., Cabrera Méndez, M., Carot, A. S., & Aquino, L. F. (2009). BIVALDI: The digital library of the Valencian bibliographic inheritance. In Theng, Y., Foo, S., Goh, D., & Na, J. (Eds.), *Handbook of research on digital libraries: Design, development, and impact* (pp. 371–381). doi:10.4018/978-1-59904-879-6.ch038

Rubeck, R. F., & Miller, G. A. (2009). vGOV: Remote video access to government services. In Scupola, A. (Ed.), *Cases on managing e-services* (pp. 253-268). doi:10.4018/978-1-60566-064-6.ch017

Russo, M. F., Kelsey, S., & Walsh, M. (2008). Online integration of information literacy in an environmental management systems course. In Zheng, R., & Ferris, S. P. (Eds.), *Understanding online instructional modeling: Theories and practices* (pp. 242–253). doi:10.4018/978-1-59904-723-2.ch015

Ruzic, F. (2009). Information-communications systems convergence paradigm: Invisible e-culture and e-technologies. In Ang, C., & Zaphiris, P. (Eds.), *Human computer interaction: Concepts, methodologies, tools, and applications* (pp. 2324–2340).

Saksena, M. (2010). Information preservation and information services in the digital age. In Ashraf, T., Sharma, J., & Gulati, P. A. (Eds.), *Developing sustainable digital libraries: Socio-technical perspectives* (pp. 133–144). doi:10.4018/978-1-61520-767-1.ch007

Santos, A. (2008). Information literacy for telecenter users in low-income regional Mexican communities. In Clarke, S. (Ed.), *End-user computing: Concepts, methodologies, tools, and applications* (pp. 1–1). doi:10.4018/978-1-59904-945-8.ch030

Santos, N., Campos, F. C., & Braga Villela, R. M. (2009). Digital libraries and ontology. In Theng, Y., Foo, S., Goh, D., & Na, J. (Eds.), *Handbook of research on digital libraries: Design, development, and impact* (pp. 206–215). doi:10.4018/978-1-59904-879-6.ch020

Saravani, S. (2009). Access and control; digital libraries; information ethics; privacy; security. In Theng, Y., Foo, S., Goh, D., & Na, J. (Eds.), *Handbook of research on digital libraries: Design, development, and impact* (pp. 16–26). doi:10.4018/978-1-59904-879-6.ch003

Sasaki, H. (2008). Multimedia digital library as intellectual property. In Syed, M. R. (Ed.), *Multimedia technologies: Concepts, methodologies, tools, and applications* (pp. 279–290). doi:10.4018/978-1-59904-953-3.ch023

Sasaki, H. (2009). Intellectual property protection on multimedia digital library. In Khosrow-Pour, M. (Ed.), *Encyclopedia of Information Science and Technology* (2nd ed., pp. 2113–2117). doi:10.4018/978-1-60566-026-4.ch332

Sasaki, H. (2009). Patent and trade secret in digital libraries. In Theng, Y., Foo, S., Goh, D., & Na, J. (Eds.), *Handbook of research on digital libraries: Design, development, and impact* (pp. 330–335). doi:10.4018/978-1-59904-879-6.ch033

Sasaki, H., & Kiyoki, Y. (2008). Digital library protection using patent of retrieval process. In Sasaki, H. (Ed.), *Intellectual property protection for multimedia Information Technology* (pp. 1–24). doi:10.4018/978-1-59904-762-1.ch001

Sasso, M. D. (2005). Evolution of a collaborative undergraduate information literacy education program. In Carbonara, D. (Ed.), *Technology literacy applications in learning environments* (pp. 117–129). doi:10.4018/978-1-59140-479-8.ch009

Sawasdichai, N. (2009). A qualitative study in user's information-seeking behaviors on websites: A user-centered approach to website development. In Szewczak, E. J. (Ed.), *Selected readings on the human side of Information Technology* (pp. 91–124).

Scarnò, M. (2010). User's behaviour inside a digital library. *International Journal of Decision Support System Technology, 2*(2), 52–59. doi:10.4018/jdsst.2010040106

Schaefer, G. (2009). Effective and efficient browsing of large image databases. In Theng, Y., Foo, S., Goh, D., & Na, J. (Eds.), *Handbook of research on digital libraries: Design, development, and impact* (pp. 142–148). doi:10.4018/978-1-59904-879-6.ch014

Schaefer, G., & Ruszala, S. (2009). Visualisation of large image databases. In Theng, Y., Foo, S., Goh, D., & Na, J. (Eds.), *Handbook of research on digital libraries: Design, development, and impact* (pp. 352–359). doi:10.4018/978-1-59904-879-6.ch036

Schmetzke, A. (2009). Accessibility of online library information for people with disabilities. In Khosrow-Pour, M. (Ed.), *Encyclopedia of Information Science and Technology* (2nd ed., pp. 1–7). doi:10.4018/978-1-60566-026-4.ch001

Scupola, A. (2010). E-services in Danish research libraries: Issues and challenges at Roskilde University Library. In Information Resource Management Association (Ed.), *Electronic services: Concepts, methodologies, tools and applications, 3* Vol., (pp. 1062-1076). doi:10.4018/978-1-61520-967-5.ch064

Scupola, A. (2010). The role of e-services in the library virtualization process. In Information Resource Management Association (Ed.), *Electronic services: Concepts, methodologies, tools and applications, 3* Vol., (pp. 1763-1770). doi:10.4018/978-1-61520-967-5.ch107

Semeraro, G., Basile, P., de Gemmis, M., & Lops, P. (2009). User profiles for personalizing digital libraries. In Theng, Y., Foo, S., Goh, D., & Na, J. (Eds.), *Handbook of research on digital libraries: Design, development, and impact* (pp. 149–158). doi:10.4018/978-1-59904-879-6.ch015

Seok, S. (2009). Maximizing Web accessibility through user-centered interface design. In Ang, C., & Zaphiris, P. (Eds.), *Human computer interaction: Concepts, methodologies, tools, and applications* (pp. 2542–2555). doi:10.4018/9781878289919.ch168

Sharkey, J., & Brandt, D. S. (2008). Integrating technology literacy and information literacy. In Tomei, L. A. (Ed.), *Online and distance learning: Concepts, methodologies, tools, and applications* (pp. 580–588).

Sharma, J. (2010). Intellectual property rights. In Ashraf, T., Sharma, J., & Gulati, P. A. (Eds.), *Developing sustainable digital libraries: Socio-technical perspectives* (pp. 223–234). doi:10.4018/978-1-61520-767-1.ch012

Sharples, M. (2009). Socio-cognitive engineering. In Ang, C., & Zaphiris, P. (Eds.), *Human computer interaction: Concepts, methodologies, tools, and applications* (pp. 677–684).

Shiri, A. (2009). Metadata and metaphors in visual interfaces to digital libraries. In Theng, Y., Foo, S., Goh, D., & Na, J. (Eds.), *Handbook of research on digital libraries: Design, development, and impact* (pp. 270–277). doi:10.4018/978-1-59904-879-6.ch027

Sinanidou, M. G. (2011). Digital libraries and Web linking. In Iglezakis, I., Synodinou, T., & Kapidakis, S. (Eds.), *E-publishing and digital libraries: Legal and organizational issues* (pp. 273–293).

Siqueira, S. W., Braz, M. H., & Melo, R. N. (2008). Accessibility, digital libraries and Semantic Web standards in an e-learning architecture. In Pahl, C. (Ed.), *Architecture solutions for e-learning systems* (pp. 137–153). doi:10.4018/978-1-59904-633-4.ch008

Soriano, J., Lizcano, D., Reyes, M., & Alonso, F. (2009). Enterprise 2.0: Collaboration and knowledge emergence as a business Web strategy enabler. In Al-Hakim, L., & Memmola, M. (Eds.), *Business Web strategy: Design, alignment, and application* (pp. 61–93).

Srivastava, S. C., Chandra, S., & Lam, H. M. (2009). Usability evaluation of e-learning systems. In Khosrow-Pour, M. (Ed.), *Encyclopedia of Information Science and Technology* (2nd ed., pp. 3897–3903).

Stamou, S. (2009). Using topic-specific ranks to personalize Web search. In Theng, Y., Foo, S., Goh, D., & Na, J. (Eds.), *Handbook of research on digital libraries: Design, development, and impact* (pp. 188–197). doi:10.4018/978-1-59904-879-6.ch018

Stefl-Mabry, J., Doane, W. E., & Radlick, M. S. (2011). Bringing the village to the university classroom: Uncertainty and confusion in teaching school library media students in the design of technology enhanced instruction. In D'Agustino, S. (Ed.), *Adaptation, resistance and access to instructional technologies: Assessing future trends in education* (pp. 381–394).

Stielow, F. (2007). Library portals and an evolving information legacy. In Tatnall, A. (Ed.), *Encyclopedia of portal technologies and applications* (pp. 554–558). doi:10.4018/978-1-59140-989-2.ch093

Strodl, S., Becker, C., & Rauber, A. (2009). Digital preservation. In Theng, Y., Foo, S., Goh, D., & Na, J. (Eds.), *Handbook of research on digital libraries: Design, development, and impact* (pp. 431–440). doi:10.4018/978-1-59904-879-6.ch044

Suleman, H. (2011). Interoperability in digital libraries. In Iglezakis, I., Synodinou, T., & Kapidakis, S. (Eds.), *E-publishing and digital libraries: Legal and organizational issues* (pp. 31–47).

Synodinou, T. (2011). The protection of digital libraries as databases: An ideal choice or a paradox? In Iglezakis, I., Synodinou, T., & Kapidakis, S. (Eds.), *E-publishing and digital libraries: Legal and organizational issues* (pp. 232–256).

Taylor, V. A., & Coughlin, C. M. (2006). A case study of one IT regional library consortium: VALE – Virtual academic library environment. In Khosrow-Pour, M. (Ed.), *Cases on database technologies and applications* (pp. 244–266). doi:10.4018/978-1-59904-399-9.ch014

Tella, A., & Issa, A. (2012). *Library and information science in developing countries: Contemporary issues* (pp. 1-335). doi:10.4018/978-1-61350-335-5

Tella, A., & Ojo, R. R. (2012). Marketing library and information services for effective utilization of available resources: The 21st century librarians and information professionals - Which ways and what works? In Tella, A., & Issa, A. (Eds.), *Library and information science in developing countries: Contemporary issues* (pp. 45–60).

Thanuskodi, S. (2012). Bibliometric analysis of DESIDOC Journal of Library & Information Technology. In Tella, A., & Issa, A. (Eds.), *Library and information science in developing countries: Contemporary issues* (pp. 303–312). doi:10.4018/978-1-61350-335-5.ch022

Theng, Y., Foo, S., Goh, D., & Na, J. (2009). *Handbook of research on digital libraries: Design, development, and impact* (pp. 1-690). doi:10.4018/978-1-59904-879-6

Theng, Y., Khoo, A., & Chan, M. (2007). Understanding usability issues in a public digital library. In Anttiroiko, A., & Malkia, M. (Eds.), *Encyclopedia of digital government* (pp. 1577–1581). doi:10.4018/978-1-59140-789-8.ch242

Theng, Y., Luo, Y., & Sau-Mei, G. T. (2010). QiVMDL - Towards a socially constructed virtual museum and digital library for the preservation of cultural heritage: A case of the Chinese "Qipao". *International Journal of Digital Library Systems, 1*(4), 43–60. doi:10.4018/jdls.2010100103

Theng, Y., Lwin Lwin, N. C., Na, J., Foo, S., & Goh, D. H. (2009). Design and development of a taxonomy generator: A case example for Greenstone. In Theng, Y., Foo, S., Goh, D., & Na, J. (Eds.), *Handbook of research on digital libraries: Design, development, and impact* (pp. 73–84). doi:10.4018/978-1-59904-879-6.ch008

Tiemo, P. A., & Edewor, N. (2011). ICT readiness of higher institution libraries in Nigeria. *International Journal of Digital Library Systems, 2*(3), 29–38. doi:10.4018/jdls.2011070104

Toikkanen, T., Purma, J., & Leinonen, T. (2011). LeMill: A case for user-centered design and simplicity in OER repositories. In Czerkawski, B. Ö. (Ed.), *Free and open source software for e-learning: Issues, successes and challenges* (pp. 147–167).

Tsigou, C. (2011). The audiovisual works as digital library content: Storage and exploitation. In Iglezakis, I., Synodinou, T., & Kapidakis, S. (Eds.), *E-publishing and digital libraries: Legal and organizational issues* (pp. 382–411).

Tsingos, T. K. (2011). Liability of hosting provider with regard to open libraries. In Iglezakis, I., Synodinou, T., & Kapidakis, S. (Eds.), *E-publishing and digital libraries: Legal and organizational issues* (pp. 430–446). doi:10.4018/978-1-60960-031-0.ch020

Tunc, T. E., & Oguz, E. S. (2012). Communicating in the age of Web 2.0: Social networking use among academics in Turkey. In St. Amant, K., & Kelsey, S. (Eds.), *Computer-mediated communication across cultures: International interactions in online environments* (pp. 91–107).

Twidale, M. B., & Nichols, D. M. (2009). Computational sense for digital librarians. In Theng, Y., Foo, S., Goh, D., & Na, J. (Eds.), *Handbook of research on digital libraries: Design, development, and impact* (pp. 552–561). doi:10.4018/978-1-59904-879-6.ch057

Ullah, M., & Mahmood, K. (2012). Pakistan Library and Information Council: A proposal. In Tella, A., & Issa, A. (Eds.), *Library and information science in developing countries: Contemporary issues* (pp. 11–31).

Upadhyay, P. K., & Moni, M. (2010). Digital library and e-governance: Moving towards sustainable rural livelihoods. In Ashraf, T., Sharma, J., & Gulati, P. A. (Eds.), *Developing sustainable digital libraries: Socio-technical perspectives* (pp. 265–285). doi:10.4018/978-1-61520-767-1.ch015

208

Utsi, S., & Lowyck, J. (2009). Digital literacy and the position of the end-user. In Khosrow-Pour, M. (Ed.), *Encyclopedia of Information Science and Technology* (2nd ed., pp. 1142–1146). doi:10.4018/978-1-59140-553-5.ch153

van 't Hooft, M. (2010). Tapping into digital literacy: Handheld computers in the K-12 classroom. In Symonds, J. (Ed.), *Ubiquitous and pervasive computing: Concepts, methodologies, tools, and applications* (pp. 886–904).

Vehviläinen, A., Hyvönen, E., & Alm, O. (2008). A semi-automatic semantic annotation and authoring tool for a library help desk service. In Rech, J., Decker, B., & Ras, E. (Eds.), *Emerging technologies for Semantic Work environments: Techniques, methods, and applications* (pp. 100–114). doi:10.4018/978-1-59904-877-2.ch007

Veronikis, S., Tsakonas, G., & Papatheodorou, C. (2009). Handhelds for digital libraries. In Theng, Y., Foo, S., Goh, D., & Na, J. (Eds.), *Handbook of research on digital libraries: Design, development, and impact* (pp. 298–307). doi:10.4018/978-1-59904-879-6.ch030

Wan Dollah, W. A., & Singh, D. (2009). Reference services in digital environment. In Theng, Y., Foo, S., Goh, D., & Na, J. (Eds.), *Handbook of research on digital libraries: Design, development, and impact* (pp. 412–420). doi:10.4018/978-1-59904-879-6.ch042

Wang, F. L., & Yang, C. C. (2009). Extracting the essence: Automatic text summarization. In Theng, Y., Foo, S., Goh, D., & Na, J. (Eds.), *Handbook of research on digital libraries: Design, development, and impact* (pp. 113–121). doi:10.4018/978-1-59904-879-6.ch011

Ward, J. (2010). Applying e-learning technologies to library information literacy instruction. In Donnelly, R., Harvey, J., & O'Rourke, K. (Eds.), *Critical design and effective tools for e-learning in higher education: Theory into practice* (pp. 227–243). doi:10.4018/978-1-61520-879-1.ch014

Ward, J. (2010). Applying e-learning technologies to library information literacy instruction. In Donnelly, R., Harvey, J., & O'Rourke, K. (Eds.), *Critical design and effective tools for e-learning in higher education: Theory into practice* (pp. 227–243). doi:10.4018/978-1-61520-879-1.ch014

Washburn, A., & Pedersen Summey, T. (2009). Marketing library services to distance learners. In Rogers, P. L., Berg, G. A., Boettcher, J. V., Howard, C., Justice, L., & Schenk, K. D. (Eds.), *Encyclopedia of distance learning* (2nd ed., pp. 1391–1398). doi:10.4018/978-1-60566-198-8.ch199

Weber, M., & Geerts, S. A. (2010). Customer involved open innovation: Innovation of new products with end users and customers. In Silva, A., & Simoes, R. (Eds.), *Handbook of research on trends in product design and development: Technological and organizational perspectives* (pp. 259–288). doi:10.4018/978-1-61520-617-9.ch014

Wecel, K., Abramowicz, W., & Kalczynski, P. J. (2008). Enhanced knowledge warehouse. In Jennex, M. E. (Ed.), *Knowledge management: Concepts, methodologies, tools, and applications* (pp. 1029–1034).

Wei, C. (2012). *Multimedia storage and retrieval innovations for digital library systems* (pp. 1–387).

Wei, C., Li, C., & Li, Y. (2009). Content-based retrieval for mammograms. In Ma, Z. (Ed.), *Artificial intelligence for maximizing content based image retrieval* (pp. 315–341). doi:10.4018/978-1-60566-174-2.ch014

Whitworth, B., & Liu, T. (2009). Politeness as a social computing requirement. In Szewczak, E. J. (Ed.), *Selected readings on the human side of Information Technology* (pp. 425–442).

Widén-Wulff, G. (2009). Library 2.0 as a new participatory context. In Pagani, M. (Ed.), *Encyclopedia of multimedia technology and networking* (2nd ed., pp. 842–848). Hershey, PA: IGI Global. doi:10.4018/978-1-60566-014-1.ch115

Witten, I. H., & Bainbridge, D. (2011). The Greenstone digital library software. In IRMA (Ed.), *Green technologies: Concepts, methodologies, tools and applications* (pp. 124-135). doi:10.4018/978-1-60960-472-1.ch110

Wu, S., & Witten, I. H. (2010). First person singular: A digital library collection that helps second language learners express themselves. *International Journal of Digital Library Systems, 1*(1), 24–43. doi:10.4018/jdls.2010102702

Wu, Y. D., Cabrera, P., & Paul, J. (2010). Librarians for tomorrow at the San José Dr. Martin Luther King Jr. Joint Library. In Pankl, E., Theiss-White, D., & Bushing, M. C. (Eds.), *Recruitment, development, and retention of information professionals: Trends in human resources and knowledge management* (pp. 62–82). doi:10.4018/978-1-61520-601-8.ch004

Xie, I. (2008). Interactive IR in digital library environments. In Xie, I. (Ed.), *Interactive information retrieval in digital environments* (pp. 116–152). doi:10.4018/978-1-59904-240-4.ch005

Yang, H. (2008). Webliography: Conception and development. In Tomei, L. A. (Ed.), *Encyclopedia of Information Technology curriculum integration* (pp. 957–962). doi:10.4018/978-1-59904-881-9.ch150

Yang, S., Wildemuth, B. M., Pomerantz, J. P., & Oh, S. (2009). Core topics in digital library education. In Theng, Y., Foo, S., Goh, D., & Na, J. (Eds.), *Handbook of research on digital libraries: Design, development, and impact* (pp. 493–505). doi:10.4018/978-1-59904-879-6.ch051

Yeh, J., Sie, S., & Chen, C. (2009). Extensible digital library service platform. In Theng, Y., Foo, S., Goh, D., & Na, J. (Eds.), *Handbook of research on digital libraries: Design, development, and impact* (pp. 27–40). doi:10.4018/978-1-59904-879-6.ch004

Yu, D. (2009). Speech-centric multimodal user interface design in mobile technology. In Ang, C., & Zaphiris, P. (Eds.), *Human computer interaction: Concepts, methodologies, tools, and applications* (pp. 997–1014). doi:10.4018/9781878289919.ch062

Yu, H., & Breivold, S. (2008). *Electronic resource management in libraries: Research and practice* (pp. 1-440). doi:10.4018/978-1-59904-891-8

Yu, S., Chen, H., & Chen, C. (2005). Dynamic metadata management system for digital archives: Design and construction. In Theng, Y., & Foo, S. (Eds.), *Design and usability of digital libraries: Case studies in the Asia Pacific* (pp. 55–75).

Zaghloul, S., & Jukan, A. (2008). Architecture and protocols for authentication, authorization, and accounting in the future wireless communications networks. In Zhang, Y., Zheng, J., & Ma, M. (Eds.), *Handbook of research on wireless security* (pp. 158–175). doi:10.4018/978-1-59904-899-4.ch012

Zaphiris, P., & Kurniawan, S. (2009). Challenges and opportunities of computer-based learning for senior citizens. In Rogers, P. L., Berg, G. A., Boettcher, J. V., Howard, C., Justice, L., & Schenk, K. D. (Eds.), *Encyclopedia of distance learning* (2nd ed., pp. 247–252). doi:10.4018/978-1-60566-198-8.ch035

Zhang, Y. W. (2008). Challenges and potentials of electronic resource management. In Yu, H., & Breivold, S. (Eds.), *Electronic resource management in libraries: Research and practice* (pp. 306–321). doi:10.4018/978-1-59904-891-8.ch017

Zhao, Y., & Yao, Y. (2010). User-centered interactive data mining. In Wang, Y. (Ed.), *Discoveries and breakthroughs in cognitive informatics and natural intelligence* (pp. 110–125).

Zipperer, L. (2009). Knowledge workers, librarians, and safety: Opportunities for partnership. In Dwivedi, A. N. (Ed.), *Handbook of research on Information Technology management and clinical data administration in healthcare* (pp. 495–506). doi:10.4018/978-1-60566-356-2.ch031

About the Author

Diane Fulkerson is the Social Sciences and Education Librarian at the University of South Florida Polytechnic in Lakeland, Florida. She was previously employed at the University of West Georgia as a Reference and Instruction Librarian. She holds an MA in History from SUNY College at Brockport and an MLS from the University at Buffalo--SUNY. Before changing careers, Diane worked in corporate America for 20 years in customer service, purchasing, and Information Technology support positions.

Index

CPSIA information can be obtained at www.ICGtesting.com
Printed in the USA
BVOW050223170212

282949BV00007BA/31/P